"Great leaders bring out the best in their teams. This handbook from two experts makes the latest evidence on team leadership accessible to anyone looking for insight in a messy and complex world."

—Adam Grant, *New York Times* bestselling author of
Originals and *Give and Take*

"Ideas about teams and teamwork are antiquated and cliché. This deeply researched, practical, and anecdote-filled book offers a thoroughly unique model and cutting-edge perspective on the complexity of teams in today's global space. Applying the principles of *3D Team Leadership* not only teaches you about teamwork, but also when and how to focus on unleashing individual potential."

—Andrea Kremer, Emmy Award-winning journalist, Chief
Correspondent, NFL Network, and Correspondent, HBO's
Real Sports with Bryant Gumbel

"In *3D Team Leadership*, Kirkman and Harris don't just tell team leaders to shift focus depending on the circumstances. With evidence, clarity, and wit, they show precisely how to do so for greatest success."

—Robert Cialdini, Arizona State University, author
of *Influence* and *Pre-Suasion*

"Given the reality of today's teams—global, remote, often 24/7—it is time for a fresh look at this topic. *3D Team Leadership* is the must-read for those engaged in and, especially, leading modern teams. It provides a detailed, example-filled breakdown of challenges and real-world solutions."

—Jon Pershke, Vice President, Strategy, Transformation, and Customer
Solutions, Lenovo

"At some point, you realize that your personal success is dependent on your ability to inspire, motivate, and guide others to their own great performances. For most of us, this starts with being a team leader. Kirkman and Harris walk you through the process of making sense of even the most complex teams, and empowering your members to achieve their own potential."

—D. Stacy Betts, Senior Director, Americas Partner Organization, Cisco

"This book provides answers to the critical question of how we should lead teams in an age of uncertainty. Digging deeply into theory and practice, the authors offer practical advice supported by pithy, real-world examples. Their archeological exploits reveal the roles and critical importance of individuals, subteams, and teams as a whole. As layer upon layer is revealed, so too is a map of how leaders need to develop."

—Deborah Ancona, MIT Sloan School of Management, author of *X-Teams*

"We are busier than ever leading multiple teams and partnering with people across global locations. *3D Team Leadership* teaches us how to direct our focus in order to work smarter, not harder. It's a valuable book for leaders who seek a practical approach and the tools to implement it."

—Sandy Ho, Senior Director of Talent Management, Carter's

"*3D Team Leadership* provides a remarkably fresh perspective on team dynamics. A must-read for any professional leading in today's global and changing environment, Kirkman and Harris demystify the art and science of team motivation and outline powerful, practical solutions to improve results."

—Jessica Steinberg, Senior Director of Human Resources, The Home Depot

"Too many people struggle to collaborate effectively as they wonder how to juggle their colleagues' competing demands. If this sounds familiar, *3D Team Leadership* is the book for you. Drawing on the best of practice and research, Kirkman and Harris provide a user-friendly framework to help you allocate and focus your time and attention across teams, subteams, and individual team members. This book helps you work smarter to get the most from your teams."

—Jeff Polzer, UPS Foundation Professor of Human Resource Management, Harvard Business School

"Working across different time zones, incompatible technology platforms, language barriers, conflicting cultural norms, and competing priorities? Kirkman and Harris provide a straightforward, evidence-based lens for understanding and maximizing performance in even the messiest team environments—with specific consideration for global teams."

—Katharyne Gabriel, Human Resources Director, YUM! Brands

"Kirkman and Harris provide a persuasive and engaging view of how today's organizations actually use teams. More importantly, they advance tried and true, evidence-backed leadership lessons in a way that will resonate with anyone who frequently works in a team setting."

—Barry Hall, Director of Strategic Initiatives, CSX Corporation

"*3D Team Leadership* is a very valuable resource for anyone teaching leadership. With the perfect balance of accessibility, on the one hand, and a firm grounding in scientific theory and research on the other, it provides a contemporary approach to real issues with teams and multi-team systems."
—John R. Hollenbeck, Michigan State University

"Effective teams are fundamental to all organizations. *3D Team Leadership* offers an organized and thoughtful leadership model with a common sense approach to teams that can help any leader. 'There is no "I" in team' will mean something new and improved to all who share the wisdom granted to us by Kirkman and Harris. This excellent, well organized, and practical text will help leaders focus and work smarter."
—Frank Rosinia, Executive Vice President & Chief Quality Officer, John Peter Smith Health System

"*3D Team Leadership* is a substantive handbook on which I can rely to make sense of any team situation. It debunks fundamental 'truths,' engages on a deep yet accessible level, and provides a roadmap to better team leadership. Kirkman and Harris show that despite what has already been said of teams and leaders, we still have a lot to discover. It's a one-stop-shop that I'm happy to have on my desk."
—Gentzy Franz, Director of People, Uptake

"*3D Team Leadership* is the best, most current, and most complete look at teams available today. Both deeply rigorous and immediately practical, the book transforms the latest research on teams into a bold and original action plan. Even in the world's most complex contexts, this book helps leaders achieve greatness."
—Jake Breeden, author of *Tipping Sacred Cows*

"With a clear and humorous writing style and lively tone that speaks directly to readers, this book focuses on how modern teams work, adding a novel twist to our traditional view."
—Tanya Menon, Ohio State University, co-author of *Stop Spending, Start Managing*

"*3D Team Leadership* provides practitioners with a new framework for understanding successful teams. By following the guidelines laid out in this book, readers will be able to place appropriate emphasis on individuals, teams, and subteams—enhancing their performance as a leader."
—M. Travis Maynard, Colorado State University

3D TEAM LEADERSHIP

A New Approach for Complex Teams

Bradley L. Kirkman
and T. Brad Harris

Stanford Business Books
An Imprint of Stanford University Press
Stanford, California

Stanford University Press
Stanford, California

Special discounts for bulk quantities of Stanford Business Books are available to corporations, professional associations, and other organizations. For details and discount information, contact the special sales department of Stanford University Press. Tel: (650) 725–0820, Fax: (650) 725–3457

Printed in the United States of America on acid-free, archival-quality paper

Library of Congress Cataloging-in-Publication Data

Names: Kirkman, Bradley Lane, author. | Harris, T. Brad, author.
Title: 3D team leadership : a new approach for complex teams / Bradley L. Kirkman
    and T. Brad Harris.
Other titles: Three-D team leadership
Description: Stanford, California : Stanford Business Books, an imprint of Stanford
    University Press, 2017. | Includes bibliographical references and index.
Identifiers: LCCN 2016057431 | ISBN 9780804796422 (cloth : alk. paper) | ISBN
    9781503603233 (ebook)
Subjects: LCSH: Teams in the workplace. | Leadership.
Classification: LCC HD66 .K574 2017 | DDC 658.4/022—dc23
LC record available at https://lccn.loc.gov/2016057431

To Allison, who makes everything I do possible and meaningful.
To Lynn, who, despite my own doubts, always believed.
—Brad Kirkman

To my favorite team: Melanie, Hudson, Annie, and Jack.
To my favorite leaders: The teachers and staff
at the KinderFrogs school at TCU.
—Brad Harris

Contents

Acknowledgments   xi

1   The Dramatically Changing Landscape of Leading Teams   1

2   3D Team Leadership   25

3   The First Dimension: The "I's" in Teams   51

4   The Second Dimension: A Team as a Whole   83

5   The Third Dimension: Subteams   118

6   Putting It All Together: Knowing When to Focus on What in Your Team   143

7   3D Team Leadership across Cultures   169

8   3D Team Leadership in Virtual Teams   201

9   What It Takes to Be a 3D Team Leader   222

10   Assessing Your 3D Team Leadership Skills   244

Notes   257

Index   287

Acknowledgments

THIS BOOK WOULD NOT HAVE BEEN POSSIBLE TO write without the influence of and friendships with the many colleagues with whom we have shared our team leadership journey over the years. We are forever grateful to Murray Barrick, Brad Bell, Jeremy Bernerth, Bill Bigoness, Gilad Chen, Ying Chen, Zhen Xiong (George) Chen, Michael Cole, Jason Colquitt, John Cordery, Stephen Courtright, Deanne den Hartog, Chris Earley, Dov Eden, Crystal Farh, Ravi Gajendran, Michele Gelfand, Cristina Gibson, Lucy Gilson, Carolina Gomez, Ricky Griffin, Stan and Nur Gryskiewicz, John Hollenbeck, Laura Huang, Susan Jackson, Timothy Judge, Steve Kozlowski, Jeff LePine, Kevin Lowe, Steve Lucas, Luis Martins, John Mathieu, Dan McGurrin, Bud Miles, Luke Novelli, Larry Peters, Ron Piccolo, Christopher Porter, Ben Rosen, Chris Rosen, Denise Rousseau, Sara Rynes, Ed Salas, Debra Shapiro, General (Ret.) H. Hugh Shelton, Piers Steel, Greg Stephens, Vas Taras, Paul Tesluk, Anne Tsui, Mary Uhl-Bien, Jack Walker, Mary Waller, and Jing Zhou.

We also give credit to a set of big thinkers whom we have long admired for their tremendous impact on our thinking and writing about teams, as this book attests. We are especially indebted to Amy Edmondson, Linda Hill, Larry Hirschhorn, Chuck Manz, and Hank Sims and to those that are no longer with us: Susan Cohen, Paul Goodman, Richard Hackman, Bob House, and Keith Murnighan.

From Brad Kirkman: I also give thanks to my former Ph.D. students who constantly push me to think differently in ways that I didn't think possible, including Richard Gardner, Brad Harris (my coauthor of this book), Andy Hinrichs, Kwanghyun (Harry) Kim, Ning Li, Sal Mistry, Troy Smith, Adam Stoverink, Brian Swider, Gary Thurgood, and Maria del Carmen Triana.

From Brad Harris: I am incredibly grateful for the support from my family and friends throughout the writing of this book. Some additional individuals (not listed above) who deserve specific thanks include Wendy Boswell, Nichelle Carpenter, Tom and Nancy Harris, Amit and Karen Kramer, Rich Lutz, Hettie Richardson, Abbie Shipp, Aaron Taylor, and, of course, my coauthor, Brad Kirkman. I also owe a ton of gratitude to my colleagues, students, and friends at the Mays Business School at Texas A&M University, the School of Labor and Employment Relations at the University of Illinois at Urbana-Champaign, and the Neeley School of Business at Texas Christian University.

The ideas for *3D Team Leadership* are a culmination of over thirty years of combined research, consulting, and teaching. We have been fortunate to work with thousands of extraordinary team leaders and members in dozens of companies on five different continents. We include our own joint research, research with our many wonderful colleagues, as well as research that we thought important to share but in which we were not direct participants. We feel lucky to be able to build on this work. The team leaders and teams we studied come from a wide variety of industries, including software development and other high-tech firms, manufacturing, insurance, governmental agencies, energy, telecommunications, fire and rescue departments, home improvement, biotechnology, and aluminum production.

We are especially indebted to the following companies that provided access to team leaders and members on numerous occasions and without which this book would not have been possible: Alcoa, Allstate, Biogen, Burt's Bees, Cisco Systems, ConocoPhillips, Genencor, Halliburton, IBM, MEMC, MetLife, Motorola, National Spinning, NetApp, Prudential, Sabre, Sara Lee, The Home Depot, and U.S. court system.

Even more important are the individuals who took way more valuable time out of their busy schedules than we deserved to work with us and share their experiences for this book. We are especially grateful to Don Allen, Greg Berg, Steve Conaton, John Deering, Alex Hall, Daniel Holmes, Bernhard Kretschmer, John McCue, Simon McPherson, Kevin Miller, Sander Pool, Beth Ritter, Nathan Snoke, Marty Turner, Maria Wadlow, and Thomas Winter.

Special thanks are owed to Louise Dandridge, Justin James, Kelly Miller, Ed Prime, Joe Provenzano, and Kelly Turner for their work in coordinating our firefighter study. We also thank Tanya Menon for her invaluable feedback on the book and Margo Beth Fleming for her excellent editorial guidance throughout the writing process. We owe special thanks to Lauren Hawkins Miller and Olivia Bartz for their editing assistance on the book.

1 The Dramatically Changing Landscape of Leading Teams

I T'S 6:26 A.M. ON A MID-AUGUST MORNING IN SAN JOSE, California. Outside, the near perfect 60-degree temperature is accented by a gentle breeze from the south. The sun is making its daily debut, and, heeding its lead, commuters all across the western United States reluctantly surrender to their snooze buttons and fire up their coffee brewers in preparation for another workday.

But, unfortunately, not Anna. Anna has been holed up in her modest second-level office at a prominent technology firm since the very early morning hours and is looking desperately at her empty coffee cup for answers that might help her meet her increasingly complex and ever-expanding obligations. Today is an example. After a brief sleep and a paltry granola bar, Anna arrived at her office around 4:00 a.m. to lead a team meeting with new product engineers in Bengaluru (formerly known as Bangalore), India; Sydney, Australia; Dublin, Ireland; and Raleigh, North Carolina. Although Anna technically has the authority to conduct these meetings during local business hours (Pacific Standard Time in California), she rotates the meeting times so that each office is given at least one convenient local time slot per business quarter. This strategy doesn't solve all cultural and geographic issues, of course, but at least it seems to boost overall engagement and fairness perceptions among her team members. Unfortunately, it also ensures that at least two members are worn down and temporally inconvenienced during the conversations—and today was Anna's turn to sacrifice.

After her new product development team meeting, Anna spends 45 minutes responding to e-mails relating to her "actual" job (an increasingly ambiguous term encompassing things like employee evaluations, sending monthly P&L numbers, and corresponding with high-level customers), then begins preparing for an 8:30 a.m. meeting with one of the company's ongoing communities of practice (the purpose of Anna's community was to generate best practices in code writing that can be disseminated throughout her company worldwide). Anna serves as an ad hoc leader of the community and is tasked with coordinating and managing ten core members (those who are relatively permanent) and somewhere between forty and fifty more peripheral members (those who move in and out of the community depending on interest level). Similar to the new product team, these members are located in many different countries and are not easily rounded up for even simple conversations. Furthermore, because it is such a large team, just making sense of the roster feels like an overwhelming task--and don't even get her started on trying to manage the actual personalities within it! Anna's most recent "go-to" play for getting things done in the community was to form and use subteams (smaller sets of teams within the overall community) to address specific initiatives, then focus on helping those subteams coordinate with one another to contribute to overall community goals.

Following her community of practice meeting, Anna grabs another cup of coffee and joins a meeting of the company's senior management team (a "privilege" afforded all senior vice presidents). Anna is not the leader of this team, but she is expected to actively contribute to discussions and action plans concerning her company's current operational issues and strategic vision. Not only are these discussions vital for company well-being, they are also important to Anna's career. They are, in essence, her chance to make a mark and impress key decision makers. As a result, Anna preps exhaustively. The meetings typically last between 60 and 90 minutes, which, on days like today, means that Anna has conducted three intensive team meetings before most restaurants even retire their breakfast menus.

Adding to all of these team responsibilities, Anna is also a member of a multicompany consortium and two to four company-specific project teams at any given time. In contrast to the ongoing teams, these project teams have limited life cycles ranging from a few weeks to several months. The special project teams, in particular, often move through various phases whereby members shift from working mostly individually and independently, then in smaller subteams, and then all together as one intact team. Although Anna is not typically the formally designated leader of these project teams, she and her colleagues often share certain leadership roles throughout each team's life span. Anna is grateful that she has only one additional team meeting on this particular afternoon, but that doesn't mean she won't be responding to other team-related e-mails, phone calls, and short video chats throughout the day (and evening).

Anna's work life is consumed by teamwork. On many days, she feels overwhelmed, even suffocated, by the prospect of managing (okay, juggling) her roles on each of her teams. They consume her time and energy, they divert her focus from her individual day-to-day responsibilities, and they even spill over into her personal life. Furthermore, she feels that her career is being decided in large part by the complex black box–like inner workings of teams—an unnerving proposition for someone used to controlling her own destiny. However, Anna knows that team-based arrangements can outperform classic individual-based ones; it was drilled relentlessly into her head during her MBA program years ago. She has also personally witnessed instances of incredible collective performance at work. In fact, her solid results on a highly visible team are a big reason that she was promoted to her current VP rank. Of course, and unfortunately, she has also recently observed just as many examples of team dysfunction--wasted time, free-riding, groupthink, nasty infighting--than the supposed synergy (that the whole is greater than the sum of the parts) her company told her teams would produce. Yet these instances have not tempered her company's desire to form new teams to address every type of challenge and opportunity. In short, teams are everywhere, and if Anna wants to continue her career ascent, she must learn to thrive in all of them.

Does Anna's story sound familiar? It should, but if not, it will soon enough. Anna's experience reflects a common tale of the thousands of leaders we interviewed and consulted with during our careers as researchers, executive educators, and practitioners. If you are someone who, like Anna, is currently leading multiple teams, while also being a member of another set of teams, and you sometimes feel stressed, burned out, confused, overwhelmed, or all of these, *this book is for you*. Our approach—what we call *3-Dimensional Team Leadership* (or "3D" Team Leadership, for short)—is designed to help you navigate what often feels like chaos in leading and working in today's teams.

3D Team Leadership, boiled down, is about focus—knowing where to devote your time and attention at any given point to maximize your and your teams' effectiveness. It's about working smarter, not necessarily harder. There are thousands of leadership books and philosophies out there, and many of them have some great, time-tested tips and strategies for effectively leading teams, but making sense of all of them or just choosing the right ones can seem flat-out impossible. In this book, we distill the most powerful leadership tools into a clear, practically useful framework you can begin using in your team leader (and member) roles right away.

Importantly, this book puts forth the two primary leadership levers that you can use to maximize your teams' effectiveness. First, there are elements of *team design* to consider, such as how work is structured, what kind of goals are set, and how rewards can be used to stimulate individual and team performance. Second, there are important behaviors associated with *team coaching* that maximizes member and team motivation and performance. Although there is at least some evidence that team design can be more important than coaching for team effectiveness[1] (or, as we like to say, a well-designed team can survive a bad coach, but you cannot coach a team out of its poor design), we will show you in this book that leaders should strive to use both to create the highest-performing teams possible.

The tools contained in this book will help you become a premier team leader and, in doing so, unleash your potential to create more value for your company, generate more professional gains for yourself and others, and reduce your overall stress. We outline three basic dimensions inherent in all teams that require different degrees of focus according to a team's current circumstances: individual team members, a team as a whole, and the subteams within an overall team. We then provide guidance to help you (1) recognize what situation your team is in, (2) know what behaviors are appropriate for that situation, and, if necessary, (3) shift your focus to different dimensions as teams move through different life cycle stages.[2]

The 3D Team Leadership model was inspired by our academic, consulting, and teaching experiences working with team leaders and members. In a nutshell, we have seen leaders make the same mistakes over and over: they are unable, or unwilling, to see the nuances of teams and, as a result, treat them as only one "thing" (usually a single, collective entity while overlooking individuals or the subteams in teams). As you might expect, they spend most of their time focusing on setting team goals, holding team retreats, coaching and motivating their teams, providing team feedback and after-action reviews, figuring out ways to help their teams be resilient when they face adversity and celebrating team success when their team achieves its goals. Unfortunately, sometimes these efforts result in frustration and inaction that actually hurt team performance.

To be clear, there is nothing inherently wrong with focusing on overall team functioning and performance. In fact, focusing on a team as a whole can be especially critical in many instances.[3] Our point, however, is that sometimes leaders can get a bit too team focused (a tunnel vision, of sorts), especially in today's business environments where we are constantly told teams can, and should, do everything. We've even heard some team leaders talk about feeling guilty if they take time to focus on their one-on-one team member relationships instead of exclusively focusing on their whole team; it's almost as if they consider it cheating on their team! But the premise of 3D Team Leadership is that there are times when you should focus on individuals within your teams, other times when you should focus on your team as whole, and still others when it might be wise for you to focus on smaller subsets of team members (we refer to these as subteams throughout the book). The keys are knowing when to shift your focus from one dimension to another and being able to answer two questions: (1) What skills and behaviors does it take for me to lead individuals versus teams versus subteams? and (2) How do I know when it is most important to focus one of the three dimensions more than the others? In today's complex business environments, the ability to *focus* has never been more important, and that is what this book will help you learn how to do.

Although many leaders are certainly intellectually capable of understanding the technical components of 3D Team Leadership, without guidance they often find it quite difficult to exhibit the actual behaviors the model requires. Using concrete, practical examples, we'll teach you how to diagnose key aspects of situations, team life cycles, and your relationships with others that will push you forward in your leadership journey. As former managers and now academics (and when we serve as department heads, managers again) who have worked in and alongside dozens of organizations over a combined thirty years, we take an evidence-based approach to discussing these tools. So, if you are serious about improving your team leadership potential, join us on a journey toward learning how to see teams as they really are—in 3D!

Teams: Looking Back and Moving Forward

Teams are inherently messy and complex. Individual members have unique skill sets, distinct worldviews, and varying levels of motivation; team composition is fluid as critical members move on to other assignments and green newcomers join in their wake; and team dynamics and goals shift over time in response to various factors. Yet everything that makes teams complicated also has the potential to make them beautiful. Research and case evidence time and time again suggest that teams have the potential to outperform, outinnovate, and even outlast comparable groups of individuals working alone.[4] As you undoubtedly know, however, this potential synergy does not occur by happenstance. Teams can also waste time, frustrate members, limit creativity, and produce subpar deliverables. One of the biggest factors that separates dysfunctional from high-performing teams is leadership.[5]

Team leadership, simply defined, is the *process of motivating and directing the actions and energy of an interdependent collection of individuals toward a common goal.* Several outstanding books have addressed the topics of teamwork and leadership over the past twenty-five years. We have benefited immensely from them and are careful here to integrate the key tried-and-true lessons of team leadership that are still relevant today. Yet without a doubt, this book is not old wine in a new bottle. Leading teams in today's business environment is dramatically different and wildly more complex than twenty years ago (or even a decade ago), and our book, importantly, is written specifically for today's teams.

To see the difference, let's take a quick look back. In the early 1990s, companies typically assigned employees to a single team, at that time often referred to as "self-managing" or "high-performing" teams, with responsibility to deliver products, services, or ideas in a relatively stable and enduring fashion. When we began working with many of these organizations, including companies like Allstate and Prudential Insurance, IBM, Sara Lee, and municipal and federal government offices, it was relatively easy to analyze and understand team functioning and performance. Typically we would ask human resource managers for a roster of teams with member names attached, solicit information from each member using surveys or interviews, analyze the data, and report the results.

These types of teams are rapidly approaching extinction.[6] Today's teams are unstable—members are constantly coming, going, and coming back to teams,[7] meaning that a team roster today is often obsolete by tomorrow. Moreover, the business world is increasingly *volatile, uncertain, complex,* and *ambiguous* (expressed by the acronym VUCA,[8] which we use throughout this book), meaning that critical team tasks cannot always be easily identified (and

TABLE 1.1. Differences between Yesterday's and Today's Teams

	Yesterday's Teams	*Today's Teams*
Stability of membership	Relatively stable	Highly dynamic
Number of teams (members)	Members on one team	Members on multiple teams
Number of teams (leaders)	Leaders lead one team	Leaders lead multiple teams
Team life span	Long term, ongoing	Short term, ad hoc
Level of interdependence	Relatively stable	Highly dynamic
Team boundaries	Clear and rigid	Unclear and fuzzy
Mode of interaction	Face-to-face	Virtual and hybrid
Team composition	Same culture	Global and multicultural

how can you evaluate the level of team performance if you don't even know the tasks that need to be performed?). Finally, teams are simply more pervasive in today's companies. Not only are more employees members of teams, many employees (like Anna) are members of multiple teams[9] (some managers we consulted with claimed membership on over ten teams in their company at a single time). Problematically, most of the books and articles that have been written to assist managers in their leadership of teams are based on the older, more stable forms of teaming. And although this material has been extremely helpful to millions worldwide, it has limited utility for the majority of us leading and working in today's teams. To help illustrate, Table 1.1 summarizes the key differences between the teams of yesterday and today.

The Importance of Leader Focus: The Key to 3D Team Leadership

Organizational life is more complex now than it ever has been before.[10] As a result, trying to find a single leadership approach for your team is futile if not outright dangerous. There are simply too many factors that can affect you, your team, and everything in between. Just think about what could be happening at this moment. Right now your best, and seemingly most loyal, team member might be quietly interviewing for another job across the country to accommodate his or her spouse's continuing education; your company's chief financial officer might be casually pitching an acquisition idea to the CEO over lunch that will drastically alter the course of your entire firm; Wall Street analysts may overreact to after-hours data from across the world and downgrade your company's buy rating (and thus hinder the ability to raise capital), which could prompt a massive "restructuring" (i.e., layoffs); or a competitor might issue a press release highlighting a new product—one that your team has been trying to develop for the past two years. You get the point. Any number of events—large or small, internal or external, work or personal—can, and probably will, affect your team. Clearly you need an adaptable leadership approach.

Those who study complexity theory (which examines uncertainty and nonlinearity in various systems, including organizations), and specifically the ones interested in leadership, have argued for several distinctions between leading in simple versus complex environments. In simple environments, leaders can use predetermined behaviors and highlight technical processes to boost performance (an administrative leadership approach). In more complex environments, however, leaders must understand that there are substantive "unknown unknowns" in their environment[11] and, moreover, they themselves have cognitive limits on how much information they can accurately process.[12] Thus, in contrast to traditional command-and-control leadership styles, they must instead work to create conditions that allow adaptive properties (e.g., problem solving, creativity) to emerge from team members.[13] Leaders, in essence, do not need to worry about being the primary source of a team's adaptability, but rather should prioritize being the enablers of their teams' adaptive capabilities.[14]

Very much related to our discussion of complexity, behavioral scientists have developed several important theories (e.g., resource allocation theory,[15] conservation of resources theory,[16] ego depletion theory[17]) that generally suggest that leaders (and their team members) cannot focus intensely on all things all the time; clearly, we have finite cognitive (e.g., self-control, motivation, brainpower), physical (e.g., strength, energy/stamina), and other (e.g., time, money) resources that must be conserved and efficiently allocated toward our myriad goals in order to be effective. So in today's environments that require us to juggle demands within and across so many teams, focusing on the right things at the right time is critical. Doing so helps you, *and your teams*, make sense of situations and optimize their efforts. Consistent with the premise that you simply don't have the resources to do it all, empowering your teams and their individual members is vital for success in complex environments. On that note, a report on global human capital trends published by Deloitte stated , "The 'new organization,' as we call it, is built around highly empowered teams, driven by a new model of management, and led by a breed of younger, more globally diverse leaders."[18] We couldn't agree more: this is the crux of 3D Team Leadership. Before going much further, we will establish some fundamental principles and terms that will anchor our discussions throughout the book.

Groups, Teams, and Everything in Between

What are the key differences between groups and teams? Does it really matter? Let's take a leader we'll call Amy, a 25-year-old up-and-comer at a major insurance company, as an example. Before starting her first job after college, Amy assumed a leadership role as a co-captain on her university's college basketball team and, afterward, attended a top business school graduate program. After graduating from b-school, her current employer deemed her a high potential (or "hi-po") employee, which meant she was given an opportunity to complete a formal management training program followed by several stretch assignments. Amy's first assignment after training was as a client services team leader overseeing twenty-seven claims-processing employees whose primary responsibility was to serve as the initial contact when customers need to file an insurance claim. Her subordinates, or what her company referred to as team members, worked primarily on the phone to gather customer information, input it into a computer system, and create unique claim reports to pass on to claims adjusters who then physically assessed the extent of a customer's suitability for an insurance payment.

Given her prior experiences (and successes), Amy was a big believer in the power of teams and considered herself an "expert" in team leadership. She now finds this term humorous. Not surprisingly, Amy's first initiative when she was formally placed in her assignment was to focus intently on establishing the "team thing" for her claims processors. She set team goals; devoted substantial time toward team building, including off-site staff retreats; and even worked with human resources to help create a modest bonus system tied to team performance that replaced a small portion of members' previously individually-based incentives. Within a few weeks, Amy (and others) could clearly see the results of her changes—and they were disastrous.

Her employees were confused and, worse, cynical toward all of what they called the "team building stuff." They didn't understand why they had a bonus tied to team goals when 99 percent of the time they worked "alone at their desks serving individual customers." Basically, there was no opportunity for team members to have any influence or impact on their fellow coworkers, regardless of their motivational intent. Amy later lamented that calling this collection of individuals a "team" in the first place (which was not her choice) was wrong—a mistake we see all the time in companies. Amy learned the hard way that groups are not teams and teams are not groups. This is the first, and perhaps most fundamental, lesson of 3D Team Leadership.

To be clear, a team is typically defined as an *interdependent collection of individuals who are mutually accountable and share responsibility for specific outcomes for their company.*[19] Members of teams with high interdependence constantly exchange the "stuff" with which they work (e.g., information, materials, ideas), have high levels of coordination and integration, and require high degrees of collaboration to get work done. In these teams, you might sometimes find it difficult to disentangle individual member contributions to the team—in other words, determine who actually contributed what in the process.

The type of interdependence just described is often referred to as *task interdependence*, because it concerns how team members work together to carry out their tasks. We should note, however, that there are two other main types of interdependence: *goal interdependence*, or the extent to which members' goals are compatible and team focused, and *outcome interdependence*, or the extent to which rewards and feedback are tied to overall team, not individual, performance.[20] Each of these is important, to be sure. Nevertheless, when we use the word *interdependence* here, we are referring primarily to task interdependence because it is the dimension you as a leader are most likely to have control over (note that we do offer some discussions on goals and reward systems throughout the book as well).

Mutual accountability means that team members are accountable not only to one another, but, importantly, *as a team* to their company. Team members also have shared responsibility for delivering something specific, and it is the whole team, not individual members, that delivers a product, service, idea, or decision. A business example might be a software development team that is writing computer code for a complex piece of software. Many hands do the writing of such code, with information moving constantly among members to accomplish their tasks. In the sports world, an example is a team of rowers moving in perfect synchronization with one another.

In contrast to teams, groups are typically defined as *people who learn from one another and share ideas but are otherwise not interdependent or working toward a shared goal.*[21] The keys here, again, are low levels of interdependence, little shared responsibility or accountability, and individuals, not entire teams, who are delivering a product, service, idea, or decision. An example might be a group of insurance salespeople working in a particular geographic territory. On a day-to-day basis, these insurance agents work primarily independently with very little coordination needed among them to sell insurance. They might share best practices, sales tips, or other information occasionally, but they do not fully rely on one another to complete their work. All income they earn, of course, gets pooled together for the benefit of the company, but the generation of those sales and income is based on the summation of individual efforts. Importantly, despite the bandwagon effect that has occurred with teaming, teams are not unequivocally superior to groups and groups are not superior to teams. Whether a team or group is better able to accomplish work depends on what type of structure is better suited to the task. For highly interdependent work, a team is often the better choice. In contrast, for more independent work, groups often surpass teams in performance.

According to the definitions we have offered, Amy was actually leading a group, not a team. Unfortunately, she was leading her group as if it were a team, which resulted in a great deal of confusion and frustration. Interestingly, Amy's mistake is quite common. After all, many companies use the word *team* to refer to any collection of individuals working in a similar capacity (e.g., sales team) or location (e.g., Midwest service team), regardless of whether those individuals actually depend on one another to successfully complete their jobs. Likewise, *team* is often used casually to motivate some sort of collective pride, irrespective of the actual arrangement of work (though, in fairness, the overapplication of the word *team* can be loosely justified because all employees do have at least some shared interest and accountability in making sure the company performs well enough to survive—their salaries depend on it!).

In their classic book, *The Wisdom of Teams*, Jon Katzenbach and Douglas Smith suggested that the practical terminology used in companies is an issue of semantics—it really does not matter what you call a collection of people in your organization as long as they are performing at a high level.[22] We agree. Our goal in this book is not to rewrite corporate organizational charts or act as vocabulary police. The more substantive point to understand, which Katzenbach and Smith also keenly pointed out, is that the conceptual distinction between groups and teams is necessary for optimal leadership. Simply put, you can call the collection of individuals you lead whatever you want (group, team, gaggle, pride, herd, coalition of knuckleheads), but you must first determine whether they operate—or should operate—as a team or a group before you determine how to lead them. This lesson is profoundly simple, but profound nonetheless.

The managers we consult with and teach in executive education courses often have "aha!" moments in response to this point. They say things like, "Oh, all this time I thought I was leading a team, so I've been doing all of these 'team things,' but what I actually have is a group. No wonder my people are confused." Or, on the flip side, "I have been treating my team more like a group, and maybe that's why I am having team performance issues."

Amy's story, we are pleased to report, has a happy ending. Once the group-versus-team distinction became apparent to her, she dropped the emphasis on teams and started focusing more on one-on-one mentoring and coaching, and she got HR to help her implement new individual performance–based incentive systems. Her focus on individuals, paired with her excellent but once misguided leadership skills, led to stellar increases in productivity and employee morale.

An important addendum to Amy's story is that leaders cannot, and should not, assume that the distinction between groups and teams reflects a clean or stable either-or dichotomy. Past work, for instance, has noted that groups and teams often go through development stages whereby they start out as groups before becoming real teams.[23] For example, in one classic development model, educational psychologist Bruce Tuckman suggested that groups move through sequential stages of forming, storming, norming, and performing.[24] Although today's teams are quite distinct from the types he studied (in fact, many of the groups he included in his review were therapy groups and groups involved in human relations training), the overall lesson here is that the quicker you can get your teams past the first three stages, the better. In another classic team development model, Connie Gersick found that MBA students who were assigned a team task in a laboratory setting typically performed at low levels of intensity until they crossed some temporal milestone, at which point they worked more fervently to finish their tasks. In her findings, this change in intensity happened when the teams had used about half of their available task time and, thus, her theory became known as "punctuated equilibrium."[25] Of course, we have seen this type of "first-half inertia" play out all the time when we assign team projects to our MBA students.

Interestingly, each of these models focused primarily on groups and teams with relatively stable membership. Yet today's teams often have fluid, revolving door–type memberships; as a result, linear models of team development may not always be appropriate. So although leaders fifty years ago may have been able to facilitate group discussions that led to quicker forming, storming, and norming processes, today's leaders may instead have to individually socialize new members on a one-on-one basis to help them see and understand team norms that were established months ago.

Beyond team development, many of today's teams also go through life cycles with either repeated patterns of episodes or stages with members moving back and forth between independent and interdependent roles. As a result, they might look very much like teams at certain time periods and very much like groups at others.[26] So rather than helping leaders like Amy determine whether they are leading a team or a group, we should instead be focusing on determining where their entity falls on the group-team continuum (we will use the terms *group-like* and *team-like* to better acknowledge this continuum throughout the book). After all, team members can work together in myriad ways that range from low to high interdependence and everything in between.

Of course, this makes things a lot more complicated for team leaders. In the simple example, all Amy had to do was figure out what type of entity she was leading based on the type of work being done—in her case, a group—and then exhibit the right type of coaching on an ongoing basis and design and implement the right performance management system. In contrast, in the more complex example in which a team's work often changes, you have to constantly evaluate what level of interdependence is optimal and then shift your coaching behavior and team design actions to match the corresponding entity (group-like or team-like); that is, you need the wisdom to know exactly what you are leading at any given time and have the flexibility and adaptability to shift your leadership approach to match.

This caveat represents a meaningful departure from the classic work on teams (including even relatively recent classics). For instance, the book *Leading Teams: Setting the Stage for Great Performances*[27] by the late Richard Hackman, who was at the time of his passing one of the foremost experts on teams in the world, long served as a premier guide for how to design effective teams. However, most of the lessons from his book were focused on teams of the past: relatively stable entities with members and leaders primarily focused on one team and little movement between the group-like versus team-like distinction.

For example, at the beginning of his book, Hackman outlined four essential features of what he called "real teams." The first essential, related to our points above, is a *team task*. Essentially a team task is akin to part of our definition of teams: a team task requires members "to work *together* to produce something—a product, service, or decision for which members are collectively accountable and whose acceptability is potentially assessable."[28] Such an either-or treatment of teams or groups assumes long-term stability in the way members work together and carry out their tasks, which may have been true in the 1980s and 1990s (when Hackman carried out most of his research), but is not necessarily true today.

The same can be said for Hackman's three other essential features of "real teams." The second feature he described is *clear boundaries*: team members are crystal clear as to who is, and who is not, part of their team. However, in today's teams, members move into and out of teams frequently and on a regular basis to respond to VUCA conditions, and team boundaries are often fuzzy rather than clear. A software engineer with whom we worked at a large technology-based storage company expressed frustration with the fuzziness of one of his teams and stated,

> One of the teams I lead is a performance automation team that builds software used by our performance teams. What that means is that with the variety of customers we have—and their rapidly changing needs—we bring people in and out of our team on a regular basis to try to serve these customers. Many team members will actually be out there working with customers, so their day-to-day work is sitting with a different team trying to figure out what they need. A lot of this team switching is informal; nobody does this for us. It's more self-organizing based on customer needs. It happens fast and very organically.

In another example, a regional manager for a large energy services firm told us, "When I look internally now, and I try to identify specific teams, it's almost like we don't have formally defined teams; it's constantly fuzzy! As business changes and grows, business development teams are constantly growing and then contracting and back again. These are mostly customer teams, so people move in and out of the teams as needed."

Hackman's third essential condition is *delimited authority*, which means that managers must "specify when a team is formed just how much authority the team initially will have and to make sure that members understand clearly what decisions are and are not theirs to make."[29] Although we agree that it is a good idea to get as much clarity as possible up front in a team's life cycle, business conditions change so rapidly today that it is not always feasible to have absolute clarity with regard to lines of authority. For example, a senior engineering manager at a high-tech company described this situation and said,

> In our world, we sometimes have a single product owner, which makes the lines of authority pretty clear. However, sometimes we have a product owner *team* consisting of multiple people. The product owner team will decide to ship a product on a certain date, and then a team leader will sometimes swoop in and change the ship date without even informing the team! The complexity of the business market in an enterprise organization is intense, and for that reason, sometimes leaders can undermine the empowerment of the team. And, unfortunately, that also undermines the team's confidence in the future.

Finally, Hackman's fourth essential condition is *stability over time*. At this point, given our discussion, perhaps it goes without saying that this might be the most tenuous of essential conditions given the dynamic nature of today's teams. Despite his citing the research evidence that teams with stable membership perform better than those that have to deal with inflows and outflows of members due to constantly changing conditions in VUCA environments, today's teams are anything but stable in their membership. Indeed, stability is a luxury many of today's teams cannot afford. A vice president of business development for a large energy services company we worked with echoed this lack of stability and said, "We are a multinational company and a multidisciplinary organization. It should come as no surprise then that our company aggressively promotes people changing positions, locations, and assignments. That means our teams change around a lot. So you're constantly in the position of having to brief people, make sure the dynamics are still working, and teams will often be unbalanced for a certain period of time. That's just the world we live in."

Reinforcing all of these newer issues, our colleagues writing about teamwork in today's companies summed it up nicely and stated: "Contemporary teams tend to overlap, with members working simultaneously on more than one team . . . [and] can therefore rarely be sure what subset of the membership will convene at any given time. In short, it can be a puzzle—or even a matter of contention—to say who is on the team."[30] We couldn't agree more with this assertion and note that it is a dramatic departure from the essential features of the teams that Hackman described. We also agree that "interdependence is a fundamental element of teams, but [we] . . . must take into account the fact that it can unfold in non-obvious ways and may well change over a team's life."[31]

Importantly, rather than being assigned a level of interdependence (or what might be called *structural interdependence*), today's members of more fluid and dynamic teams are just as likely to choose varying levels of interdependence, depending on changing task needs or business conditions (or what might be called *behavioral interdependence*). Based on these assertions, a key recommendation is to "relax the definitional elements of what makes a real team and explore what is interesting in contemporary collaboration."[32] Ten years after the publication of *Leading Teams*, Hackman himself acknowledged as much and stated, "The time is right to rethink how we construe and study [teams] because the balls are in the air and in ways that pose direct challenges to traditional conceptual models and research methodologies."[33]

From our experience, we should all be in agreement that the nature of teamwork has changed dramatically in the past twenty-five years, and perhaps exponentially in just the past decade. We also agree that most of the current research has not caught up to practice in this regard. That was the impetus for our book. We believe that the approach we offer here, 3D Team Leadership, advances a highly effective and evidence-based approach to leading today's teams. In large part, the success of all 3D team leaders rests on their ability to focus on the right things at the right time for the entities they lead. Indeed, Hackman put this eloquently: "Coaching, then, is not just a matter of helping a [team] deal with problems and opportunities that come up. Instead, it involves giving focused attention to where a team is in its temporal life cycle— and then providing the kind of assistance that is likely to be especially helpful at that particular time."[34] Unfortunately, given the complexity of today's teaming, such advice is tough to follow. We next review the various tensions of team leadership that make this advice so challenging to implement.

The Classic (But Still Relevant) Tensions of Team Leadership

One of the most important elements of teamwork that makes such seemingly straightforward advice so difficult to translate into action is the notion that team leadership consists of a set of seemingly intractable tensions (or

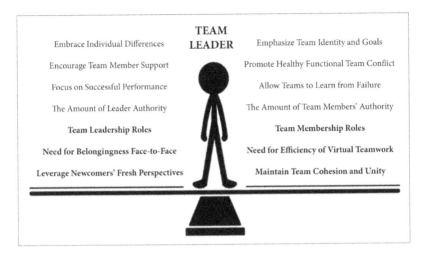

FIGURE 1.1. The Tensions of Team Leadership: Striking a Balance

Note: The tensions in boldface type represent the new tensions identified in our work; the others are more established (but still relevant) tensions from Linda Hill's Harvard Business School note, "Managing Your Team."

paradoxes) with which you must grapple. As we will argue throughout this book, the 3D Team Leadership approach will equip you with the tools you need to reduce unnecessary strains. Some of the most critical tensions are classics that were originally articulated decades ago but still ring true today. Others are relatively unique to today's teams. We describe the seven most pressing tensions, starting with four classics and then moving on to three unique ones for teams today. These are summarized in Figure 1.1.

One of the foremost experts in leadership today, Linda Hill of Harvard Business School, articulated the classic tensions of leading teams in her Harvard Business School note entitled, "Managing Your Team"[35] as well as her book, *Being the Boss: The 3 Imperatives for Becoming a Great Leader*.[36] The first paradox is *embracing individual differences while simultaneously emphasizing team identity and goals*.[37] Because teams are composed of individuals, there are two potentially competing forces here, particularly in Western countries that place more emphasis on individuals compared to groups. That is, although most people desire to be a part of groups and teams and have a sense of belonging to them, they also simultaneously desire to be unique and have a sense of themselves as individuals. Those who study social identity theory, which refers to the part of an individual's self-concept that is determined by both group or team membership as well as the emotional significance of the membership,[38] acknowledge the fundamental tension between the human need to be both similar to and also different from others simultaneously.[39] Such research demonstrates that people will achieve an optimal sense of social identity and demonstrate the highest degree of team loyalty if a team can provide individuals with a sense of belonging and distinctiveness simultaneously.[40] This begs the question: How much emphasis should be placed on motivating, recognizing, and rewarding individuals versus motivating, recognizing, and rewarding entire teams?[41]

A senior engineering manager at a high-tech company we worked with talked about the delicate balancing act for getting a win-win when it comes leading individuals and teams:

> You certainly grow individuals, but you're also thinking about the team at the same time. I spend a lot of time on one-on-ones—so much so that most of my people say they've never had a leader spend as much one-on-one time as I do, but I think it's critical. I do this with each of my direct reports every other week. I also have team meetings to reinforce team goals and achievements. To keep the balance, I constantly pay attention to where individuals want to grow, but at the same time I also focus on where the team is going. It's not seamless; sometimes you have to be creative. I always remind individuals what the team goals are in my one-on-ones. These meetings are really the lifeblood of how I manage. I have to figure out how to plug individuals into the overall team dynamic so that individuals are successful and the team is successful. I try to find particular tasks that raise the individuals' visibility, even if it's outside a given project.

The second tension is *encouraging team members to support one another while simultaneously creating conditions under which members can confront one another and have healthy levels of functional team conflict*.[42] Clearly, if team members are too supportive, they will be reluctant to disagree with or criticize one another's ideas. Such reluctance would lead to the typical pitfalls associated with team decision making such as groupthink,[43] conflict avoidance,[44] or the common knowledge effect, known as situations in which team members simply discuss information that is already commonly known because they are afraid that bringing up unique or unpopular information or ideas might put them at risk for ostracizing by fellow team members.[45] Conversely, if team members get too confrontational, what might start out as healthy, functional, task-based conflict might turn into unhealthy, dysfunctional, relationship-based conflict.[46] If teams move too far in either direction, it will be very difficult to steer them back from one side to the other. You have to find a sweet spot between support and confrontation.

A regional manager at a large energy services company we worked with described the benefits of creating a certain amount of tension in a team:

> I am a huge fan of friction for teams. I think when team members challenge each other, it's extremely beneficial. I don't mind a few complaints coming across my desk. What that means to me is that people are fully engaged and looking for new ways of doing things. We are a heavily matrixed organization, which is essentially there to create friction and challenge. I guess we're used to challenging each other without it becoming personal, and we try to keep it more business focused. In fact, when I'm leading a team meeting, I'll always point out one or two people who consistently challenge me on things; I openly identify them in the meeting. That way, I'm giving the group permission to challenge me and each other.

The third tension is *focusing on successful performance while simultaneously creating learning experiences that come from making mistakes and failing.*[47] In today's hypercompetitive VUCA business environments, companies are typically focused on creating and sustaining the highest levels of performance possible. Pressures from shareholders often create a short-term focus in many publicly held companies that works against the notion of allowing learning from mistakes and failure. The problem here is that there is general consensus that much more lasting and deep learning occurs from failure compared to success.[48] In fact, Stanford University professor John Krumboltz (along with his colleague Ryan Babineaux) even created a continuing studies course, Fail Fast, Fail Often (which they also turned into a book), to emphasize that happy and successful people spend less time planning and more time acting and, as a result, making mistakes and failing.[49]

This is also related to the work on individuals' goal orientations, which suggests that some individuals are motivated by a learning-goal orientation; that is, they try to develop their competence by building new skills and mastering new situations.[50] Other people have a performance-goal orientation, which means that they seek out situations that they can perform well in and, as a result, avoid negative judgments. The former will not be as afraid as much as the latter to stumble every now and again as long as they are learning something valuable. Although some aspects of these orientations are personality driven (i.e., traits), people can also be primed to have a stronger orientation for one or the other in particular situations (i.e., states).[51] Thus, leaders can play a role in encouraging a specific orientation.

Of course, if you were to encourage too much risk taking in order to enhance learning and too much failure ensues, you run the risk of damaging your career and reputation, as well as your team's. However, if you focus only on performance to the exclusion of any failure-based learning experiences, your teams will likely be unable to adapt when business conditions change. You have to figure out how to balance a focus on performance, success, and creating shareholder value (if you're in a public company) versus creating the conditions that allow team members to learn from their mistakes.

Although some of the leaders with whom we work tell us that making mistakes and failure are not really tolerated in their companies ("the cutting edge is the bleeding edge" was a particular phrase that emerged), others found ways to create more tolerance for these kinds of learning experiences. For example, a manager in a large energy services company said,

> We're a team of engineers; we're very analytical, very precise, and too much of that can lead us to analysis paralysis. I don't think any of us are expecting perfection by any means. All solutions will be flawed to some extent. I'd rather have a slightly flawed solution that we can learn from now rather than perfection much later. We've actually been incorporating some Silicon Valley thinking into our projects now—you know, the whole "minimal viable product" concept. We take things to market, find out what works and what does not work. We make mistakes from time to time. We learn a lot of valuable things along the way.

The fourth tension is *balancing leader authority with team member discretion and authority*.[52] This concept is similar to Hackman's delimited authority, which refers to specifying which decisions will be made by team leaders and which ones will be in the hands of team members. This paradox is best described by the notion of team empowerment. Team leaders can retain most of the decision-making authority in their teams, which would result in a very low level of team empowerment. Or these leaders can decide to empower their teams to make most of the team's decisions, which would allow the leaders to turn their attention to more external team matters.

The most important questions underlying this tension are: "How much empowerment should a team ultimately have overall?" and, "On which particular areas or dimensions of team responsibility will a team take most control and on which areas will that team's leader retain more authority?" Even before the arrival of teams in great numbers in the late 1980s and early 1990s, leaders struggled with the issue of how much authority to give to those who work for them. In fact, in our work with companies, this seemed to be the most troubling tension for most managers. One vice president of business development at a large energy services company said, "This is where I struggle the most sometimes—not decision making so much but problem solving. I will give them decision-making authority, but if a problem lands on my desk, I have to catch myself from blurting out a solution I know is right. I have a tendency to come up with solutions rather than letting them do so."

In a similar vein, a senior engineering manager at a large technology company said, "My one-on-ones are my way to get alignment on this issue with my team members. I try to remain disciplined with respect to staying out of decisions, at least for those that are less impactful. If the stakes are higher, then I'll push back and ask them to reevaluate. If I've learned anything through this process, it's that empowerment is so important. It's what makes them stay late and work on weekends and own the destiny of the project."

The New Tensions of Team Leadership for Today's Teams

Our work with today's teams suggests that leaders must figure out how to manage at least three additional tensions. The first is *simultaneously balancing team leadership roles and responsibilities in some teams with team membership roles and responsibilities in other teams.* We have already pointed out that people are likely to be on many teams, sometimes as team leaders and other times as team members. If a person is taking on leadership roles in one or more teams and yet is a member of other teams, there is an inherent tension in trying to balance these roles across the various team types. Perhaps even more basic than the challenge of managing time commitments and role transitions (leader to member and back), evidence also tells us that people commonly suffer from "attention residue,"[53] which makes it hard to shift focus from one task to another. Simply put, our attentional resources are sticky, and our minds can stay with one team even though our body is present on another.

Exemplifying this puzzle, a manager at a large energy services company with whom we worked said, "I do this multiple times on a daily basis! As a result, it is very hard to shift this mind-set. I'm managing up and down about half the time. I get impatient and I want to take over. What I do to correct this is make a deliberate effort to shift my mind-set and ask the leader of the team, 'What do you need from me on this project?' That helps me shift from leader mode to follower mode; it's a mental switch."

A senior engineering manager at a large technology company said,

> You never really stop being a leader. It comes down to what's needed in any given situation. When I'm designated the team leader, I'm much more disciplined in terms of setting agendas, alignment, communication—all those things; but when I'm a team member, I'm mostly interested in the outcomes. I can step up and lead occasionally, but I really mostly work with the leader to help the project succeed. My natural personality is to not have to be out in front all of the time. As long as the right outcomes are occurring, I'm comfortable.

Although leader-member tension often occurs *across* different teams, it could also conceivably occur *within* a single team. The notion of shared or emergent team leadership has grown in popularity in both organizations and the academic management literature.[54] Shared leadership suggests that different team members will emerge as team leaders at different times depending on the nature of the tasks at hand or where the team is in its performance life cycle. As a result, leaders might evolve into members, back into leaders, and so forth. How a person is able to shift between these roles and balance the tensions that accompany this shifting is an area in great need of additional examination. For now, based on our work with many of today's companies, we can say for sure that it represents one of the most important, and difficult-to-manage, tensions for team leaders.

The second new tension in today's teams is *balancing the need for belongingness associated with face-to-face teamwork against the requirements for efficient teamwork associated with more technology-based, virtual approaches.* Indeed, this is one of the most commonly addressed issues among executives when we discuss best practices for managing virtual teams—teams that work primarily using technology-based communication tools rather than large amounts of face-to-face contact. We are asked: How much face-to-face interaction should I create in my team? How often should we have face-to-face meetings? When should I insist on some type of videoconferencing tools versus audioconferencing? We discuss answers to these questions later in the book, but for now it is safe to say that trying to balance the amount of face-to-face teamwork versus virtual working represents an important tension that leaders of today's teams have to navigate. For example, a region manager from an energy services company said,

> Right now, my team is spread out through North America. I'm going to have to make the sacrifice to go to them . . . that really builds trust and credibility . . . it's so beneficial. I try to keep in mind that there is so much value in face-to-face contact, and I try not get too caught up in the cost. I often ask them if we need face-to-face, and then I respond. I encourage them to come to me as well. We operate on an out-of-sight, out-of-mind situation. I tell folks that they need to cheerlead for themselves and make their contributions known. You can't do that over technology very well.

A final tension in today's teams is to *leverage newcomers' fresh perspectives with the pressure to get them quickly acclimated to an existing status quo.* As we have noted, membership in today's teams is dynamic. People shift on and off teams on a whim and, even more generally, employees shift companies more than they ever have in the past. Member turnover can be problematic, of course, because it disrupts the norms and flow that teams need to perform at a high level, but on the flip side, adding new members can also be valuable. Evidence shows, for example, that being a newcomer can be extremely stressful, but in this stress, newcomers can generate creativity[55] that combats groupthink and look at problems from a different point of view. In addition, new team members are often assigned because they have specialized expertise or experience that addresses a gap in a team's current composition. Given that fighting against turnover is increasingly futile in today's environment, particularly given the influx of turnover-prone millennials (those born between approximately 1980 and 2000) into the workforce, leaders must be prepared to leverage it in the best way possible for their team.

Organization of the Book

As we hope we have made crystal clear by now, the complexity of teaming in today's environment is increasing exponentially. Moreover, there are constant tensions that can make leading (and working on) teams feel impossible at times. Rest assured, though, that it doesn't have to be this way. Our book will show you how to cut through the complexity of teams by using a clean, sensible framework. It will help you filter out the seemingly endless noise of teamwork and pay attention to the meaningful cues you'll need to guide your leadership behaviors and decision making. By honing your focus, you will unleash your own leadership potential as well as the true power of your teams.

The rest of our book proceeds as follows. In Chapter 2, we provide a more detailed description of what we mean by 3D Team Leadership and give examples of the concept. In Chapter 3, we provide a more thorough understanding of the first of the three dimensions of 3D Team Leadership: the individuals on a team, along with a set of recommendations for maximizing individual performance in team settings, particularly with regard to empowering individuals. In Chapter 4, we discuss the second dimension of our 3D model, a team as a whole, and we focus on how to maximize overall team performance with a special emphasis on team empowerment. In Chapter 5, we tackle the third and final dimension of our 3D Team Leadership approach, the subteams within an overall team, and we use recent evidence from work on multiteam systems to help you understand how to manage multiple subteams and their interrelationships. In Chapter 6, we bring all the dimensions together and discuss how you can effectively manage each of the three dimensions; importantly, we provide guidance as to how you can recognize when you should focus more intently on which dimension. In Chapter 7, we go global with our 3D Team Leadership model and describe how to adapt it for use in different countries or with teams composed of people from different countries. In Chapter 8, we add still another layer of complexity by discussing the role of virtual teaming and how it affects your use of the 3D Team Leadership model. In Chapter 9, we address the needs of individual team leaders and provide practical tools for helping you build the key competencies that will enable you to become a highly effective 3D Team Leader. In Chapter 10, we discuss the broad applicability of our approach and introduce a series of self-assessment tools designed to measure your effectiveness at using the 3D Team Leadership model, as well as team assessments for measuring the health of the teams you lead.

2   3D Team Leadership

I N TWO-PLUS DECADES OF WORKING WITH THOUSANDS of team members in hundreds of teams across dozens of companies, we have repeatedly observed three major pitfalls that severely limit a team's potential to be effective. The fascinating underlying reasons behind these pitfalls are hardly unique to today's teams, but they continue to emerge in new ways. Luckily, they can be quite easy to diagnose once you start paying attention.

The first pitfall we have encountered is that leaders and companies promote an entirely "there is no 'I' in teams" ideology (and we acknowledge the joke that there is a "me" if you rearrange the letters!). In essence, those who endorse this approach expect individuals to sacrifice their own interests and goals for the good of a team. Those who speak out too much or try to advance their own agendas are often told, "You're not a team player!" or given mandates to "fall in line or else." It's hard to blame leaders and companies who adopt this mindset. After all, the idea that collective goals should usurp individual ones is likely rooted in good intentions and, moreover, ingrained in leaders well before they ever accept their first jobs; just think about some of the all-time great movies espousing teamwork, like *Apollo 13*, *Braveheart*, *Hoosiers*, and *Remember the Titans*.

The problem, however, is that a constant "we over me" mind-set is neither realistic nor optimal in companies today. Employees now often balance charters from multiple teams, receive evaluations and rewards based on different metrics (including individual performance), and, frankly, are more likely to move on to other companies if they feel undervalued as individuals. The point here is not that we should be promoting individualistic mercenaries; it is, rather, that the best leaders know when and how to give due attention to individuals and their team as a whole. Illustrating this point, a high-performing team member in an insurance company told us:

> In a team I was in a couple of years ago, I told my team leader that I would like to start doing some additional work that relates to my own personal career goals, some things that would lead me closer to my long-term ambitions. I enjoyed working on this team a lot, but it was kind of stifling me and keeping me away from some of the goals I had set for myself when I originally took this job. And his reaction was like, "What are you talking about? We get things done in teams in this company, and we don't put our own agendas ahead of our team's agenda. Aren't you being a little selfish here?" So I started looking online for positions elsewhere, kind of casually at first, but then I guess I just lost interest in working for him and that company. I left a few months later. To me, it seemed like they ignored what I, as an individual person, wanted to accomplish. It was just teams, teams, teams.

This example is important because it highlights the hidden effects of neglecting individuals. This employee, who by all accounts was a value-adding member of her team, likely responded to her leader's feedback in a way that indicated she learned her lesson—at least initially. For instance, she tabled her requests for individual development opportunities and fell in line with the team-first mentality without complaining. It's what she didn't do, however, that gets easily lost in the story. When members become fearful of being accused of not being a team player, they often shut down, withhold valuable dissenting opinions, and easily agree to potentially devastating false consensus in critical decisions (i.e., groupthink, or our personal favorite term for this, *groupidity*,[1] for group stupidity). Some employees, including the one in this example, eventually leave their team and company—usually after months or even years of reduced contributions and unseen withdrawal.

The second pitfall, which we also mentioned in Chapter 1, is that many companies create teams in name only. They bring members together with tremendous, albeit fleeting, excitement and hope that, through some great magic, value-adding synergies will materialize. However, instead of breakthrough thinking, superior customer service, or higher quality products, these "teams" stagnate or, even worse, disintegrate in ways that cost organizations months of lost time and thousands of dollars in mistake-correction efforts, not to mention disgruntled employees.

One of the most common examples occurs when well-meaning managers ask employees to behave like a team without the power or foresight to alter an individual-based reward system. A similar phenomenon occurs when managers halfheartedly set team goals in a project's initial stage, but then fail to follow up with any meaningful thrust such as publicly recognizing teamwork behaviors, altering performance evaluations, or providing team-based feedback. Consequently, most employees eventually and often quickly end up viewing teamwork as a sham, or "token teaming." The main issue here is that excitement, hope, and outright magic are hardly the primary fuels for effective teamwork. The best-performing teams are the product of hard and mindful work—not the least of which is upfront efforts to properly design and use a team for a common goal.

We witnessed an example of this pitfall in one of the governmental agencies we consulted with a few years ago. The agency had hired us to help their employees performing mostly clerical jobs operate in a more team-like fashion. We quickly set out to establish what the teams would look like, how members would work in an interdependent manner, and demonstrate how teamwork would benefit them with greater productivity and efficiency. After working there for several months, we thought we had gotten the organization to embrace the team concept, so we left that job to work on projects in other companies. About six months later, we got a panicked phone call from the person who originally hired us proclaiming that the "team thing" was over. He asked if we could come back in to assess the damage.

What we quickly discovered was that all of the team design features that we had helped to put in place were not there anymore. Employees were not holding team meetings, they went back to working rather independently in their jobs, and the team bonus system we had helped set up had been completely abandoned. It was no wonder, then, that the teams were not working. Our recommendation to the organization was that teams were not right for them because management was not willing to do the hard, uncomfortable work to maintain proper team functioning. The big lesson is that if a company or leaders want true teamwork but aren't willing to forgo their tendencies toward assigning, evaluating, and rewarding individual work or aren't willing to work through some of the initial messiness, they are playing a fool's game.

We'll be the first to acknowledge that change can be unpleasant, especially at first, but a little grit and openness can make a world of difference.

The third pitfall is the tendency to overlook the relationships between smaller subsets of members—we refer to these as subteams—once an overall team is up and running. Many leaders, for instance, take the approach that members need to "figure it out on their own" for their teams to function properly. Although classic research on groups and teams does suggest that individuals tend to experience uncomfortable interactions early in their formation[2] and some types of disagreement can be beneficial,[3] too much conflict can produce unhealthy subteam divides. These divides, sometimes referred to as *faultlines*[4] because they indicate where teams are likely to fracture, can emerge from seemingly innocuous factors, such as departmental membership or geographic location, or deeper-level issues including fundamental disagreements on strategy or team processes. The outcomes associated with us-versus-them faultlines also vary. They can be obvious, such as outright arguments and altercations between factions, or remarkably covert, including microaggressions or silent disengagement from substantive discussions. The latter, problematically, is sometimes mistaken for group consensus. Despite their mostly negative connotation, subteams can also be leveraged for good for some types of tasks.[5] Many of the effective leaders we have studied and worked alongside not only strive to mitigate and bridge potentially harmful faultlines but also proactively construct and harness subteams that work concurrently on complementary tasks during some team life cycle stages, which can aid an entire team's progress toward its overarching goal.

As an example of improperly managing subteams, we often use a case with our MBAs and executives published by the Ivey Business School at the University of Western Ontario that tells the story of the Leo Burnett company, the venerable ad agency behind such popular brand icons as Kellogg's Tony the Tiger, the Pillsbury Dough Boy, the Jolly Green Giant, and the Marlboro Man.[6] After landing a lucrative contract from a cosmetics company to develop a global advertising strategy for new age-defying skin care product, Leo Burnett set up a global virtual team consisting of three satellite subteams: one in London, England; one in Toronto, Canada; and another one in Taipei, Taiwan. After starting things off right by having a face-to-face kickoff meeting in Toronto and conducting videoconference meetings every two months, the team appeared to be working well. The leader of the team, who was based in

London, also traveled to Toronto and Taipei occasionally to approve the creative ad designs and provide support.

Trouble started to arise, however, when conflicts emerged between the Toronto and London subteams, which had split their responsibility for various parts of the ad campaign. These subteams worked rather independently from each other, developing parts of the advertising materials that did not fit together in a seamless fashion. To make matters worse, there was almost no communication, and hence no learning opportunities, between the Taipei and Toronto subteams outside of the bimonthly videoconference meetings. Over time, communication became even less frequent, devolving into occasional e-mails here and there. What the leader of this global virtual team did not realize is that subteam faultlines occurred right where you would expect them to, along geographic location lines, and no coaching was done to encourage or facilitate between-subteam collaboration. To make matters worse, because advertising awards (like the ones given out at the Cannes Lions Ad Festival held annually in France) are typically bestowed on the local offices housing the subteams (even though Leo Burnett still gets the credit overall), there was nothing in place from a team design perspective to bind these subteams together. On the contrary, these subteams were almost set up to compete with one another. We use this case to demonstrate how easily an overall team composed of subteams can fracture and end up operating like several separate teams. Unfortunately, we have seen this scenario play out over and over again in the companies with which we work.

Why do we see leaders stumble into the three pitfalls so frequently even when they seem fairly obvious on the surface? There are multiple answers, of course, but one of the most powerful explanations is that the most commonly used leadership training and development resources, popular press leadership books and practitioner articles do not offer a consistent or comprehensive framework suitable for leading today's complex teams. Most team leadership books, for instance, are focused almost solely on leading teams as a whole; that is, they only answer the question, *How can leaders more effectively motivate and manage groups of people working interdependently?* Unfortunately, this is only one of the questions relevant to today's teaming.

Though this focus is certainly useful at least some of the time, we contend that it has led many leaders to underemphasize the importance of individuals and subteams that make up overall teams. With only modest exceptions, the broad body of work on team leadership has yet to fully embrace this complexity of teaming.[7] Rather, many studies rely on older behavioral leadership frameworks—including task-based leadership (classically referred to as "initiating structure"), relationship-based leadership (referred to as "consideration"), and change-oriented leadership (referred to as "transformational")—that were developed before the widespread use of teams.[8] So when managers seek out best practices, whether in popular books or articles, they're likely to find incomplete, and sometimes even competing, messages.

What's the solution? As our book title suggests, we believe the answer is 3D Team Leadership; that is, you must be aware of and be able to focus on *all three dimensions of a team*—the individuals in a team, a team as a whole, and the subteams within an overall team—at the right time and in the right situation in order to maximize team effectiveness. Our model, rooted in both evidence and practice, not only explains how to overcome individual and subteam-centric problems to achieve optimal team performance but also how the individual and subteam dimensions can be leveraged for the good of a team as a whole in some circumstances. Of course, there's always a catch: our work suggests that it is difficult, if not impossible, for anyone to focus on all three dimensions simultaneously. And even if you could focus on all three entities, you'd run the risk of sending confusing messages. This is akin to the adage, "If you focus on everything, you're actually not focused on anything." The trick is knowing when, and then how, to focus on each of the team's major dimensions—and that's exactly what we're going to help you figure out in the remainder of this book.

Not surprisingly, we are not the first to wrestle with the idea that you might need to emphasize different dimensions at different times. In fact, this issue has been a problem in contemporary team leadership research for over half a century. We are, however, the first to explicitly integrate the most powerful theories and frameworks of team leadership into a simple yet prescriptive model suitable for leading today's most complex teams. Rest assured, this book's intent is not to describe every theory of team leadership in painstaking detail; our goal is to simply provide enough context for you to have a rich and immediately applicable perspective.

We'll start with one of the most fundamental team leadership perspectives: *functional team leadership*. Functional team leadership broadly suggests that team leaders' primary purpose is to make sure "that the group fulfills all critical functions necessary to its own maintenance and the accomplishment of its task."[9] Boiled down, leaders are most effective to the extent that they do whatever the team needs whenever the team needs it[10] (also referred to as a "leader as completer" approach).[11] Despite the unquestionable conceptual breadth of this theory for explaining why some leaders are more effective than others, its application often lacks the practical specificity needed to serve as a leadership "how-to" (some have even lamented that the theory can seem rather like the chicken and the egg—we don't know which leaders are functional until after we see the outcomes).[12] Nonetheless, understanding the general notion that a leader should seek to satisfy team needs provides a nice starting point for being an effective team leader.[13] The 3D Team Leadership model will give you the practical skills to diagnose and respond to your teams' many unique needs.

Though this may sound overly simplistic, most of the leaders with whom we have worked have typically been good at managing only one, or at most two, of the dimensions we describe. For example, some leaders are great at motivating teams as a whole, but they struggle as one-on-one coaches and mentors. Conversely, other leaders are great at getting the most out of their individual team members but stumble when trying to motivate the collective to reach higher levels of performance. Only in the rarest of situations have we found leaders who have demonstrated the awareness and skill to effectively manage the subteams within an overall team. To this end, the most common reaction of leaders is to fight like heck against subteam emergence, even though it can often be inevitable and, in some cases, even outright useful. Figure 2.1 illustrates the three dimensions of 3D Team Leadership: the individuals on a team, a team as a whole, and the subteams within an overall team.

A Team Is Not One Thing; It's Actually Three Things

Breaking down teams into multiple dimensions is not an entirely new idea. Over a quarter of a century ago, management consultant Larry Hirschhorn wrote *Managing in the New Team Environment: Skills, Tools, and Methods*[14] (the book was republished in 2002).[15] Perhaps not coincidentally, Hirschhorn's work emerged about the same time that teams started their mass infiltration into companies. During this time, many companies were enamored by the potential to increase productivity by shifting away from tall, hierarchical, bureaucratic structures to flatter, more agile ones. However, those who lived these events firsthand will remember that these transitions were often fraught

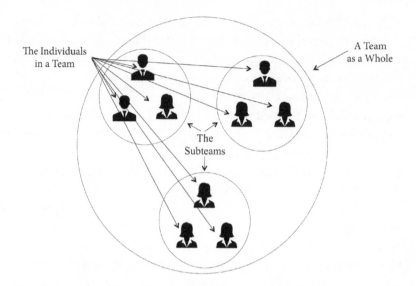

FIGURE 2.1. The Three Dimensions of 3D Team Leadership

with peril as many organizations encountered significant psychological and behavioral resistance on the part of employees *and* managers; the difficulty for both to understand new roles; and complications stemming from new systems, policies, and structures that were needed to accompany new organizational charts.[16]

Also important to note is that the shift toward team-based work was not always motivated by altruistic, synergy-seeking reasons. Transitions to teams were often subterfuge for cost cutting, meaning that many employees likely considered "teamwork" a synonym for more ominous concepts like "reengineering," "trimming the fat," and "cross-training," with the goal being that you could be replaced at some point by one of your teammates. As a result, teaming in companies was met with great cynicism from managers and employees alike during its formative years as a widely used organizational practice.

In an effort to clarify the benefits of teaming and help managers understand their new team leadership roles better, Hirschhorn conceived of a triangle of relationships inherent in all teams. Sitting at the three points of the triangle were (1) the leader of a team, (2) an entire team itself, and (3) various individuals on the team. He used the triangle to suggest that leaders must simultaneously manage two important relationships: a leader's relationship with his or her team as a whole and a leader's one-on-one relationship with each individual member. To be able to manage both types of relationships, he suggested, leaders needed "binocular vision."[17] Hirschhorn, however, had no way of conceiving what three decades of rapid change in business environments would mean for understanding how to manage not only two, but as we will argue, three different types of relationships in a team. Our approach builds on some of Hirschhorn's points, but it also features several fundamental differences—and we feel advancements—that are purposefully suited for teams in today's companies.

To begin, Hirschhorn's model considered teams as stable entities performing highly interdependent tasks over a lengthy period of time. As a result, leaders could work on cultivating these relationships slowly while worrying about only one team, or maybe two at the most. These relationships could be built primarily face-to-face, so leaders could have the benefit of richer communication by way of tone of voice, body language, and facial expressions. Although this *is* how many teams operated three decades ago, stability is now a distant remnant. Teams today are vastly more complex.

Hirschhorn did not incorporate the third type of relationship that we argue is crucial for today's teams: the leader's focus on, and relationships with, the various subteams contained within an overall team. In fairness, subteams are likely much more common now than they were several decades ago. For example, in today's environment in which employees often serve on numerous teams, they often use demographic, departmental, or even company overlap as a de facto identity marker, which can then create faultlines. You have to be especially mindful to manage harmful faultlines between members and be opportunistic about using subteams to complete smaller but still interdependent tasks on larger projects. In this sense, team leadership now extends beyond Hirschhorn's original vision of leading individuals and a team as a whole; that is, many team leaders today end up overseeing a large team system consisting of multiple, smaller teams within it.[18]

Next, Hirschhorn believed that leaders should balance their focus on their team as a whole and each individual on their teams. Although we agree that leaders should, in a general sense, be mindful of each of the dimensions within a team, the 3D Team Leadership model emphasizes optimization over mere balance in terms of allocating a leader's focus. Recall from Chapter 1 that we briefly introduced the premise that leaders have finite cognitive and physical resources that must be allocated efficiently in order to maximize their effectiveness. Based on this view, we believe that it is unreasonable for most leaders—and especially leaders who have already decided to invest their limited time to read a leadership book!—to ratchet up their efforts to focus on even more than they are currently.

If you're like Anna in Chapter 1, for instance, you do not have any more time or effort to give. Furthermore, it's possible that your team members are also maxed out in terms of devoting resources toward their work, so they'll appreciate your more focused direction as well. Assuming most motivated leaders are already giving near-maximum effort, asking them to spread their focus across multiple entities is a risky proposition. For example, what if efforts to increase your focus on one or two entities ended up reducing the attention toward the focal entity that your team needs the most? Then you really have a problem on your hands.

To be clear, we are not suggesting that your focus can be on only one dimension. Indeed, as we will detail much more in this book, you will want to allocate some of your resources to multiple foci when you are anticipating a transition from one interdependence level to another. Our point, rather, is that *the allocation of your leadership resources should match the ideal interdependence level of your team.* For instance, if your team is working on a simple task that requires low interdependence now but will eventually move to more complex tasks in the future, your focus might be 75 percent on individuals, 20 percent on your team as a whole, and 5 percent on the potential subteams within your overall team.

You might be thinking, *Why would I want to invest anything in subteams if I don't know for sure that'll ever use them?* Some of our own research addresses this question. While working on an extensive review of the factors that help teams perform proactively, we found evidence that leaders might be well suited to lay the basic groundwork for different types of behaviors even if they are not relevant at the moment.[19] In this sense, you can consider your leadership efforts like an investment portfolio, whereby even modest diversification can protect you from unexpected, albeit inevitable, changes in your team's task or environment.

Very much related to the above, your resources as a leader will vary as a function of your physical energy, demands from other parts of your job (e.g., you will have fewer resources available for leading your team when your boss asks you to turn around a massive presentation at the last minute), and myriad other factors. When your available resources are strained, the 3D Team Leadership model can help you choose from different leadership tactics. For example, if you have 30 minutes free in an afternoon, you might choose to conduct a single team meeting rather than two individual coaching sessions if your team is currently trying to complete a complex project. With that on the table, we now define and describe each of the three facets of 3D Team Leadership.

The "I's" in Teams

Many leaders have become so enamored with using teams to complete a variety of tasks and solve problems that they overemphasize the collective team to the detriment of the individuals in it. In this sense, common axioms like "we over me" and "there is no 'I' in team" can spur overly simplistic, impractical, and even dangerous corporate ideologies. There are several reasons why overlooking individuals can inflict undue harm to your team. At the most basic level, and as we alluded to in Chapter 1, many tasks are better suited for less interdependent groups of individuals versus highly interdependent teams. Artificially imposing teamwork principles on noninterdependent work can result in wasted time coordinating, avoidable interpersonal and task-related conflict, free riding or slacking, and countless other "process losses."[20] When a task is ill-suited for highly interdependent teamwork, leaders who focus too much on a team as a whole will likely do more harm than good.

At a deeper level, some evidence suggests that overemphasizing teamwork can even be oppressive to employees. For example, in an examination of self-managing work teams in the early 1990s,[21] researchers found that in contrast to what was expected based on popular wisdom—that self-managing work teams would provide individual team members with greater freedom and autonomy (and thus more motivation) compared to the prior, more bureaucratic structure the company had used—employees actually felt more constrained by a "form of control more powerful, less apparent, and more difficult to resist."[22] This type of oppression, referred to as "concertive control," comes from "a substantial consensus about values, high-level coordination, and a degree of self-management by members or workers in an organization."[23] Simply put, many team members who used to have one boss overseeing their work responsibilities now felt as if they had nine or ten bosses (their fellow team members) telling them what to do. As a consequence, team members felt suffocated rather than set free by the new, overemphasized role of team-based work.

Although the choice to implement self-managing work teams is sometimes a structural decision, these findings convey two important lessons for team leaders. First, by shifting too much responsibility to an overall team, some individual members will embrace, and even abuse, their newfound power. In reaction to these individuals ("the oppressors"), other members may strive to conform rather than offer divergent viewpoints that may add value to their team. As a leader, you thus play a critical role in protecting the value-adding potential of each individual member to your team's overall charter.

A second, and perhaps more intuitive, lesson is that placing too much focus on team goals, priorities, and accomplishments can cause individuals to feel overlooked and underappreciated. Speaking to this issue, a regional manager at a large energy services company told us:

> I just had this situation two weeks ago. We are allowed to give stock awards to select employees every year based on individual performance. After I made my award decisions, a guy came into my office very upset. He wanted to know why he didn't get an award this year. He reminded me that his team had been very successful, and he was actually right, but he still felt overlooked for his individual performance. So I had to admit that I completely focused on the success and goals of the team and overlooked the individuals in that team. I don't think I did any one-on-one coaching with that team; I was more focused on the whole team. After he calmed down, we ended up setting specific goals and objectives for the next year—the specific things he'd be evaluated on.

So despite the fact that his team did well, this particular team member still felt overlooked and underappreciated.

In a similar vein, a manager at a large high-tech company said:

> We had a situation with a relatively inexperienced manager who overrotated on all the team goals. People wanted to leave the team and not go the extra mile for that leader. It turns out that this guy was focused on business goals and not enough on the individuals in the team. There was a lack of people development, and he just ignored the balance between business and team goals and developing and coaching his people. I understand he was getting pressure from upper management to meet those goals, but he will never meet any of them by ignoring the needs and interests of the people in his team.

So what might account for leaders' tendency to minimize the "I's" in their team? The answer, not surprisingly, is multifaceted. One common explanation we've encountered is that some leaders hold a profound (and incorrect) belief that devoting attention to individual team members directly and unequivocally undermines the core principles of effective teaming. Speaking to this, our numerous interactions with managers suggest that many leaders not only place too much focus on their team as a whole, but do so quite proudly. Moreover, many of these same leaders also seem to believe that by openly promoting an exclusive team-first focus, they were strategically positioning themselves for promotions into higher levels of management, which is consistent with many organizations' focus on teams. For example, a vice president of sales and business development at a large energy company recalled a particular leader who

> let her preconceived notions of what the team should be get in the way of letting individuals shine. She was too disengaged, and even though she acted like she wanted input from the individual team members, in the end, you'd see the output, and she didn't take any member input into consideration. That particular leader was too busy managing upward to take time enough to build high-quality relationships, even though she was capable of doing it.

Unfortunately, leaders with this mind-set are not playing with a full deck, so to speak. As we saw in Chapter 1, they are failing to realize the complexity of a key paradox in teams: embracing individual differences while simultaneously emphasizing team identity and goals. The perpetuation of the myth that team leaders should have a near unwavering focus on a team as a whole (Hirschhorn's work excluded) is particularly curious. For instance, many team leaders also justify their company's emphasis on teamwork by saying things like, "Teams allow us to combine individuals with a diversity of viewpoints, ideas, experiences, and backgrounds," and, "Having unique individuals on a single team allows the whole to be greater than the sum of its parts." Indeed, research supports these arguments.[24] We agree. If there is no potential for a team to create synergy, there probably isn't even a need for a team; a group, or even a single individual, would probably do as well or even better. Thus, one of the most important ways you can help create the conditions for synergy to occur is to make sure individual inputs are surfaced, heard, integrated, and valued.[25]

Of course, other leaders fall short of embracing the individuals in their teams for nonideological reasons. Sometimes it might be because they have been rewarded or recognized for their team leadership focus in their current or previous company, particularly if their organization is overly enamored with teams. As a result, they have a lot of difficulty working against these past tendencies (i.e., practice makes permanent). Another reason is that they might lack the confidence, skills, or knowledge breadth to be effective one-on-one mentors, coaches, and sponsors. For example, a manager at a high-technology company told us, "I think personality matters to some extent. We have a lot of introverts in engineering, and they shy away from people. The tendency is to just get away in a closet somewhere; they're just not that interested in the one-on-one stuff. And these people are at least decent at team leadership, but the one-on-ones make them uncomfortable."

A managing counsel at a large energy company also highlighted cultural differences as a cause for mishandling the "I's" in his team:

> I lead a team located in South America, and all the team members are female and Latina. I'm a white male born and raised in Texas. The cultural identity is very different. So I can be very short in an e-mail, and that's not good. I need to add more nuanced language and be generally more careful about how I say something. When I'm talking with them one-on-one, I can't say "yes" or "no" directly. I need to be subtler. My skill set is still improving on this, but I think the key is willingness to learn and adapt.

A Team as a Whole

Although many leaders tend to overemphasize their team as a whole at the expense of individuals and subteams, it is not uncommon for us to observe and hear about leaders who largely neglect their overall team. In these cases, leaders generally treat their team as a collection of individuals and devote their time toward one-on-one coaching, mentoring, and sponsoring rather than trying to identify and solve team needs. They do not set team goals, establish strategic frameworks to guide their team's decision making, implement team bonuses, or design and monitor the amount of interdependence members use to complete tasks. In essence, they lead a "group" under the guise of a "team." For example, a vice president of business development for an energy company we worked with said:

> There was this manager I had in the past, and I worked for this guy for six months, and the whole time he didn't have even one team meeting. Other teams were having them at least once a week. He really struggled with managing the team; he didn't really do it at all, only individuals. And this was of no

benefit to our company because there was no synergy or sense of accomplishment. I don't think he was comfortable being a team leader.

Not surprisingly, employees quickly identify this as a sham and end up ignoring their manager's (or company's) toothless expectations to behave like a team; they know individual efforts are the valued currency to gain rewards and recognition and, consequently, continue to behave individualistically. Yet these practices compromise all of the potential benefits of actual teamwork: that teams can generate synergy. We suspect that some leaders fail to focus enough on their team as a whole for several reasons.

One of the biggest reasons stems from a lack of skill development. We highlight skill development here rather than knowledge deficiency or innate ability because most leaders we talked to in this category actually understand what they should be doing. In fact, although many leaders today have read books or attended executive education classes on team leadership, they still feel unnatural taking the necessary steps with their own teams. And some leaders, at an intuitive level, believe that focusing on the building blocks of their teams, the individuals, is more effective than working with the overall product. As an example, a senior director in a governmental agency with whom we worked said:

> Earlier in my career, I struggled a lot with doing all of the things I needed to do to use my team leadership skills effectively. I did okay with the individual team members. . . . We had systems in place for individual performance evaluations, management by objectives, training opportunities, and individual career paths. But I just couldn't wrap my head around doing much of this for the team as a whole. I mean, you can't promote an entire team, can you? And wouldn't individual members who might have worked harder during a particular period get upset if I gave a whole team a negative performance review? Over time, I've learned that these were excuses. . . . What I really couldn't admit at the time was, "I didn't know how to lead a team."

In addition to skill deficiencies, some leaders have deep-seated attitudes and values that explain their reluctance to focus on their team as a whole. Research on national culture, for instance, suggests that, on average, leaders from Western countries are more comfortable focusing on individuals, whereas leaders from Eastern and Latin American countries take a predominantly group-centric view (e.g., families, teams, country).[26] Given that these value-based dispositions are often instilled in us from an early age and are reinforced over time through rich traditions, they can be understandably hard to disentangle from leadership behaviors.

Beyond cultural differences, some managers also cited perceptions of generational differences as a possible cause. One employee, for example, noted:

> I had a team leader working for me who was from Generation X, and she was leading a team of all millennials. She hated the team thing—she didn't hold any team meetings or promote any teamwork at all. The only problem was that the millennials on her team seemed to love all that stuff. So they were pretty frustrated for a while. I finally encouraged her to pay more attention to team leadership. She eventually adapted pretty well, and things improved.

We hesitate to draw too many conclusions about the role of generational differences and team leadership, however. Wharton Business School professor Peter Capelli, one of the foremost thought leaders in HR, concluded that efforts to bridge generational gaps are often fruitless "time wasters,"[27] and, to his point, there is still a lot of controversy about the evidence for generational differences.[28] As one example, to assess generational differences, some researchers sent out surveys measuring things like values or attitudes; then they used respondents' ages to separate the data into categories like veterans (i.e., the Greatest Generation), baby boomers, Generation X, Generation Y (millennials), and now Generation Z (born 2000 and later, although we have seen some use 1996 as the cutoff between millennials and Gen Z). However, using age ranges to create the generational categories means that age and generation are confounded. Ideally, you would want to hold age constant by examining survey data from veterans when they were 25 years old, boomers when they were 25 years old, and so on. Then you could conclude that differences were in fact due to generation, not age.

That said, different generations of workers might have at least slightly different reactions to teamwork worth considering, presumably because they were raised at different times and in some cases have had dramatically different exposure to significant historical events (e.g., wars, economic depressions, technology changes). In one of the few studies that has provided a comprehensive review of the research evidence on generational differences and work attitudes, the results showed that Generation X, and especially Generation Y, are consistently higher in certain individualistic traits than previous generations.[29] Those who have witnessed millennials' (and Gen Z's) obsession with taking selfies with their phones would probably agree that they at least appear more narcissistic than previous generations.

If you took this information at face value, you would conclude that you should focus more on the "I's" in your teams at the expense of your over-all team if you are leading mostly millennials. However, other research has shown that age changes in narcissism are larger than generational changes, that is, narcissism decreases as people grow older; *translation*: children are selfish, but they tend to grow out of it.[30] The bottom line here is that although millennials do want to be recognized as individuals on their teams (ignore them at your own peril, because they will seek work elsewhere), growing up constantly exposed to teams in organized sports and in school means that they also value their place on a team and derive an important sense of mean-ing from being part of something bigger than themselves. Of course, using broad buckets like generations (or genders, cultures, ethnicities) to make assumptions about individuals' preferences or predispositions is always a risky proposition. There is still no substitute for getting to know your team members personally.

Subteams

Now we come to a key component of teams that is unique to our 3D Team Leadership model: subteams, or the smaller sets of team members contained within an overall team. As noted at the beginning of this chapter, individual team members frequently identify strongly with a smaller faction of their teammates. These groupings often occur naturally through social identity processes[31] and can serve as a key way for members to make sense of the team context; in some cases, they can even promote team learning behav-ior.[32] Members sometimes associate with others based on surface-level demo-graphics (e.g., age, race/ethnicity, gender), functional or geographic location (e.g., accountants versus information technology, North America versus Europe), or even deep-level belief systems (e.g., values). Less readily acknowl-edged, however, is that you as a leader can exert major influence on whether intrateam boundaries result in problematic faultlines or powerful subteams that boost overall team functioning.[33]

Subsets of members on many project teams are often constructed to carry out specific team tasks, especially when the size of the overall team gets really large. For example, on a software development team, two or three members might work interdependently to write a certain section of code. Concurrently, another two or three members might be charged with testing and debugging that code (and so on). The best leaders are aware of their various subteams and understand that they must pay attention to multiple sets of relationships, such as the ones members have with one another within each subteam and those between each of their subteams.

Sounds complicated, doesn't it? Well, it is. In fact, a team composed of multiple subteams represents a more complicated level of interdependence than even a highly interdependent overall team. We refer to this more intense level of interdependence as *multilayered interdependence* because, as a leader, you will need to attend to layer upon layer of different types of interdependence. For example, within each specific subteam, members work interdependently with one another (very much like a small overall team), which we call *within-subteam interdependence*. However, at some point, subteams typically have to coordinate their efforts and work interdependently with the other subteams, which we call *between-subteam interdependence*. Finally, there is the interdependence that connects an overall team (composed of the various subteams) to its external environment, or what we call *across-subteam interdependence*. We hope that it is apparent by now why we refer to this as *multilayered* interdependence!

To be sure, if the subteams are relatively small and unlikely to have their own subteam leaders, then it will be your responsibility as the overall team leader to manage all of these different sets of relationships (within, between, and across subteams). As subteams become larger, however, they may be more likely to have actual subteam leaders (these can be formally identified or emerge on a de facto basis, though overall team leaders must be wary of the latter). To maximize your effectiveness, you will likely be relying more on each subteam's leadership to manage the relationships between individuals within each subteam, which will then allow you to focus more on the relationships between and across the subteams. That does, however, introduce another layer of management, which can create problematic coordination and communication issues.

Importantly, you should be proactive in establishing subteams ahead of appropriate tasks based on factors like members' knowledge, skills, and abilities. Be wary of trusting members to divide up on their own, as they will often choose to do so based on nonsubstantive differences. Although harmful divides between members must always be a concern, knowing when to focus on and use subteams often requires you to have a core understanding of your team's life cycle stage. And, similar to our points regarding the other two dimensions, you must also be careful not to focus on subteams so much that they usurp the priorities of your team as a whole or cause individual team members to feel overlooked.

High-tech industries, especially those that focus on software development and project-based information technology, have made significant strides in understanding how to best use subteams. As an example, consider the following description of teaming from a senior engineering manager at a large technology firm:

> We use an Agile model [an approach to project management that uses flexible and iterative, rather than sequential and lockstep, phases] for many of our teams, and those teams definitely have subteams. We call those subteams "sprint teams," and they meet daily in what we call "stand-up meetings." In this process, team leaders have to let the subteams do their thing; they have to be empowered. In the old days, leaders could be more directive, but it's much more complicated now. When you have multiple subteams, as a leader you have to worry about one subteam doing something the other subteam is not aware of. You have to have the right balance of communication, and it's a leader's job to put the right mechanisms in place to make sure there is enough coordination between the subteams. It's always hard to find the right level of communication; you don't want too much, but you don't want too little either. Our Agile sprint teams have five to nine members, so things can get complicated pretty quickly. It's all about empowerment now. You might have sprint teams where you communicate the overall goals, but the authority and responsibility has got to be with those teams.

A vice president of business development at an energy company echoed this and said, "It's all about two things: empowerment and communication. When you lead an overall team, you might have time for less empowerment, but when subteams are formed, you have to empower! And with communication, you need constant feedback. When subteams go off track, you need to have your finger on the pulse to get them back on track."

As the examples illustrate, focusing too much on the individuals on a team or a team as a whole can harm the potential for team success because some of that potential rests with subteams working effectively within an overall team. Related, both people we quoted commented on the need for leaders to empower their followers, and the subteams specifically, to ensure success.

Managing a traditional team is hard enough, but throw in several subteams and you've got an entire complex system of potential problems and multilayered interdependence to consider. It would be difficult—okay, impossible—for you to do it all by yourself. Subteams must be empowered to resolve their own issues and find the best ways for the entire team to be successful. The best leaders just facilitate that process.

The leaders with whom we have worked struggle with subteams for numerous reasons. The most obvious and common reason, based on our evidence and observations, is that providing direct, explicit leadership focus to subteams within an overall team is a relatively new concept—and probably a counterintuitive one too. Although work has gotten more and more complex over the past several decades and, coincidentally, team membership has grown and spans more boundaries than ever before, leaders often have not had any specialized training on the unique needs of subteam leadership. Thus, they lack the awareness and skills needed to lead complex multisubteam systems and consequently mismanage or altogether neglect subteams.

A senior manager's experience summed this problem up well:

> I had a manager who was very technical, and he was charged with leading four remote subteams, and each subteam had a different way of doing things. He could never seem to bring the subteams together to get any type of common process or alignment. He didn't spend time with off-sites, and he didn't bring people from the different subteams together at all. He had great technical skills, but he just seemed lost with the subteam leadership. He eventually left the company.

Even when leaders are willing to acknowledge the existence of meaningful subteams, they are not always willing to provide leadership to them. The reasons for this unwillingness vary. Some leaders may be fearful of acknowledging that different subteams are operating because they think doing so will somehow compromise the overall goals of their team; others may be overwhelmed by the prospect of managing multiple subteams (again, this is complex!); and finally, some leaders may become disinterested, or "lose a little steam," when thinking about subteams and the granular, detailed work best suited for such arrangements. For example, a vice president of sales and business development at a large energy firm told us, "Sometimes leaders seem to forget they have subteams. They lack the passion for the subteams' work. They forget they have to integrate with other subteams to tie it all together. I almost think leaders become disinterested and unwilling to manage the subteams because if they get too far down into the subteams, they will lose their passion and lose sight of the overall team goals."

An important point here is that nearly all teams are susceptible to divides between members,[34] regardless of whether their leaders care to acknowledge such factions. However, only the best leaders realize that they play critical roles in managing and leveraging these divides for the betterment of their teams. We next discuss how the material in this book can be applied to teams that feature shared leadership in addition to a single, formal leader.

Using 3D Team Leadership in a Shared Leadership Environment

The idea of leadership coming only from one individual is not always an accurate reflection of how team leadership really works, especially in today's environment. Indeed, as we briefly mentioned in Chapter 1 when discussing the tensions of team leadership, the concept of shared leadership has grown in importance and popularity. Shared leadership on a team exists when leadership behaviors emerge from various team members at different points along a team's life cycle.[35] Shared leadership is critical in today's teams because (1) rarely can a single person handle all of the leadership responsibilities in a VUCA environment, (2) knowledge teams are typically staffed by people with high levels of expertise who are usually eager to take on leadership responsibilities, and (3) flatter organizational structures necessitate leadership emerging more so from within teams rather than from a formal leader nested in a traditional hierarchy.[36]

Our 3D Team Leadership model can be applied to teaming environments with high levels of shared leadership just as well as it can be applied to teams with a single, formal leader. The major difference is that leadership activities and behaviors have to be coordinated among those carrying out different leadership responsibilities. And these activities and behaviors can be broken up and assigned in many different ways, perhaps based on individual leader strengths or a team's task requirements.

One of the teams we worked with in the energy industry used our model in a team with a great deal of shared leadership. Greg, the formal team leader, described it this way:

In our company, management really wants us to focus on grooming team members to become team leaders and executives. In fact, we have a lot more junior folks that have joined the company in the last ten years due to technology breakthroughs and new opportunities. But the problem is that there is a gap between all of those relatively new people and the more senior folks we have. There really aren't that many people in the middle. We have a kind of "two-hump camel" distribution when it comes to seniority. We in the industry refer to grooming these younger folks to replace the more senior ones as the great "crew change."

One way to develop the junior people faster is to throw a lot of leadership challenges at them quickly. But we do this in teams so they also have a lot of support from their team members and also their other leaders and mentors. So, in one of the teams I lead, I put Erin in charge of doing all the team leadership stuff we need, like team building, team coaching, setting team goals, and so on. I've gotten feedback on my performance reviews in the past that I'm great at leading individual employees, but I struggle with doing the same things for my team. So having Erin take on the team leadership role serves two purposes. One, it helps to overcome my challenges when it comes to leading teams. Erin can do it much better than I can. And, two, it gives Erin a chance to develop her leadership skills much more quickly than if I tried to provide all the leadership. It's working really well breaking it up this way.

Thus, sharing some of the responsibilities inherent in the 3D Team Leadership model can serve to both play to the strengths of each individual and help to develop other members.

There are, of course, challenges that occur when using the 3D Team Leadership model in a shared leadership fashion. Greg talked about these challenges:

When I first started asking Erin to take on more and more team leadership responsibilities, we got our wires crossed quite a bit. I don't think we spent enough time up front discussing exactly what leadership responsibilities were hers and which ones were mine. We had an agreement at the beginning that I would focus on individual motivation and leadership, and she would focus on team motivation and leadership. But the problem is the differences are not always clear-cut. For example, sometimes she would do a lot of one-on-one mentoring and occasionally some mentoring for the subteams. And then I would do the same thing only to find out that she had provided slightly different direction and advice. So, it wasn't that Erin shouldn't have been doing the one-on-one stuff ever; it was more about her coming back to me at some point and saying, "Hey, I gave some advice to Brent that I thought you should know about just in case it comes up in your discussions with him." Not doing that caused some real headaches in the beginning. So I would strongly advise anyone wanting to use 3D Team Leadership in this kind of a situation, you better make sure that you are constantly communicating and coordinating with those people in the team taking on leadership responsibilities. Otherwise, you're in for a lot of unnecessary confusion. Believe me, I lived it.

Greg's experience suggests that 3D Team Leadership can be effectively used with teams that practice shared leadership just as well as it can with a single, formal leader of teams. The main concern with shared leadership, however, is the amount of coordination needed between leaders. This, of course, is a known challenge inherent to shared leadership that extends well beyond our 3D Team Leadership model. Indeed, shared leadership does add an extra layer of complexity to our model, but again the advantages are that you don't have to do all the leadership tasks for your team (a frequent necessity in VUCA environments). Team members can develop leadership skills and abilities while they are team members, not just when they are formally appointed to leadership positions. Our energy companies refer to the latter advantage as "keeping the leadership pipeline full." Even if your team relies on shared leadership, you as an individual can help guide some of the critical coordination and communication functions with your newfound 3D Team Leadership skills.

Before moving on, we briefly describe how each of the next three chapters lays out the fundamental building blocks of 3D Team Leadership: the individuals in a team, a team as a whole, and the subteams within an overall team.

The Building Blocks of 3D Team Leadership

So far, you have learned that the most successful team leaders are those who know when and how to effectively manage the three dimensions inherent in most team environments: individuals, a team as a whole, and subteams. We have also discussed that most of the team leaders with whom we have worked are adept at managing only one, sometimes two, but rarely all three of the dimensions well. Instead, they typically have a "go-to" style that they use in just about any situation, especially when they are under pressure and time constrained. In today's teaming environment, that's a recipe for disaster.

What you will learn next in Chapters 3, 4, and 5 are the practical, action-oriented team leadership skills for leading each dimension of your team. Chapter 3 provides a step-by-step guide for how to motivate and lead individuals in team contexts. Team contexts bring their own unique set of conditions and challenges, even if you are focused on primarily leading and motivating individuals. For those who tend to focus insufficient attention on their team as a whole, Chapter 4 is key. If you need to learn more about how to effectively lead subteams or just want to better understand their nuances, pay particular attention to Chapter 5.

Something else important to remember when seeking out the most helpful parts of this book to fit your specific situation is, again, knowing what you are leading. For example, if you are leading what is generally recognized as a stable, ongoing group—that is, a collection of people who learn from one another and share ideas but are not interdependent and are not working toward a shared goal—then Chapter 3 can help. If you are charged with leading what is generally recognized as an ongoing team with higher levels of interdependence, the leadership actions described in Chapter 4 will equip you to do your job better over the long haul. If you are leading what is generally recognized as an ongoing team with multiple subteams that display multilayered interdependence, Chapter 5 provides an essential how-to guide.

However, many of you are or will be leading teams that make transitions over time: from individuals to teams to subteams in an unpredictable fashion. Our advice is to familiarize yourself with all of the material and recommendations in Chapters 3, 4, and 5. Something else to remember before reading these chapters is that a team's members will not always pick the right level of interdependence on their own. It is not uncommon, for instance, for members of virtual teams to defer to mostly individual-based arrangements because it is easier than trying to communicate across multiple time zones. Unfortunately, this means that members and their teams lose out on the potential benefits that come from collaboration—which is the very reason we use virtual teams in the first place.

On the flip side, members of some teams prefer to work in highly interdependent arrangements because they enjoy the relationships they have with one another. However, when tasks are relatively straightforward, these teams often fail to outperform standard groups of individuals because they spend more time socializing and overthinking or discussing than actual work. Thus, one of the key leadership functions is *to identify which type of interdependence enables the team to optimally accomplish its mission at any given time (i.e., from low to high to multilayered).* After identifying the proper arrangement, you can then shift your focus and, when necessary, make team design changes by, for example, establishing formal reporting guidelines or assigning specific individual roles to members.

The process of identifying the appropriate level of interdependence is multifaceted. You need to rely on your own judgment and expertise, of course, but you must also probe for your team's pulse, which can come from directly soliciting member feedback or making more indirect assessments of the team's performance (e.g., monitoring member attitudes, benchmarking against other teams). At a base level, you should aim to understand the complexity of your team's current task when deciding on an optimal interdependence arrangement, with higher levels of complexity typically dictating more highly interdependent arrangements.[37] Once the level of task complexity is gauged, you can then choose how you will structure and incentivize your team's work. We'll provide you with some common, telltale signs to look for in the following chapters that will help you diagnose your situation. As we have discussed in this chapter, focusing on different dimensions—individuals, a team as a whole, and subteams within an overall team—can reinforce the optimal work flow arrangement and thus contribute to superior team performance.

Finally, different teams might vary on their optimal interdependence arrangement *even if they are assigned the exact same tasks.*[38] For example, when a team has one or more experts in a particular domain, they may work most efficiently by assigning relatively independent tasks to the experts rather than working in a collaborative fashion.[39] However, when a team doesn't enjoy a particular expertise in a domain of interest, its members may need to work together intensively so that they can evaluate and discuss the merits of multiple solutions. Very much related to this point, teams can also learn over time, meaning that a task that is considered complex at an early performance episode may eventually become routine as it gets repeated in later episodes.[40] Thus, determining the level of interdependence that is appropriate for your team involves more than just diagnosing the characteristics of a particular task in isolation; it also requires that you account for the knowledge, skills, and abilities of your team members in your team's current state.

As you read Chapters 3, 4, and 5, we ask that you assess yourself on each of the behaviors and skills discussed in these chapters. Eventually we hope you will use a multirater feedback system with the measures found in Chapter 10 to do a more formal assessment of your 3D Team Leadership competencies. As you read each chapter, ask yourself: How well do I perform these behaviors? Am I paying enough attention to each dimension in my leadership of teams? Do I change my focus on the different dimensions as my team's needs change, or do I tend to stick with a singular focus no matter the situation? Am I flexible enough to be a true 3D team leader?

Be honest with yourself and, if necessary, embrace the discomfort. Indeed, no learning or growth will occur in your leadership repertoire if you are not truthful about the various leadership approaches and behaviors described in the rest of this book. Our hope is that you will soon be viewing your team in 3D and reaping all the satisfaction that comes from harnessing the power and beauty of great teamwork.

3 The First Dimension: The "I's" in Teams

"THERE'S NO 'I' IN TEAM." "YOU'RE NOT A TEAM PLAYER." Sound familiar? Chances are, you've heard—and maybe even said—phrases like this before. Innocently enough, they insinuate that a focus on individual interests always comes at the expense of some important team outcome. Yet this mind-set often reflects an oversimplified, and frankly unrealistic, view of teaming today. Indeed, our extensive research, interviews, and consulting experiences confirm that a singular focus on a team over individuals can be a perilous leadership strategy.

Unfortunately, these strategies are everywhere in companies and are often viewed as gospel. They operate at an almost subconscious level and guide leaders' actions, symbolic behavior, what they say, and approaches to processing information and viewing problems. So what's wrong with these practices? Two things. First, as we described in Chapter 1 (remember Amy, our young high-potential leader at the insurance company), not all tasks are suited for teamwork. As the great teams scholar Richard Hackman was fond of saying, "So far as I know, not a single great novel, epic poem or symphonic score has ever been written by a team."[1]

Second, neglecting the individuals on a team can result in members feeling insecure (what is often referred to as psychologically unsafe)[2] and mentally withdrawing from their jobs.[3] Ultimately this can have compounding costs. Evidence suggests that many employees silently quit—in terms of speaking up and being engaged—well before they actually leave their job.[4] Because people often have numerous roles on a lot of teams and must constantly shift their priorities from one team outcome to another, all while trying to demonstrate their own individual value so that they can enjoy a successful career, these concerns are likely more important today than they have ever been. Thus, even seemingly harmless "we-over-me" leadership approaches, like throwing around the phrases at the start of this chapter any time individualism emerges, can hurt your unit's effectiveness.

Why do some leaders believe that the needs and interests of individuals on a team should unequivocally be sacrificed for team interests? There are many explanations, of course, but we have observed three recurring reasons. First, many of us (academics, managers, students) simply take it for granted that teams should take precedence over individuals. Maybe we're just uncomfortable acknowledging that individual contributions play such a big part in our everyday lives. Doing things for the "good of the team" or "sacrificing self-interest in the name of teams" is a way of life at work today. To be sure, there are many instances when a team should take priority over individuals; again, we're just saying it shouldn't be this way all of the time.

Second, and related to the first reason, is a belief in the widely regarded myth that focusing on a team over individuals promotes fairness and important developmental stages of a team. Yet failing to differentiate among individuals can hinder team success and can be perceived as unfair to top-performing members. Of course, as we discuss later in this chapter, focusing on individuals is a nuanced practice with some slippery slopes too.

Finally, many leaders are uncomfortable having difficult conversations with individuals and struggle to manage conflict and reconcile differences between members. Indeed, the most common form of handling conflict in many organizations is avoidance: "If I pretend it's not there, hopefully it will just go away." To this end, telling someone that he or she is "not a team player" is often used as an ineffective substitute for active conflict management.[5] Well-managed team conflict, however, can sometimes serve as a starting point for the kind of breakthrough thinking that separates the best teams from the rest. In this light, fully engaging individual team members and embracing their unique ideas is vital for tapping into the upside of teaming.

In the remainder of this chapter, we provide practical advice for leading individuals in team contexts. As we said in the previous chapter, the words *in team contexts* are not accidental. For example, working in teams, even those with relatively low levels of interdependence, gives members plenty of opportunities to observe or hear accounts of how you interact with your other team members. As much of the research on motivation shows, people tend to compare themselves with others to figure out their relationship with you, and then they form judgments about how fairly you are treating them.[6] Thus, it behooves you to think about your actions and behaviors toward each of the "I's" on your teams in order to build highly effective and productive teams as a whole.

Focusing on the "I's in teams takes precedence over a team as a whole in two types of situations. First, individuals should be the primary focus in an ongoing team with relatively low levels of interdependence—or, more accurately, a group. Importantly, we are assuming here that the level of interdependence is relatively stable whereby the group will not eventually change into a team. Recall that many organizations refer to groups as "teams" because the term is popular and "sounds right." However, leading a group as if it were a team creates all sorts of confusion among members and, depending on the nature of the task, often results in inferior performance.

The second situation in which a focus on the "I's" in teams takes precedence over a team as a whole is when a team follows some sort of life cycle and a particular stage in that life cycle calls for more independent, group-like work (not uncommon in teams that use multiple stages or phases, like software development teams). Note that this is very different from the situation we just described: an ongoing group with relatively stable, low levels of interdependence. In that situation, you need to identify that you have a group and then adjust your behaviors to focus primarily on the "I's" in your group. However, leading an entity that switches between groups and teams is more complicated. You will need to know, at any given time, exactly what you are leading. Once identified, you will need to switch your focus[7] to the individual dimension as the situation calls for it and initiate team design changes and coach individuals to a greater extent than your team as a whole. This, of course, requires you to engage in meaningful reflection and forethought.

Best Practices for Leading and Motivating the "I's" in Team Contexts

Although research on leading and motivating individuals has been accumulating for well over 100 years, what we offer here is a focused, hands-on set of practices for leading and motivating individuals in team contexts. We'll cover topics related to both intrinsic and extrinsic motivation. Intrinsic motivation is basically what the term suggests—motivation that comes from within individuals. It is driven primarily by an individual's interest in or passion for the work itself and therefore is not based on drivers outside the person, like money or a promotion. And although you cannot directly cause individuals to be intrinsically motivated (after all, it comes from within), you can create the conditions under which they experience an internal fulfillment in carrying out valued tasks.

In contrast, extrinsic motivation consists of motivation that comes from outside an individual. Such motivators could include things like pay raises or bonuses, opportunities for promotion, competition, external praise, and even negative sources like fear of punishment or criticism from others. Unlike intrinsic motivators, extrinsic motivators tend to have shorter-term, less permanent effects. As David Russo, former head of human resources at the SAS Institute located in Cary, North Carolina (a repeat winner of *Fortune* magazine's best places to work in the United States), once said, "A raise is only a raise for thirty days. After that, it's just somebody's salary."[8] Although extrinsic rewards tend to have shorter-term effects and sometimes get a bad rap, make no mistake, they are still highly important in companies. Speaking to this point, a report by the Society of Human Resource Management noted that employee pay was the number one driver of employee satisfaction,[9] which is of course related to motivation.

The relationship between extrinsic and intrinsic rewards can be complicated, so we cannot just tell you about all the potential levers to pull—both intrinsic and extrinsic—and turn you loose on your team. For instance, some evidence suggests that adding extrinsic rewards to a task that people already find highly intrinsically motivating can actually end up undermining their intrinsic motivation.[10] The overall evidence, however, shows that intrinsic and extrinsic rewards go hand in hand to produce high levels of individual motivation as long as they are aligned toward promoting the same goals.

In the following sections, we discuss how each of these concepts, to some extent, can be used to effectively motivate the "I's" in your teams and thus improve overall team performance. One important point, however, is that we focus more on intrinsic than extrinsic techniques due to their longer-lasting and generally more powerful effects on performance. We believe this approach is appropriate for several reasons: (1) employees today are expressing a strong desire for meaningfulness in their work, an intrinsic facet; (2) you may not always have the formal power to change extrinsic reward systems easily; and (3) teams often move through different tasks and life cycles so fast that trying to change extrinsic reward systems quickly enough is impractical, if not impossible.

Empowerment Really Is the Gold Standard of Individual Intrinsic Motivation

Prior evidence, including some of our own research, clearly supports the notion that empowerment is one of the best intrinsic motivators for individuals. But we can guess what you might be thinking: *Here we go again—more talk on the greatness of empowering your employees even though, in reality, it often doesn't work.* We get it. Just the word *empowerment* can cause cynical reactions in a lot of the companies with which we work, and rightly so. There are so many examples of failed empowerment experiments that it's no wonder many leaders just aren't open to the idea, and even if they do practice it in some way, they avoid the use of the word altogether to reduce others' skepticism.

What are some of the roots of the cynicism directed toward empowerment? At its base, there is a lot of confusion about what *empowerment* really means. Is it a feeling? An experience? A structure? A set of leadership behaviors? If this were a multiple-choice test, the answer would be "all of the above" (and more). Empowerment, in practice, is complex. For our purposes, we will define it using the most widely accepted and evidence-based definition that exists today. In essence, we'll separate the wheat from the chaff and get to the heart of what empowerment really represents: a powerful form of intrinsic motivation.

Another reason empowerment invites a great deal of suspicion in companies is that even if everyone agrees on a definition, plans are often so poorly implemented that they're doomed from the start. An effective empowerment program requires a lot of hard work upfront, and some leaders are often, sadly, either unable or unwilling to put in the work that would make it successful. For example, some leaders are unwilling to empower their employees for fear of letting go (they might have a high need for control or need for power complex, of sorts). They think, *If my individual performance is going to be judged by the performance of this team, then by gosh, I'm going to have my hand in as much of the process as I can!* At the opposite end of the spectrum are leaders who have better intentions but fail to do the hard work up front to empower individuals; instead, they set their team members out to wander in the wilderness. Our colleagues Tanya Menon and Leigh Thompson call this type of laissez-faire approach to leadership "macromanagement" (*read*: hide in your office and avoid your people), the opposite of micromanagement. Both are disastrous for empowerment.[11]

Unfortunately, there is a fine line between empowering leaders and those who are more laissez-faire that often goes unseen.[12] Richard Hackman gave a fitting example for how leaders should think about sharing their authority when he said: "It is entirely proper for senior leaders to say, in effect, 'This is the mountain we will climb. Not that one, this one. Although many aspects of our collective endeavor are open for discussion, choice of mountain is not among them.'"[13] Thus, just because you are an empowering leader does not mean you will relinquish your instrumental role in helping the individuals on your team succeed; you will keep them focused on the mission, proactively make changes and suggestions, and more generally keep a pulse on what individual team member needs should be met.

So, to be clear, empowering leadership is not easy. You must be prepared for and willing to accept that your team members may choose to do things differently than you would have done yourself. The trade-off, however, is that when they're empowered to do it their way, they'll work harder, longer, and with more conviction. Another benefit of empowerment is that it will allow you to focus more intently on bigger-picture leadership functions while your team members work through the complex, and at times chaotic, nature of today's tasks. In this sense, empowering your followers is one of the most efficient ways to maximize your limited resources. When it is done correctly, your empowered team members will amaze you by how much they can accomplish.

The influential business writer Ken Blanchard's aptly named book *Empowerment Takes More Than a Minute*[14] (published almost fifteen years after the best-selling *The One Minute Manager*[15]) is a testament to the importance of working hard at empowerment. Making sure empowerment programs work properly takes way more than a minute! We next provide an evidence-based approach for empowering the "I's" in team contexts, and we start by providing a clear definition of empowerment.

Why Are People Still Confused about What Empowering Individuals Really Means?

When we ask our executives to provide a definition of *empowerment*, we hear about as many definitions as the number of people we ask. And as we noted already, some people are fairly cynical about empowerment. The most common definition of empowerment we hear is *to transfer power from leaders to those around them.* After all, the word *power* is in the word "em*power*ment" itself. This definition suggests that a leader loses power so that other individuals may gain it. There are two problems with this view. First, the definition is overly narrow. As you will see, the term means a great deal more than one person giving another more power. Second, this definition also assumes that empowerment is a zero-sum game or some sort of fixed pie: if you give someone else more power, by definition, you must lose power. However, the evidence shows just the opposite: by empowering others to tackle more ambitious challenges, you will be freed up to take on more of the actual leadership responsibilities of your role rather than doing others' work for them. In other words, giving up some power can, paradoxically, make you more powerful than you ever thought possible.

The evidence-based definition of empowerment we use implies that people have perceptions and judgments about the tasks they perform and the work they do. These judgments, in turn, determine how intrinsically motivated they feel. Importantly, people make judgments about four distinct aspects of their work:

- How much *choice* they have over what they do
- The degree of *impact* their work has on others around them and their company
- The level of *competence* they experience when performing their tasks
- The extent to which they feel a sense of *meaningfulness* when working

Figure 3.1 shows the four dimensions of individual empowerment. Note that these dimensions combine to create individual empowerment, but they also themselves are mutually reinforcing (e.g., increasing choice also increases impact).

The first dimension of empowerment is *choice*, defined as the extent to which people have self-determination or control over carrying out their work.[16] Although empowerment does not equate solely to choice, this is the

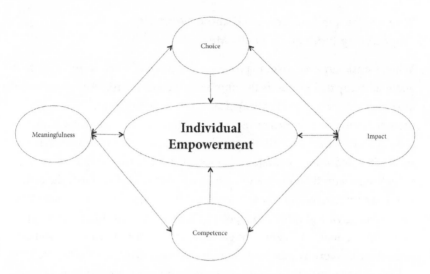

FIGURE 3.1. The Dimensions of Individual Empowerment

dimension that is most commonly associated with empowerment. In fact, some people use the terms *empowerment* and *choice/autonomy* interchangeably. This is a big mistake. Giving someone a great deal of choice over a meaningless task with little or no impact in which a person feels very incompetent does not constitute an effective empowerment experience. People need more than power to be truly empowered. Despite this, the role of choice is not to be underestimated in any empowerment effort.

The second dimension is *impact*, or the extent to which a person's work is perceived as making a difference in a company.[17] People typically want to feel that what they do matters at work. The key here, then, is feedback: people need clear information on their work's level of impact within a company. We have probably all experienced times in our working lives when we felt as though we were doing fairly mundane, routine tasks that lack a sense of impact in our companies and, consequently, for ourselves. Of course, all of us still do some of these tasks from time to time. However, we have all also probably experienced the opposite: when we perform tasks that really matter, we can stand back and truly see the results of all of our hard work. There is a high degree of intrinsic satisfaction in that.

The third dimension is *competence*, or the extent to which people can carry out their work skillfully when they attempt to do so.[18] We can all think of times when we did not feel competent in certain tasks we attempted. In fact, that's why neither of us plays golf—too much consistent incompetence on display! A low level of perceived competence typically results in an aversion to taking on tasks we do not feel we can do well. And by avoiding certain tasks, we never really get to even attempt to develop competence at them. In contrast, a high level of perceived competence is usually associated with proactivity, high levels of effort, and persistence in the face of obstacles.[19] Thus, experiencing competence is a direct precursor to feelings of intrinsic motivation.

The last dimension is *meaningfulness*, or the extent to which people care, on an intrinsic level, about the work they do.[20] Of all four dimensions of empowerment, this one is the easiest to spot. When people are performing activities that are meaningful to them, they exhibit many visible clues. Everything from their facial expressions, body language, the excitement with which they talk about their ideas, and their interactions with others communicates meaning. When people do intrinsically meaningful work, they typically do not need any other source of motivation. They often perform at extraordinarily high levels of effort and persistence, even in the face of seemingly insurmountable obstacles, and have a greater sense of well-being and happiness than those doing less meaningful work. In fact, a comprehensive study of motivation found that above all other factors, meaningfulness was the most powerful force linking how work is designed (discussed below) to important outcomes like performance and job satisfaction.[21] And today's employees are seeking meaning in their work more than ever before.

Reality or Hype: What Does the Evidence Say about the Benefits of Empowering Others?

You don't simply have to take our word for it that empowering individuals in team contexts works. The evidence is in regarding the effectiveness of these four dimensions of empowerment in producing valuable outcomes for leaders and individuals, and it's overwhelmingly positive. A comprehensive analysis of almost 150 research studies across a variety of industries, occupations, and geographic regions demonstrated that people who are more empowered are more satisfied with their jobs, more committed to their companies, feel less strained, and are less inclined to quit. Empowered individuals also exhibit better job performance, are more innovative, and make better organizational citizens (they act in ways that go above and beyond their formally required job duties).[22] So although we do have some anecdotal evidence that empowerment programs sometimes fail to live up to their originally intended objectives,[23] when implemented correctly, *empowerment works* in today's companies that value innovation, creativity, proactivity, and an entrepreneurial mind-set.

What Leader Behaviors Are Critical for Empowering Individuals in Teams?

By now it should be clear that you should be very interested in empowering the individuals you manage on your teams because empowered employees have superior performance as well as a healthy set of other work-related behaviors and attitudes. Now you're probably wondering: What should you actually do to get your employees to experience high levels of individual empowerment? If empowerment is really all about intrinsic motivation—something that you cannot actually directly affect—how do you set the stage so that employee empowerment actually occurs? There are three main ways that you can accomplish this goal: (1) displaying empowering leader *behavior*, (2) creating empowering *structures and systems*, and (3) building high-quality empowering *relationships*.

Five Ways to Display Your Empowering Leader Behavior

You can behave in certain ways that help lay the foundation for individuals to experience empowerment. Almost two decades ago, we developed a measure of empowering leader behavior and examined it in several different companies. We found that people who had more empowering leaders actually felt more empowered, and ultimately, these employees were more productive and were happier with their jobs.[24] We have included this measure in Chapter 10 so that you can assess your own empowering leader behavior or, better yet, have people around you assess your behavior. Shortly after we developed our measure, other researchers independently developed another measure of empowering leader behavior and examined it in a variety of companies.[25] Both evidence-based approaches agree that five leader behaviors are critical for increasing the level of individual empowerment in organizations.[26] Although we originally intended these measures of leader behavior to be applied to teams as a whole, they have also been shown to be applicable to individuals in team settings.[27]

The first behavior is *role modeling*, or leading by example. If you've been formally appointed to a leadership role or just organically fell into it, and especially if you rightfully earned that position through superior performance, your team members will probably be looking to you for clues about how they should behave. Don't underestimate that opportunity. We spoke about this topic with a senior director for digital strategy and transformation in a high-technology company with whom we worked. This director believes in the power of role modeling the empowerment behavior he expects from his individual team members. He provided the following example:

> Just today, in fact, I set out to go and meet with the chief digital officer of our company. I didn't ask my boss for permission, but I did let him know I was going to do it. I share stories like this with my people, and I tell them how much I appreciate the fact that my boss lets me do this. If you want to go and talk to senior people, go do it! Every now and again, somebody will mess this up and look like an idiot, but that's okay too. Of course, you're then going to get a lot of coaching. I expect people to own their s—t. If it goes well, great; if it doesn't, you still own it. I want to be 100 percent consistent with this.

This director's anecdote demonstrates several key aspects of role modeling. For one, leading by example automatically entails that you display the desired behaviors yourself. When he took action to speak with his company's chief digital officer, he was clearly acting out the empowerment behaviors he wanted to see from his own team members. Second, sharing empowerment stories is important. Actions speak louder than words, for sure, but that doesn't mean you should avoid sharing your experiences in ways that help employees draw connections. By verbally relating his own experience, this director ensured that his team members not only knew about the experience but also understood how they could take similar action. And third, an emphasis on *consistent* role modeling of desired behaviors can help you show members you are serious about empowerment. Thus, leading by example can be a powerful way to set the conditions for greater individual empowerment.

The second behavior is *encouraging and allowing individuals to participate in decision making*.[28] Another leader at a high-technology organization discussed the way in which he allowed one of his team members to be more active in decision making:

> I have a team member who used to be an analyst, but she wanted to be more strategy oriented. So I started bringing her into more conversations about

strategy. And I invited her to challenge me. I told her that you need to be willing to argue with the boss. But from my perspective, it takes a leader who has a certain level of self-confidence and self-esteem, which will allow you to invite conflict and input, and people can tell you you're wrong, and you will have to be okay with it. Some people leave my team because they want to be "lawn furniture." Those who learn that I expect participation in decision making and disagreement, they're the ones who stay.

Therefore, by emphasizing the critical role of team members' participation in decision making and by actually giving individuals the opportunity to exercise such behavior, you can increase individual empowerment in your teams.

The third behavior is *providing effective coaching* so that individuals can become confident in their empowerment experiences.[29] Coaching can be tricky and requires that you tailor your efforts differently for each individual team member; being fair, in these cases, does not necessarily imply treating everyone the same way. Coaching trends have gone through several fads over time, but some common underlying facets of effective coaching stand the test of time. For one, an effective coach must truly believe that her or his people are capable of positive change. Although some individuals have deep-seated beliefs about this ability to change, the evidence shows that employees are generally malleable.[30] Second, coaches must be willing to encourage learning-goal orientations and give individualized feedback that helps individuals craft specific goals and build self-belief in their ability to accomplish those goals.[31]

A director of sales in a large technology-oriented company described his experience in coaching his new Australian team member, who had taken three years of leave after the birth of her first child:

> I called her three weeks before she came back and told her I was delighted to have her back at the company. I wanted to make sure she didn't have a reaction like "This guy doesn't know me or trust me," so I had to set the scene and make sure she knew I was familiar with her skill set. I had a team member in Singapore help her get back into the flow since she was located in Australia. I gave her an assignment where she led a team tasked with developing an application for virtual sales training. I gave her my vision and also coached her on how to handle the vendor. I spent a lot of time coaching her on the job on how she can evolve her role. After so much time off, I was really happy she reintegrated so well back into the company.

As this leader's anecdote shows, coaching can be a critical component in increasing the likelihood of individual and, subsequently, team empowerment and success.

The fourth behavior is *sharing important and strategic information* with individuals. Although you often have to be judicious in the types and amount of information you share with your team members due to confidentiality issues or company-sensitive information, team members will likely experience higher levels of individual empowerment when they feel like insiders to your company's important and strategic information. A high-level executive at a technology-based company reinforced the importance of information sharing:

> I do this every day. I might have a tendency to share too much information actually. It's not always clear where knowledge stops and gossip starts. But if my people are better informed, then we can have better debates and discussions. I explain the company strategy every day and how it ties to the macroworld. And even if my ideas aren't fully formed yet, I still share information about what I'm thinking and what the higher-level people in our company are thinking. In fact, I've shown them fifty iterations of our new digital strategy. They embrace the fact that this is an evolving story, and they need to know that we are in the process of socializing the strategy.

Sharing such information with team members, though likely differing in level and amount depending on the team, is crucial for individuals to experience greater empowerment.

The final behavior is *displaying a high level of concern and caring* for individuals. Showing respect for people, ensuring that they feel a sense of dignity at work, and making sure that they know that you have their best interests at heart goes a long way toward making your individual team members feel empowered. The director of sales said, "My Australian team member actually did a professional kickboxing match. She won the fight, which, knowing her, I expected, but she ended up in intensive care; she ruptured her spleen and almost died. She was so concerned about missing work, but I told her not to worry; something similar had happened in my family, so I said she should take care of herself; I will take care of things on this end; don't work full time; take it slowly."

Another high-technology team leader echoed the importance of a personal touch and said, "I personally care for my people. I'm comfortable having an emotional connection to them. I can be close, but I can still be objective about making decisions about career and bonuses. I probably have more people in tears sharing deeply moving issues with me than many leadership books say you should have, but in a good way. I think it boils down to self-confidence and being genuine and authentic." Ultimately all companies, divisions, and teams are made up of people. When you show great concern and care for individuals, you will give your team members the confidence they need to branch out and act on their own empowerment opportunities. To be clear, expressing empathy and concern for others comes more easily for some people than others (no judgment here), but the evidence shows that even the most challenged individuals in this regard can improve.[32]

Table 3.1 provides practical examples of the five empowering leader behaviors.

Leveraging Your Company's Structures and Systems to Make Them More Empowering

In addition to the various leader behaviors just described, there are two structural features associated with higher levels of individual empowerment: *sociopolitical support* and *work design*.[33] Regarding the first, there are three main interventions to enhance your individual team members' perceptions of this form of support.

First, individual team members need to feel as though they work in a *supportive organizational climate* that promotes empowerment, and you can play a big role in fostering such climates. For example, having a great number of empowering leaders working to make sure individual team members feel comfortable taking risks and being proactive in their jobs can foster perceptions of a supportive climate. As a result, you need to make sure you are encouraging all of the actions associated with individuals' display of empowerment. Importantly, and what makes this distinct from empowering leader behaviors, is that all leaders in a company to the extent possible must collectively, not singularly, work together to promote such a climate by integrating and coordinating their empowering leader behaviors. In order to have a strong supportive climate, all hands need to be on deck.

A manager at a high-technology company talked about the importance of creating "air cover" for his team members to take risks:

I get feedback that I support people taking risks. People's bosses sometimes chicken out when they get challenged about their follower. A few weeks ago,

TABLE 3.1. Empowering Leader Behaviors Targeted at Individuals in Teams

Empowering Leader Behaviors	Examples
1. Role model	Take an individual team member to a meeting and show that person how you take initiative in the presence of your own boss.
2. Encourage and allow individuals to participate in decision making	Assign an individual team member to be a devil's advocate or inquisitor; encourage that person to disagree with you and poke holes in your ideas. Don't punish this person if he or she makes good points; instead, use what he or she said.
3. Provide effective coaching	Take time out to develop unique coaching strategies for each team member individually.
4. Share important and strategic information	Beyond information that is strictly off-limits, make individual team members feel like insiders by openly sharing important information.
5. Display a high level of concern and caring	Ask one of your team members to think of a request that might make something in his or her personal life better. If it's a day off to attend to a personal matter, a slightly longer vacation, or going to flex-time for a few weeks, say yes.

we were doing transformational change, and one of my team members who was in charge of a certain group of customers forgot about including them. One of our executives had a meltdown. I could have had my team member shafted for that, but I went to the executive and I said, "Yes, we missed this one group. Thanks for letting us know; we'll address it." I didn't yell at my guy and throw him under the bus. You will always go to battle for those in your team, even those you don't like.

Clearly, this leader works to create a supportive climate for his team members. When combined with similarly empowering leader behaviors from others, a company can develop a strongly supportive organizational climate.

Second, individual team members need to have a high level of *perceived organizational support*, or a recognition that their company values and cares about them and has their best interests at heart. As we noted previously, having team members who feel psychologically safe can lead to a host of positive team outcomes.[34] One team member in a health care organization we spoke with talked about the importance of this type of support:

I always knew that I had the support of my boss and my teammates to take risks and do things that were a little, I guess I would say, unorthodox—for example, when I wanted to change the way I handled a certain process in my team, which actually involved getting people from other teams—both upstream and downstream—to buy into the change because it affected the whole process of what we do. After getting encouragement from my team leader and teammates, I approached a couple of higher-ups about the idea. I had done my homework, but I was still nervous about presenting my plans because again it was not the normal way we typically did things. And in the meeting, they asked a lot of questions—I was sweating, but I knew deep down my ideas were better than what we were currently doing. Not only did these guys buy in, but they asked me to make the same presentation to their bosses. Now my approach is being adopted by the whole company. That's what the words *organizational support* mean to me: it means the company cares about my opinions."

Thus, when individuals feel that their company will support them, they will take bold risks that could have lasting positive effects. Without such perceived organizational support, however, individual team members will likely not bring their new ideas to light, and the company may ultimately lose out on a potentially great change or opportunity.

Finally, individual team members need to feel that their company has *a high level of trust* in them. A high-technology manager located in Europe said:

We make sure they know the company trusts them by allowing them to participate in decision making. I make sure to keep explaining my own decision making to them, so I might say, "Here was my rationale for getting to a certain place," especially with unpopular decisions. It's part of my own growth to explain decisions to them, so I can get honest feedback. I send my folks out to do important things to build their confidence and competence, even when others in the company might rather have me there instead. I take three-week vacations, not like a day or two like you guys in the United States, so I have to tell my team members, "You are my fully empowered stand-in; see you in three weeks."

Trusting your individual team members to make decisions, act as representatives, or lead others might sound unnerving because much of your performance may rest on the success of these individuals, but it is absolutely critical to empowering the individuals on your teams. In addition, by trusting your team members, you will help them develop the ability to take on greater responsibility, which frees up your time and allows you to focus on your most important tasks.

In addition to sociopolitical support, the other key feature of an empowering structure is having a *work design* that supports empowerment. There are five key elements for designing empowering work experiences: skill variety, task identity, task significance, autonomy, and feedback.[35] First, skill variety is the extent to which a job requires a large number of different activities and behaviors so that an individual can use various skills or knowledge bases. In other words, does an individual use many or few skills to carry out work? An example of a job with high skill variety might be university professor, who teaches classes, conducts research, writes papers, leads and serves on committees, and presents papers at conferences. Some of the tasks are more extraverted in nature, requiring extensive interaction with colleagues and students. Other tasks are more introverted in nature, such as sitting at a computer and running statistical analyses. In contrast, a job with low skill variety might be a college instructor whose sole responsibility is to teach the exact same courses every semester. Of the four dimensions of empowerment, skill variety is most closely tied to producing feelings of competence and meaning.

Second, task identity is the extent to which a job requires the accomplishment of an entire product, service, decision, or output. Essentially, is an individual involved in all or substantial portions of producing the output or just a small part? For example, the Saturn Motor Company was well known for enhancing task identity for their autoworkers by creating small cells of employees who were responsible for assembling an entire vehicle. In contrast, some automotive manufacturers still use long assembly lines, often highly automated these days, in which employees perform only a very small part of vehicle assembly, representing low task identity. Of the four dimensions of empowerment, task identity is most closely tied to producing feelings of competence and impact.

Third, task significance is defined as the extent to which a job influences the work or lives of other people or the company as a whole. In other words, is an individual carrying out tasks that are visible and influential for others or doing work that is more behind the scenes and lacks an immediate, tangible impact on others? As an example, a colleague of ours is a pediatric cardiac surgeon who on a day-to-day basis has the lives of children in her hands. One can imagine the level of significance she feels when she can inform anxious parents about a successful surgery. Of course, every hospital setting has various behind-the-scenes individuals who perform important tasks that might not have immediate significance for the people around them. Of the four dimensions of empowerment, task significance is most closely tied to producing feelings of meaning and impact.

Fourth, autonomy is defined as the extent to which the task allows individuals to have the freedom, discretion, and independence for how and when they carry out work. Is an individual allowed control over the various aspects of his or her job, or constrained in decision making by other job aspects, such as a boss or the routinization of the task? Importantly, note that autonomy is both an aspect of job design *and* one of the actual dimensions of individual empowerment, a similarity that trips a lot of people up. The difference lies in the fact that for job design, work is set up in such a way that allows an individual to have a lot of choice and discretion. As a result, autonomy in this sense is an aspect of work structure. In contrast, when viewed through the lens of individual empowerment, autonomy refers to the actual experience of freedom and discretion, which would, we hope, be the result of structuring work in an autonomous fashion. Creating an autonomous work structure and then having an employee actually experience autonomy as a result of that structure is not always guaranteed, however. Many varying factors (e.g., a controlling boss, an employee's unwillingness to accept responsibility) might cause an individual to not actually experience the feelings of being autonomous despite an enabling work structure.

Sales jobs are often structured so that salespeople have a great deal of autonomy in deciding when, how, where, and what tasks they will carry out on a day-to-day basis. The sales support roles of assisting salespeople, however, have much less autonomy because support work is often tightly coupled to the ebb and flow of the sales activity of those in the field. Of the four dimensions of empowerment, not surprisingly, autonomy in job design is most closely tied to producing feelings of autonomy as an empowerment dimension.

Finally, feedback is defined as the extent to which a job produces clear and consistent information about how well an individual is performing his or her work. Basically, is an individual constantly aware of his or her performance level on a day-to-day basis, or are there substantial time lags in gaining that information? For example, a laboratory technician who tests samples of tissue for viability receives ongoing, immediate feedback about the results of his work. In contrast, a laboratory researcher who conducts experiments on tissue samples and submits the results of her work to academic journals might get feedback only every few months. Of the four dimensions of empowerment, feedback is most closely tied to producing feelings of competence and impact.

Taken together, to create high levels of individual empowerment, you can focus on redesigning jobs to enhance skill variety, task identity, task significance, autonomy, and feedback. But you're probably wondering, "Just how viable is enhancing all of these aspects of job design for your employees?" One piece of good news is that jobs in the knowledge economy often come with these design aspects already baked in, particularly when compared to manufacturing or many service jobs. Moreover, some companies are beginning to reduce, or eliminate altogether, the formal and bureaucratic role of HR in designing jobs, which can provide you and your team members with significant latitude in determining how work is done.[36]

Despite these promising avenues, a comprehensive review of work design practices recently concluded that many companies still fall quite short in terms of optimal work design.[37] Moreover, even when organizations report that they have enriching work designs, their employees often see things quite differently (and much more cynically). When work is designed around heavy routinization or automation, or in companies in which an HR department maintains strong oversight for specific job redesigns, you may experience significant headwinds when trying to alter how employees can approach their work. In these cases, having a solid HR business partner can be extremely helpful in facilitating design changes, and so we recommend cultivating this relationship extensively. Try to help those in HR see your point of view, understand theirs, and work together to find value-adding solutions that can supplement your efforts as a team leader. Sharing the knowledge you've gained in this chapter is an excellent starting point.

Beyond partnering with HR, you might also have to get creative in order to enhance job design. For example, you could use job sculpting to tap into individuals' life interests even if their immediate jobs do not take them into account. Life interests are "long-held, emotionally driven passions, intricately entwined with personality and thus born of . . . [a] . . . mix of nature and nurture."[38] Job sculpting thus creates a match between individuals and jobs so that their deeply embedded life interests can be expressed. Some successful techniques for job sculpting include these:

- Asking employees to write down their opinions about career satisfaction
- Listening carefully and asking questions that draw out deeply embedded life interests

- Adding a new responsibility that helps to tap into a life interest
- Changing assignments to match life interests to responsibilities if possible
- Considering a more major move such as a complete job change or even an amicable separation if necessary[39]

You should not assume that you as a leader are solely responsible for helping individual team members sculpt the characteristics of their jobs to make them more empowering and intrinsically motivating. Another line of research has demonstrated that employees will engage in job-changing behaviors themselves—something that has been referred to as "job crafting."[40] Indeed, team members are not just passive entities waiting to be motivated and led; rather, they are actively shaping and reshaping their job responsibilities in a self-motivating way. Whether you rely on job sculpting, crafting, or some other means to change a job's design, the bottom line is that *empowerment matters*. As a result, do whatever you can structurally to make sure that the "I's" in your teams experience the fullest amount of empowerment possible.

Moving beyond empowering behaviors and structures, we also know that team members' empowerment is affected by the larger systems in which they operate. Our experiences suggest that lacking an organized and coherent system that promotes empowerment is the biggest cause of failed empowerment initiatives in companies. So what's the trick? If you ask us to pinpoint one issue, at the top of our list is "clarifying expectations." Without this, empowerment efforts get off track from the very beginning. Your vision of empowerment will likely differ from that of individual team members, and if these differences are not properly discussed, never the twain shall meet.

An effective empowerment system largely encompasses one-on-one conversations, broader communications, and other more peripheral information channels working together to communicate the same set of expectations to employees. Classic organizational behavior research describes the "sensemaking" processes that employees go through to determine their best courses of action at work.[41] At base, these processes suggest that employees will look to their supervisor, coworkers, and others in their company to determine what options are available to make sense of uncertainty and, by extension, the most likely outcome of each option. This process will happen again and again over time, with employees constantly updating their assessments of what outcomes are likely to emerge from each behavioral option. So employees may decide that they'll follow their supervisor's push to act empowered at some early point in time, but if they later find out that their company does not reward this course of action in their annual review, they may opt for more cautious approaches going forward. Clearly you want to make sure they're getting the most direct and consistent message from every possible source you can control.

One of the most important conversations to have early on in any empowerment discussion centers on detailing a job's tasks and how those tasks contribute to a company's strategic objectives. This serves several purposes. For one, this is your chance to explicitly highlight the match between what you want your employee to do and what the company expects from that person; if there's any inconsistency, you can work to reconcile it. Second, related to helping an individual with sensemaking, this conversation could also show people how valuable their job is to their company. Third, and importantly, you can use this conversation to highlight the possible constraints employees are likely to face when carrying out their newly empowered tasks. When people know some of the most common challenges, they can better frame strategies for moving ahead and avoid feeling blindsided later. Knowing challenges ahead of time makes it less likely that they question their own ability later (e.g., "I don't know why I fell short. It must be a 'me' problem!"), as they can instead contribute shortcomings to a common and expected headwind (e.g., "Okay, I knew that might come my way, and now I'm ready to try again!").

Some common challenges you might want to discuss directly with individuals upfront include issues relating to costs and time, resource availability, participation level of other parts of the organization, and, related, any key stakeholders who require buy-in before something can move ahead. Of course, it is also important to be sure their skill sets are properly matched to a job and determine how their progress will be monitored, especially if you are giving them a stretch assignment.

The first meeting or two that you have with individual team members is crucial. In that initial conversation, you need to make sure that your employees completely understand the answers to the following questions:

- What exactly are you asking them to do?
- Why does what you are asking them to do matter? How does it contribute to the big picture?

- Who else in the organization will need to be involved to get the tasks done? What messages you will be sending to these people?
- What will a truly successful outcome look like?
- How will they keep you in the loop, and how often?
- How much authority do they have to take action and make decisions?
- What are the major resource constraints?
- What is the system for monitoring their progress?

These questions will help you create an effective empowerment system and serve to establish the clear boundaries, expectations, and communication systems needed for employee success. If it isn't already apparent, we'll say it again: empowerment takes way more than a minute! However, by using these techniques, you will also experience what we call the "pay now or pay much more later" phenomenon: if you put in the hard work for creating an effective empowerment system upfront, you will reap the benefits further down the road. We summarize the ways in which you can create empowering structures and systems in Table 3.2.

Building High-Quality Relationships Can Also Jump-Start Your Empowerment Efforts

So far we have discussed the behaviors needed to build an effective empowerment program, as well as the structures and systems that are critical for supporting such a program. What we have not discussed yet, however, is the importance of building high-quality empowering relationships with each of the "I's" on your teams—what researchers call "leader-member exchange (LMX)." A substantial body of evidence links the quality of the relationship between leaders and team members to valuable outcomes. In fact, a comprehensive analysis of almost 250 studies found that employees reporting higher relationship quality also performed their jobs more effectively, were better organizational citizens, and had lower turnover.[42] Those same employees were also more committed to their company and were more satisfied with their jobs and leaders. In addition, these employees see their companies as being fairer and their work roles as having less ambiguity and conflict. Critical to our focus on empowerment here is that *the link between relationship quality and employee empowerment was the second strongest relationship in the entire study* (just behind that of relationship quality and satisfaction with supervisors).

TABLE 3.2. Creating Empowering Organizational Structures and Systems Targeted at Individuals in Teams

Empowering Organizational Structures and Systems	Examples
1. Supportive organizational climate	Make sure that all individual members in your team know that you have their back. Encourage other leaders to support your team members and defend them if those leaders do not.
2. Perceived organizational support	Reinforce to individual team members that the overall organization will support them in their goals and pursuits. Make all team members aware of the various support programs in place for any issues or problems.
3. Organizational trust	Provide all team members with opportunities to take risks and do not punish for them. Build a network of trust by expanding the number of mentors for team members.
4. Work design: Skill variety	Constantly expand each individual team member's skill repertoire by creating new tasks and responsibilities that build new skills. Coach team members on the most valuable skill sets to develop.
5. Work design: Task identity	Involve each team member in as many of the steps of completing a product, service, decision, or output. Try not to restrict team members to accomplishing only a small piece of a task.
6. Work design: Task significance	Make sure each team member knows how his or her efforts tie into the big picture.
7. Work design: Autonomy	Ensure that all team members have the appropriate level of autonomy and discretion when performing their jobs. Design the job itself so that autonomy is "baked in."
8. Work design: Feedback	Have team members meet with internal and external customers. Get feedback from these meetings, and pass it along.

The evidence on LMX seems rather straightforward: build good relationships with all of the individual members on your team so that they perform better, feel better, and react more positively in general. However, such advice is easier said than done. In fact, a preponderance of evidence shows that in reality, leaders naturally build high-quality relationships with some (but not all) team members, perhaps subconsciously based on factors such as perceived competence, similarity, likability, or even prior performance.[43] Why does this happen? As we noted in Chapter 1, it's most likely all about resources. One particularly valuable resource in short supply is time. Because leaders are often busy juggling team demands with those of their individual day-to-day jobs, they must be selective in how they allocate their time for building high-quality relationships. In addition, leaders must efficiently allocate their emotional and cognitive resources. Unfortunately, some members prove more taxing than others, and frankly, it's hard to build high-quality relationships with people you can't really stand!

Related to these constraints, many of the practical takeaways from this research are misconstrued in ways that ignore the fact that individuals are often embedded in teams (however, the theory was originally constructed with groups and teams in mind).[44] Thus, some leaders may arrive at a simple conclusion: use their finite resources to build high-quality relationships with only those members performing the most important tasks. In some ways, this isn't an altogether bad strategy. Some evidence, for example, supports building different quality relationships based on the importance of individuals' roles within a team.[45]

Yet this approach is also somewhat oversimplified in that it does not explicitly acknowledge that team members are constantly evaluating the relationships of their peers with their leader to determine where they stand in their team and, by extension, how they feel about their role. Much research, including our own, suggests that differentiating relationships among team members can have harmful effects on individual outcomes, including employees' being less engaged[46] and having increased perceptions of unfairness,[47] which may hinder overall team performance in the long run. So, what do we make of this? Should you spread your limited resources evenly and try (likely in futility) to build high-quality relationships with everyone on your team—or instead be selective and focus only on the "most critical" relationships? We think the answer is both—and, no, this isn't as impossible as it might sound.

As it turns out, leaders and followers often evaluate the quality of their mutual relationships based on different criteria. Leaders, not surprisingly, tend to assess quality based on work-related factors (e.g., performance), whereas followers are often more concerned with interpersonal treatment (e.g., being treated with dignity and respect).[48] This fact is important because it presents leaders with an opportunity to attain the best of both worlds. For example, you may be able to optimize team performance by differentiating quite liberally—and thus preserving valuable resources—based on work-related factors. Examples might include assigning more important tasks to higher-performing individuals or providing more coaching to members who are struggling to keep pace. Related, when team members have concurrent roles on other teams or other significant work responsibilities, you should ask them how their roles on other teams are going and, when possible, be considerate of competing time demands.[49]

Apart from this work-related differentiation, you can simultaneously be mindful of treating all members equally based on interpersonal factors. Finding a brief moment to ask a member how his or her day is going, inquiring about important life events, and other personal acts of concern are small gestures that can potentially make a big difference in maintaining the fairness perceptions that keep members engaged. (This is essentially equivalent to one of the empowering leader behaviors already discussed: displaying a high level of concern and caring.) Indeed, the evidence shows that individuals are more willing to tolerate, and even embrace, differentiated relationships in teams so long as they perceive the overall context to be fair.[50] In the absence of perceived fairness, however, members may display lower levels of commitment and satisfaction and will be more likely to want to leave their team.

We should also acknowledge that most of the professionals with whom we have worked admit to having ebbs and flows in their daily schedules in which some days are less busy than others. So beyond the prescriptions above, we advise you to take advantage of your relative downtime by investing in your individual relationships with team members. Examples from our observations and interviews with effective team leaders include taking a team member to lunch to check in on how he or she is doing on a project or, better yet, refusing to talk about work-related matters at all; recognizing team members informally for their contributions, preferably in the presence of more senior leaders; engaging in small acts of kindness like remembering birthdays, asking a specific question about family members, or attending a nonwork event in which the team member is participating (e.g., a half-marathon, their child's soccer championship); asking a team member to volunteer with you at a community event; or simply stopping by a team member's work space every now and again just to catch up. These investments may seem small and not really feel like conventional "work," but they can pay big dividends in terms of creating the individual empowerment your team needs to achieve success.

Beyond Empowerment: How You Can Use Extrinsic
Motivation to Get the Most Out of Your "I's" in a Team

Although we have spent the bulk of this chapter on intrinsic motivation—
specifically that created by empowerment—we also recognize the importance
of extrinsic motivation for the "I's" in your teams. In contrast to the ubiquitous "we-over-me" mentality, many extrinsic reward systems in practice still
place a major emphasis on individual contributions. However, when considering the case of rewarding individuals in team contexts, some approaches are
more effective than others. Because there are many great books on individual
performance management,[51] we focus here on what we believe are the most
crucial elements for enhancing performance management for individuals *in
team contexts*. In fact, the biggest mistake we see companies make today is
that they fail to provide any rewards or recognition for the team component
of individual performance. A lot of managers talk about the importance of
teamwork and collaboration, but their company reward systems are set up to
encourage only individual performance and recognition.

A great example of this is the forced ranking system popularized by GE in
the 1990s (and since abandoned) that a substantial, though declining, number
of companies still use. [52]Sometimes pertly referred to as the "rank-and-yank"
system, forced ranking requires that managers categorize their employees
using a fixed percentage, typically modeling the categories of 10 percent as
underperforming, 50 to 60 percent as passing, and the remaining 30 to 40
percent as high performing. The result of such a system, however, is anything
but teamwork. In fact, a forced ranking system is actually laser focused on
fostering competition among team members, encouraging such behavior as
ingratiating oneself with a leader, shameless self-promotion, and perhaps even
bad-mouthing or sabotaging the work of others in order to attain the limited rewards promoted in the system. In short, it can bring out the worst in
people. A related concern is that employees rarely follow a standard bell curve
in terms of performance, which means that forcing them to fit one artificially
and unfairly gives the illusion that some employees are falling short in terms
of their contributions.[53]

Due to the numerous bad effects produced, Microsoft abandoned its forced
ranking system altogether in in favor of a system that promotes collaboration
and teamwork.[54] At about this same time, Yahoo picked up the rank-and-
yank model, presumably as way to get rid of lower-performing employees.

However, the forced ranking system perfectly reflects the underlying message in the classic article, "On the Folly of Rewarding A, While Hoping for B."[55] Author Steve Kerr points out that one of the most common management reward follies is hoping for teamwork but rewarding for individual effort. In addition to dropping the formal rank-and-yank system years ago, GE also has surprisingly acknowledged that it was abandoning formal annual reviews altogether and will move to providing performance information using an app, presumably driven by millennials' desire for more frequent feedback and love of technology.[56]

So what gives? Why are we still rewarding for individual performance while simultaneously asking for teamwork and collaboration when we know that people often do things for which they get rewarded and evaluated? Part of the answers lies with culture. In the individualistic cultures characteristic of the West, people want to be recognized and rewarded mostly for their individual, not collective, contributions. Our organizations are in part a reflection of national culture, so we cannot abandon individual-based reward and recognition systems, particularly in the West.

What we have seen produce great results in many of the companies with which we have worked is building in a subset of rewards and recognition based on an individual's teamwork behaviors. Notably, these do not need to involve huge changes to current performance management systems. Something as simple as adding a few survey items on teamwork behavior to an evaluation system can work. In one of the more widely used, evidence-based survey measures of assessing individual performance, a four-item section on teamwork behavior supplements the dimensions of general job performance, career progress, innovation, and organizational citizenship behavior.[57] Despite its simplicity, many organizations to this day have yet to add a teamwork component to their evaluation systems. However, most team members, especially in Western cultures, pursue their own distinct agendas if there is no actual measure of teamwork behavior put in place.

A possible worst practice for managing the "I's" in teams is favoring team-based over individual-based performance incentives. Although it might make sense on paper to assume that "if you want people to act like a team, you should pay them as a team," most of the research evidence suggests otherwise.

For example, in the late 1990s, Levi-Strauss replaced its denim jean sewers' piece-rate pay system of compensating each person based on the number of jeans she or he produced over a specified time period with a team-based pay system of dividing workers into teams of ten and paying each individual based on an entire team's output.[58] After making the switch, things got so heated at a plant in Tennessee that the company had to hire off-duty sheriff's deputies to be posted at the entrance to the plant to keep the peace. This clearly shows that individual team members want to be compensated primarily for the work they do themselves, especially in highly individualistic countries. If companies want to add team bonuses on top of individual pay, this is not a problem. But carving out a portion of a team member's individual-based performance pay and replacing it with team-based performance pay will not work. Just ask Levi-Strauss, which now makes a much smaller number of jeans in the United States (which, admittedly, was also the result of large-scale outsourcing of the U.S. textile industry, not just bad incentive systems).

Another important aspect to consider for an effective, teamwork-rewarding extrinsic motivation system is that it is not enough to simply score someone on how much teamwork behavior he or she exhibits. The evaluation and performance of the desired behaviors must also be tied to each company's reward system, preferably with salary increases or bonuses, or both. A high-technology team leader described his company's system for incentivizing teamwork by saying, "Everyone can recognize anyone on the team with a cash award. If it's a hundred bucks or so, you just give it; you don't need approval. You can do up to a thousand dollars with management approval. Team members can grow their network this way, and it's a mechanism to build support for teamwork. I like to see people use this outside our team; it helps build support for your team too." Giving cash awards or other extrinsic rewards for teamwork on top of an individual's base pay can thus be an effective way to motivate individuals in team contexts.

In addition to reward systems, the importance of nonmonetary recognition programs should not be overlooked. In a series of studies we conducted looking at both employee-of-the-month awards and team leaders publicly recognizing high-performing individual team members, we found that individual recognition actually had spillover effects.[59] That is, when an individual team member received an employee-of-the-month award or was formally recognized by a team leader in front of peers, the performance of that individual's fellow team members also increased, and, more important, so did the overall team's performance. The effect was even stronger if the recognized team member was an important and central member of the team. Although rewarding individual team members monetarily might breed unhealthy competition or resemble the rank-and-yank evaluation system, recognition appears to operate differently. Thus, it is perfectly acceptable to single out an individual top performer because such recognition will raise all boats in terms of fellow team member and overall team performance. An important caveat, of course, is to ensure the recognition is fair and will not result in harmful disruptions in the team's working patterns.

A comprehensive goal-setting program is also a key determinant of a high-quality extrinsic motivation system. The acronym S-M-A-R-T goals (pertaining to goals that are specific, measurable, achievable, relevant, and time-bound) is frequently heard in many companies to the point that one wonders if this is just another faddish term without much evidence behind it. However, based on many decades of research in the management and applied psychology fields, some scholars argue that goal setting is the most powerful theory of motivation we have.[60] Thus, the evidence would support setting SMART goals in organizations to promote excellent performance. Still, setting such goals tells you only what characteristics the goals themselves should have. It says nothing about the content of the goals. And just like rewards and recognition, most of the language used in the contents of SMART goals tends to be targeted more toward individual-focused behavior and outcomes, omitting a focus on teamwork behaviors and results.

It is also important to note that you sometimes have to work hard to find common ground between individual and collective goals. A best practice here is to develop a set of cascading goals from the team level down to the individual level. Individual team members will have to clearly see how their individual goals fit into the bigger picture of their team's objectives. Otherwise, members will either be confused about the mismatch between individual and team goals, or they will focus more of their energy on their own distinctive goals and thereby compromise team performance.

The last point we make about extrinsic motivation is that many people are on more than one team, some temporary and some more permanent. Nonetheless, this reality does not change the fact that extrinsic motivation will be a key driver of an individual's performance on all of these teams. Thus, you will have to be creative in terms of simultaneously designing reward, recognition, and goal-setting programs for multiple team membership complexities.

These types of reward systems are recent and evolving, and one of the leaders we work with in a high-technology company reflected this point:

This is really difficult. You come together on initiatives; we set objectives based on initiatives, and when an initiative is successful, we tie rewards to the goals that were accomplished in the initiative. So our performance reviews have to cover multiple teams. We collect feedback from each team and provide it back to each individual. So this way, I can get a more well-rounded picture of what the person has contributed to each team. It's part of our HR process now: we get to go out and collect information from many cross-functional teams.

Multiple team complexities are now a key characteristic of today's companies, and leaders need to be able to set up their extrinsic motivation systems in such a way that enables the success of all involved.

As the previous quote suggests, it could be useful from time to time to collect information about an individual team member's performance from his or her team members. Although the popularity of peer evaluations has ebbed and flowed over the years, there are certain things you can do to make them more valid and useful.[61] First, make sure the team members you are asking to review a focal individual have adequate opportunity to observe his or her performance. Not every member of a team has an equal chance to get a good sense of whether a fellow team member is performing well. Second, make sure your peer evaluation survey items or questions you ask in an interview are a true reflection of the most important things you want to see from your team members. Related, a good rule of thumb is the more behaviorally oriented your measures are (meaning, do not try to assess someone's personality or non-job-related aspects), the more valid the evaluation will be. Third, a single peer evaluation system is not likely to be applicable company-wide, so leave room for modification based on idiosyncratic criteria. Finally, take into account the relationships team members have with one another as you begin to review and incorporate peer evaluations. With regard to the quality of relationships between leaders and team members, team members themselves often have different quality relationships with their teams (sometimes referred to as team member exchange, or TMX,[62] rather than leader-member exchange, or LMX). So, you might find some hints of bias depending on relationship quality.

When taking into account the variety of intrinsic and extrinsic motivation tools available to you, an obvious concern is how you know which motivational tool to focus. There is no simple right answer we can give for everyone, as every team is different and, moreover, most teams are constantly changing. That said, you can learn a lot by engaging in your own sensemaking processes. Recall that we have described this as asking yourself a series of questions aimed at developing a range of options and assessing (and constantly updating) probabilities regarding their potential outcomes.[63] At first, you may have to rely on somewhat indirect cues, such as observing how your team members react to different tasks or whether they're willing to take ownership. If you see that your team members never really break out of old routines despite your best efforts, you may be well served to look at what extrinsic messages they're getting.

Another approach, which is supported by the evidence on external boundary spanning[64] and environmental scanning,[65] is to look beyond the borders of your team to find necessary information that can better inform your internal processes and functioning. For example, you might evaluate the external environment to find out whether other team members in your company are demonstrating high levels empowerment or, alternatively, whether individuals on other teams are similarly struggling to act in empowered ways. If the former, your team may be lacking some of the intrinsic gusto they need, whereas in the latter, perhaps more extrinsic forces are to blame. Be prepared in these early stages to make some mistakes; it takes time to tune your levels. A key for mitigating downsides of these mistakes is to communicate constantly and respectfully to your team members about why you made the changes you did, be empathetic to team member concerns (remember LMX!), and admit and own up to your own mistakes.

Fortunately, your ability to diagnose team needs and, by extension, what motivational tools you need to use will get easier. To this point, heeding the advice we offer in this chapter will not only help you achieve short-term results, but will also help you refine your sensemaking to be more accurate over time. For example, when you work to build high-quality relationships with your team members or rely on more rigorous performance feedback, you can get a better sense of how your team is working and where members might be seeing some deficiencies or tensions. The trust and psychological safety you engender with your team members not only helps them engage with their day-to-day tasks but will also translate into their being willing to give you valid or critical advice.[66] They may, for instance, admit that they have not been taking ownership over certain aspects of their job because they don't feel that the company rewards that part of their job or because they've been getting mixed signals from elsewhere in the company. Similarly, as you learn to be mindful of the larger system in which your team is operating, you'll be more attuned to how messages from outside the team (e.g., company-wide communications, promotion and bonus decisions) create a match or mismatch with your own messaging. In these cases, you can step in and reconcile mixed messages, provide support, and coach them toward positive change. Taken together, you should look to your team members and the broader environment to determine the motivational tools with the most impact that you can use.

In this chapter, we covered several key reasons you should be concerned with motivating the individuals on your teams, and we provided practical advice and many examples from the team leaders with whom we work that you can use to do so. Intrinsic motivation techniques such as displaying empowering leader behavior, creating empowering structures and systems, and building high-quality empowering relationships; or extrinsic motivators like recognizing and rewarding individuals on teamwork behavior, adding on team bonuses, and setting individual- and team-aligned SMART goals will all allow you to set the stage for individual empowerment to occur. By leveraging these factors, you can better manage and guide your teams, and ultimately your company, to enduring success.

4 The Second Dimension: A Team as a Whole

IN CHAPTER 3, WE DISCUSSED THE IMPORTANCE OF focusing on the "I's" in teams that have either relatively low and stable levels of interdependence (i.e., more like a group) or life cycles that include stages in which team members sometimes work relatively independent of one another. For many leaders, this is a counterintuitive, albeit critical, lesson. In this chapter, we'll shift gears and focus on providing you with the hands-on tools for leading *a team as a whole*.

There are two main instances when a team as a whole takes precedence over the individuals and subteams within it. The first is in an ongoing team with relatively high levels of interdependence—what might be referred to as a "real" team. Importantly, the assumption here is that the level of interdependence is relatively stable; that is, the team will not eventually change into a group. If led properly (a big if), teams tackling interdependent work will almost always produce superior outputs compared to a similar number of individuals working independently, particularly for complex tasks.[1]

The second situation, and an increasingly common one, occurs when a team needs to shift from relatively low interdependence to a more collaborative effort as part of a life cycle progression. In contrast to the prior scenario—where leaders simply need to identify that they have a real team and then adjust their behaviors to focus mostly on the team as a whole—leaders in the second situation need to be able to recognize the transitions from group-like to team-like work and switch their focus accordingly. This, of course, requires leaders to be constantly mindful of how their team is completing tasks (and how their team should be completing tasks).

Best Practices for Leading and Motivating a Team as a Whole

Well over a century of research has examined the effects of good leadership on individual outcomes like performance and job satisfaction. By contrast, the evidence addressing the leadership of groups and teams is much younger. For instance, social psychologists began examining small groups in earnest only in the 1960s and 1970s. Two decades later, in the 1980s and 1990s, research on organizational teams became more widespread and has remained strong ever since. In this chapter, we build from the accumulating evidence to offer a focused set of practices that can be used to coordinate and motivate teams as a cohesive unit. We start with a primer on team basics, then move toward a more updated approach that takes into account the fact that today's teams are highly dynamic and that leaders and members are often part of multiple teams simultaneously. Similar to Chapter 3, we also discuss the underlying intrinsic and extrinsic motivational drivers underlying great performances in today's teams.

As we discussed in prior chapters, teams, in their simplest form, represent two or more individuals working interdependently toward a shared goal. Their primary virtue, and hence why companies use them, is that they have the potential to produce synergistic gains that exceed what can be achieved by an equal or larger set of individuals working independently.[2] Of course, teams do not always achieve these gains. As Richard Hackman said, "I have no question that a team can generate magic. But don't count on it."[3]

So what sets the good teams apart from the bad ones? There are nearly infinite possibilities, but at base it comes down to two distinct, albeit related, factors: the way in which team members work together and the energy behind the way the team works. In our framework, the way in which team members work together reflects how they go about completing their tasks, that is, the specific activities, or processes, that convert a team's "raw materials" into "finished goods."[4] By contrast, the energy component of our framework is meant to capture the psychological and motivational aspects of a team, sometimes referred to as emergent states or simply states.[5] With this framework, it is possible that two teams could approach their tasks in the exact same way (e.g., same meetings, same outlined steps for completing work), but one team might do so with more vigor and commitment, thereby generating superior performance. Similarly, it is possible that two teams may be equally motivated toward goal pursuit, but one team organizes and approaches its tasks more efficiently than the other. Thus, it is important for leaders to consider both processes and states to ensure optimal performance.

Let's start with the way in which teams work—their processes. Our colleagues and team experts Michelle Marks, John Mathieu, and Stephen Zaccaro developed a taxonomy of team processes. Within this framework, they argued that teams frequently move through episodes in which they might plan and strategize for some time (i.e., transition phases) and then work intensively on team tasks (i.e., action phases) and eventually repeat the iteration any number of times.[6] This could be like an airline cockpit crew that spends time planning for an upcoming flight (a transition phase), then actually taking off, flying, and landing an airplane (an action phase), and then doing an after-action review (back to a transition phase).

Consistent with this model, there are three basic types of team processes. The first type, *transition processes*, includes activities like analyzing a team's mission, specifying goals, and formulating a strategy. The second type, *action processes*, typically follows transition processes and includes activities like coordinating the sequence of actions among members, monitoring a team's resources, and assessing a team's progress toward goals. Finally, the third type, *interpersonal processes*, operates across both transition and action phases and includes activities like resolving conflict and maintaining healthy member relationships on a team.

Not surprisingly, as a team leader, you should actively monitor your team's processes and, when necessary, step in to meet team needs.[7] In some cases, this may be as simple as helping your team develop appropriate goals or resolving conflicts between two or more team members. In other cases, it may be more complex and require more substantive interventions aimed at altering how your team coordinates its tasks. This is particularly important in today's teaming environment where team tasks change frequently in both their overall scope and complexity.[8]

Helping to establish healthy processes is especially important when your team is first formed (or when a substantive influx of new members join). Indeed, teams typically decide very quickly—even in the first few minutes!— how members will conduct their work without much specific thought as to whether the approach is appropriate;[9] in many cases these decisions are born from members' previous experiences on other teams or simply as a matter of convenience. As we noted previously, members often want to "divide and conquer" (either individually or using subteams) when a more collaborative, interdependent team approach is actually needed. Unfortunately, these initial interaction patterns are sticky, which means they can last a long time and be difficult to change.[10] Thus, you need to set the proper tone early and guide your team toward healthy changes throughout its life cycle.

Consistent with this logic, your role in helping your team establish healthy processes is critical when members do not yet have a common implicit understanding for how they are supposed to behave during the team's action phases, referred to as shared mental model.[11] Teams with well-developed shared mental models can process information more effectively and clarify members' expectations for accomplishing tasks, which allows you to direct your leadership efforts toward other important aspects of your team, such as building team empowerment. To help your team develop a healthy shared mental model, you should invest time early on in your team's life cycle toward team briefings that you lead before and after important tasks or projects are completed[12] and, related, be mindful to lead your team in thoughtful discussions about task strategies.[13] If you inherit a team that is already up and running, your first job will be to diagnose what type of shared mental model already exists in the team, if any, and then take steps to change it if needed.

Of course, teams can vary wildly in how they approach their work, and in today's VUCA environment, there may not be a single best way to approach tasks (or the "best way" may not be known). In addition, due to constantly changing tasks and revolving-door team rosters, continually developing and redeveloping shared mental models can be an overwhelming prospect. Luckily, just like we noted for individuals in Chapter 3, you can empower your team's members to initiate many of these processes themselves. This is where the energy (or team emergent state) component comes in to support healthy team processes. We next discuss ways in which you can motivate and empower your team as a whole to generate the type of energy your team needs to be high performing.

Empowerment Is Not Just for Individuals; It Works for Teams Too

The evidence for the positive effects of empowerment on individual outcomes such as job performance and satisfaction is undeniable. What might be less apparent to you, however, is that similar outcomes can be achieved by empowering an entire team. Interestingly, individuals respond very positively, in both behavior and attitude, when you empower your teams as a whole.

There is even better news: team empowerment also improves both an entire team's performance and its internal team processes (such as communication and decision making), yielding a kind of two-for-one effect in companies. In order to help you implement this sort of empowerment in your own teams and thus reap its many benefits, we first discuss an evidence-based definition of team empowerment that parallels individual empowerment. Importantly, despite the fact that there are similarities between individual and team empowerment, there are also some crucial differences worthy of discussion.

What Is Team Empowerment, and How Is It Different from Individual Empowerment?

Although the four-dimension definition of individual empowerment—choice, impact, competence, and meaningfulness—got significant traction in 1990s, there was an almost complete absence of attention toward empowerment in teams. This was especially surprising given the widespread adoption of teamwork in many companies worldwide at the time. Although some of the companies we were partnering with talked very generally about empowering their teams, they nevertheless couldn't articulate exactly what that meant. Frustrated by the lack of a common definition and evidence on team empowerment, we decided to embark on a two-decade research program ourselves designed to (1) find out what empowerment really means in teams, (2) determine whether teams with more empowerment performed better than those with less, and (3) if that were true, determine how leaders can actually create more empowerment in their teams.

Our evidence-based definition of team empowerment relies on the notion that team members have collective perceptions and beliefs about their overall team tasks, which in turn determine how intrinsically motivated team members feel as a team. Importantly, these perceptions have to be shared by all team members (or at least a majority) for team empowerment to truly exist. After all, if there are no shared beliefs about team empowerment (i.e., everyone in a team sees it differently), then all you probably have is individual empowerment and no real sense of team empowerment. Our work showed that team members make collective judgments about four distinct aspects of their team's work:

- how much *autonomy* an overall team has
- the degree of *impact* an entire team's work has on others (e.g., individuals, other teams, a company, clients)
- the level of *potency* members experience when performing team tasks
- the extent to which team members feel a sense of *meaningfulness* when carrying out team tasks.

Figure 4.1 shows the four dimensions of team empowerment. Note that each of the four dimensions combines to create team empowerment, but the four dimensions themselves are also mutually reinforcing (e.g., increasing autonomy will also increase impact).

The first dimension of team empowerment is *autonomy*, defined as the degree to which team members experience substantial amounts of freedom, independence, and discretion in their team's work.[14] Autonomy is akin to the individual empowerment dimension of choice. And while many people equate team empowerment with team autonomy, autonomy alone is not enough for a team's members to be truly empowered. In fact, our own work shows that although giving a team more autonomy does lead to at least some valued team outcomes, it is only when you add impact, potency, and meaningfulness to the mix that teams truly experience the type of valued outcomes we really care about.[15]

It is important to note here that although some people might assume that increasing individual autonomy for every member of a team automatically increases overall team autonomy, this is not exactly true. After all, individual autonomy is the degree of freedom an individual believes she or he has in carrying out a task or making a decision. Team autonomy is the degree to which a team's members collectively believe they have a sense of freedom in carrying out their tasks or making a team decision. The key difference is that with team autonomy, a team's members have to share the amount of decision-making latitude in their work with one another—which, by definition, might actually result in decreases in individual autonomy. For example, when an individual has complete choice about working independently, that person can decide entirely on his or her own how or when to do something and there is no need

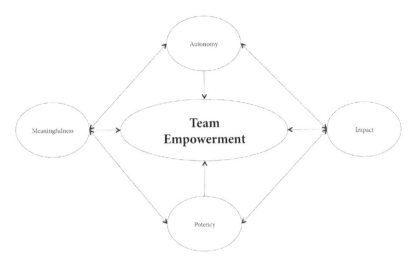

FIGURE 4.1. The Dimensions of Team Empowerment

to discuss options with fellow team members or share in any decision making. In teams, however, members might have to give up at least some of their individual autonomy in order for their team to reach a shared decision about how or when to act. In short, although a few members on a team might have a high degree of choice individually, the team as a whole might have a relatively low level of autonomy. Similarly, even though a team might have a high collective sense of autonomy, the individuals on that team might be constrained from making totally independent decisions.

Similar to individual empowerment, the second dimension of team empowerment is *impact*, or the extent to which a team produces work that is significant and important for a company.[16] Members of most teams want to believe that their work is worthwhile and that it has substantial benefit to stakeholders both inside and outside their company. As with individual impact, feedback from stakeholders is important. The more a team's members believe that their work really matters—and not just symbolically—the more intrinsically motivated they will feel, and thus they will be more likely to persist in their tasks even in the face of obstacles.

Despite the fact that the term *impact* is used for both individual and team empowerment, they do not mean exactly the same thing. When an individual experiences a sense of impact, that individual realizes that his or her independent actions have a significant effect on stakeholders. On the contrary, when a team experiences impact, its members realize that the collective efforts of their team are having a substantial effect on a company's stakeholders. And just like autonomy, a team could have a few members who are experiencing high levels of individual impact even though the team's members do not necessarily share in a collective sense of impact. Similarly, an entire team might be accomplishing tasks with a high level of collective impact, even though the individuals on that team do not experience impact independently. Given that individuals increasingly belong to multiple teams and might feel that they need to choose between which team gets their full investment, working to explicitly establish and clarify members' perceptions of their team's impact is in your best self-interest (although, of course, we'd hope that all teams in our companies are high-impact teams).

The third dimension of team empowerment is *potency*, or the collective belief of members in a team that it can be effective.[17] Potency is akin to the individual empowerment dimension of competence and is a broad concept that constitutes a belief that applies to a wide variety of team tasks, not just a single or small subset of tasks. It is similar to confidence but less amorphous in that it is tied to specific beliefs about work. When a team's members feel a collective sense of potency, they believe that nothing can stop the team from being successful. When we were interviewing high-potency teams in various companies and observing them in action, we saw that members act differently; they literally stand taller, are more at ease with one another, are quick to smile and laugh with one another, and display a sense of confidence that is palpable. In contrast, we observed that members of low-potency teams have poor body language and facial expressions, sometimes appear beaten down, seldom smile or laugh with one another, and generally display a lack of confidence.[18] In our experience, you need to interact with a team for only a few minutes to get a read on the likely level of team potency.

As with the other dimensions, team potency is not the same thing as individual competence. Indeed, adding up each member's level of competence and averaging them to get a team total will not yield an accurate assessment of team potency. Just because each member of a team has a high level of perceived competence does not automatically translate into all members feeling a collective sense of potency. The 2004 U.S. Olympic men's basketball team is a good example. This team was widely considered to have some of the most talented individual players of any other team in the tournament, with a roster that included current and future National Basketball Association hall-of-famers like Allen Iverson, Tim Duncan, LeBron James, Carmelo Anthony, and Dwayne Wade. Yet for all their individual talent and competence, they still demonstrated remarkably underwhelming team performance (relative to expectations) and ended up losing to Puerto Rico, Lithuania, and Argentina en route to a bronze medal. Especially relevant to our point here, their collective potency seemed to visibly deteriorate at various points in the competition. They just didn't seem to have that collective belief that they could win, even though they were all superstars in their own right.

Now imagine just the opposite scenario. Think about a basketball team composed of moderately talented individual players without any clear superstars. Thanks in large part to coaching, this team plays well together, understands how and is willing to integrate each player into a cohesive game plan, and selflessly works to get the ball to the player in the best position for a high-percentage shot. Using teamwork, this team defies the odds and, as a result, enacts very high degrees of collective potency. If you ask individual players about their own individual level of competence, however, they probably wouldn't be as forthcoming. They understand that when you put a particular set of team-minded individuals on the court, the team wins together. They might not be the most confident of individuals, but together they know that they can compete effectively on any given day. Clearly, team potency and individual competence are distinct things, and the level of one does not necessarily determine the level of the other.

The fourth and final dimension of team empowerment is *meaningfulness*, or the degree to which a team deems its tasks as important, valuable, and worthwhile.[19] Like impact, *meaningfulness* is the generally recognized term for both individual and team empowerment. And similar to individual empowerment, meaningfulness is the most important dimension for team empowerment. In addition, although meaningfulness is related to impact, it is still distinct. For example, a team might complete some tasks that are personally meaningful to that team's members but have little impact on company stakeholders. Conversely, a team might perform tasks that matter to a company but hold little intrinsic meaning for the team members. So although many meaningful tasks are likely to also have impact (and vice versa), this does not have to be the case. Still, the fact remains that when team members experience a collective sense of meaningfulness in their work, they are likely to get so wrapped up in what they are doing that they lose sense of time or forget how hard they are working (or maybe they even wouldn't call it work at all!).

Just as with the other three dimensions, individual and team meaning-fulness are not interchangeable experiences. Although one or two individual team members may believe that their own tasks are meaningful, the entire team may not share a collective sense of meaning. And, conversely, a team's level of overall meaningfulness might be high, but there also could be one or two members who are just going through the motions and experiencing a low level of individual, personal meaning.

Through understanding the four elements of autonomy, impact, potency, and meaningfulness and how they differ from the dimensions of individual empowerment, you should be able to better discern how team empowerment forms and which aspects your team might be lacking. Next, we turn to why developing these factors is so important for companies.

The Evidence for Team Empowerment: An Empty Promise or an Important Performance Lever?

We personally helped introduce an evidence-based approach to understand-ing team empowerment in the workplace almost twenty years ago and have since been delighted by the amount of additional work that has been carried out by others in the management and applied psychology fields. Indeed, our treatment of team empowerment has been generally accepted as the most reasoned approach to understanding empowerment in teams. Therefore, we can say with confidence that—like individual empowerment—the positive evidence for the impact of team empowerment on meaningful outcomes in companies is overwhelming.

In fact, there have now been several comprehensive analyses of the effects of team empowerment in organizations that ultimately show that more empowered teams perform better and have members who are more satisfied with their jobs.[20] Further analyses showed that this is true *regardless of the type of team* (e.g., service, manufacturing), meaning that team empower-ment is widely applicable and useful. In addition, the positive effects of team empowerment on team performance were actually stronger for larger, com-pared to smaller, teams.[21] Given the evidence that suggests that teams often experience problems related to members' slacking off and reduced coordina-tion as they grow in size,[22] it is reassuring to note that leaders of larger teams might be able to offset some of these issues by increasing team empowerment.

Do Individual and Team Empowerment Coexist
Peacefully, or Do They Work against Each Other?

Given our previous warning that empowering a team might in some ways detract from individual empowerment, we decided to test this possibility in a Fortune 500 home improvement retailer using each store's freight team, whose members unload items from trucks, and its receiving team, whose members put merchandise out on the floor.[23] In one of the rare studies to simultaneously examine individual and team empowerment in the same teams, we found that maximizing team empowerment did not, as we had originally thought, reduce individuals' empowerment levels in teams. Quite the contrary, in fact. Although leaders' actions for enhancing team empowerment were directed toward their teams as a whole, these same actions actually spilled over to produce both *higher individual empowerment* and *higher individual performance*.

Even when we looked at cases in which individuals had low empowerment and thus lower individual performance (as the evidence for individual empowerment would predict they would have), we found that being part of a highly empowered team reduced these harmful effects. Thus, empowering a team as a whole *can actually offset the harmful effects of low individual empowerment on performance*. The upshot of these findings is that all else equal, you might be well served to focus on team empowerment a bit more than individual empowerment because team empowerment appears to have a two-pronged set of positive effects on individuals *and* teams. We note that similar effects have been found for broader unit empowerment, such as company departments or divisions, in addition to teams.[24]

Finally, we found that team empowerment had stronger positive effects for those teams whose members worked more interdependently (i.e., real teams) compared to teams whose members worked more independently (i.e., groups). This is just what our 3D Team Leadership model would predict. At the points in a team's life cycle when you have real teams, focus more on team empowerment; when you have groups, focus more so on individual empowerment.

What Else Does My Team Need to Be Successful?

Although the evidence shows that team empowerment is an important type of team state that is essential for increasing the intrinsic motivation of a team as a whole, we would be remiss if we did not mention two other key team states that are important for today's teams to really be successful:

- *Team trust*, defined as the common belief among a team of individuals that team members make a good-faith effort to behave in accordance with any commitments, are honest in whatever negotiations preceded such commitments, and do not take excessive advantage of one another even when the opportunity is available[25]
- *Team psychological safety*, defined as the extent to which a team as a whole is safe for interpersonal risk taking[26]

At this point, you might be asking why we are singling out team trust and psychological safety when there are many other potentially important team states that could be discussed (e.g., cohesion, healthy norms). Our justification is rooted in the importance of coping with and leveraging diversity in today's VUCA environment. Specifically, teams today have no choice but to be diverse in as many ways as they can (function, expertise, experience, tenure, nationality, and demographics like age, race/ethnicity, education) because a complex world calls for divergent opinions and viewpoints. However, as the evidence shows and probably your own experience as well, diverse teams do not always live up to their promise, and in some cases, diversity creates harmful conflict.[27] If conflict becomes too high in a team, that team will likely fracture and never deliver the kind of synergy that leaders so desperately need.[28]

A key factor in whether a diverse team lives up to its promise, or stagnates and fails, is the extent to which its members' perspectives, opinions, and ideas are openly discussed and integrated in ways that produce better, more holistic solutions.[29] After all, differences are beneficial only if they can be used for the good of a team. Two of the most important drivers of both surfacing and using different types of information and perspectives, as you probably guessed, are team trust and psychological safety.

In fact, in a comprehensive review of over 100 studies, trust was found to be an above-average driver of team performance relative to other factors, particularly in teams with high interdependence (i.e., real teams, as our 3D Team Leadership model would predict) and in teams that have members with unique skill sets (i.e., skill differentiation), echoing its importance for more diverse teams.[30] Similarly, comprehensive reviews of psychological safety have demonstrated that it is also important for team performance, including those outcomes that are necessary in a VUCA environment, such as creativity, innovation, quality, learning, breakthrough idea generation, information sharing, and work engagement.[31] Evidence, perhaps not surprisingly, suggests that creating trusting and safe environments for your team is especially important when members are on multiple teams (an increasingly common occurrence), when members feel stretched thin by their varying team roles, and when their full effort is contingent on believing that team members will meet their commitments and act in good faith toward the team's goals.[32]

In order to allow a team's members to demonstrate innovativeness in their work, members need to feel that they can take risks with their fellow team members. In Chapter 1, we discussed the tendency for team members to share only information that is already generally known (i.e., the common knowledge effect).[33] Such an effect can then lead to a "hidden profile," in which a team reaches a suboptimal decision even when a highly promising solution is actually within its grasp.[34] Again, the primary reason that team members fall prey to the common knowledge effect is that revealing unique or novel information can actually make team members feel vulnerable to disrupting the good feelings of a cohesive team, as fellow team members might be made uncomfortable with such information.

To reduce the fears and concerns associated with hurting team cohesion and thus avoid the common knowledge effect, team members need to strongly believe that their fellow team members will accept their input, even if it might have the potential to create discomfort in the team. Again, team trust and psychological safety are critical for cultivating such beliefs. For example, a high level of team trust generally means that team members feel comfortable being vulnerable with one another.

As a team leader, you can play an important role in developing your team's trust from the onset. There are two main types of team trust you should try to influence. The first type, and the one that most of us are familiar with, is relationship-based trust.[35] This type of trust is just what it sounds like: trust built on the personal relationships members form with their fellow team members. Obviously you can't force relationship-based trust onto your teams, but you can help set the stage by allowing team members to spend time together socially, either informally or through more formal team-building activities. Relationship-based trust creates long-lasting bonds that can help instill a sense of confidence for offering up new and novel ideas in teams.

The second type of trust is task-based trust.[36] Just as the name implies, this type of trust is based on the reliability, dependability, and conscientiousness that team members display when working interdependently. In some ways, task-based trust is even more important than relationship-based trust. For example, even if team members already have great affinity for one another, if they do not keep their promises when it comes to completing their work, that team will not likely be capable of functioning well for very long. But team members don't necessarily have to be best buddies with one another to have a successful team so long as the members are reliable in following through and meeting task or client needs. Of course, in an ideal world, we would all love to have teams with high levels of both types of trust. But in a pinch, we would take task-based over relationship-based trust every time.

Before we provide a detailed discussion of important leader behaviors, we briefly highlight a few ways you can specifically help your teams build task-based trust. The first and most obvious way to affect trust is to actively role-model the behavior you expect from your team members. This could include things like responding to team member requests and needs in a specified period of time, consistently following through when you make a commitment to your team, and keeping your promises to avoid increases in cynicism. Second, you can coach members on exactly what other members expect from them, such as avoiding long lags in responding to fellow member requests, having unexpected shifts in priorities, or failing to follow through on previous commitments. Finally, a team charter, or a detailed written document that spells outs various aspects of team functioning, can be helpful because it explicitly identifies what the team norms are so that members understand the specific behaviors that will generate high levels of team trust.[37]

Increasing the level of psychological safety is another way that you can reduce team members' fears about sharing unique ideas and approaches with fellow members. Although it likely goes hand in hand with trust, psychological safety goes a bit further in that it relates specifically to interpersonal risk taking in teams, which again is the essence of a team's ability to generate the type of breakthrough thinking so critical in today's VUCA environments. And although words like *psychological safety* can sound a bit too "touchy-feely" for many, we do not mean to imply that team members should feel safe enough to share their deepest, darkest secrets or delve into their inner lives with their fellow team members (they can certainly do that on their own time if they wish). What we are talking about is creating an environment in which team members can feel free enough to offer their out-of-the-box thinking that can lead to value-added ideas. So if it makes you feel more comfortable, you can call psychological safety something like "creating a feedback-rich culture" or "a learning organization," as Rachel Mendelowitz of the McChrystal Group recommends, to make it more palatable.[38]

To build team psychological safety, you should be consistently accessible, ask for team members' input, and encourage team members to discuss their own mistakes in a constructive manner.[39] In addition, interventions such as team charters or structuring activities can help build members' psychological safety, especially during their early interactions.[40] For much more information on building psychological safety in teams, we highly recommend the book by Harvard Business School's Amy Edmondson, *Teaming: How Organizations Learn, Innovate, and Compete in the Knowledge Economy.*[41] For now, our general overview of the topic will be sufficient for the purpose of this book.

What Can You Do as a Leader to Increase Empowerment, Trust, and Psychological Safety in Your Team as a Whole?

By now, we hope it is clear why you should be very interested in empowering and building trust and psychological safety in the teams you lead. Teams with these healthy states have superior performance as well as a healthy set of other team- and individual-related behaviors and attitudes. But now, of course, the question is: *What should you do to actually get your teams to experience high levels of team empowerment, trust, and psychological safety?* If these important team characteristics are really all about collective intrinsic motivation—something that you cannot directly affect—how can you create an environment in which team empowerment, trust, and psychological safety are likely to occur? Based on the evidence, there are three main ways that you can accomplish this goal: (1) displaying empowering *leader behavior directed at teams* (often referred to as *team coaching*), (2) creating empowering *team structures and systems* (often referred to as *team design*), and (3) exhibiting team-focused aspects of *transformational leadership.*

Five Ways to Demonstrate Empowering Leadership to Your Team

In Chapter 3, we discussed the five leadership behaviors associated with increasing individual empowerment. Because these five dimensions were originally conceived of (and tested with) teams rather than individuals, we have a lot of evidence to suggest that these same five empowering leader behaviors will lead to higher levels of team empowerment, trust, and psychological safety.[42] However, it is important that *the behaviors be directed at a team as a whole* rather than at the individuals within that team. We now provide examples of each of the behaviors as they relate to a focus on team, not individual, empowerment.

The first behavior is *role modeling*, or leading by example. One of the managers with whom we work, a quality assurance automation architect for a technology-based firm, said:

> When my team is working on the functionality of a piece of software, I first try to clearly define the various "chunks" or "'pieces" of functionality, and then I give them complete freedom as to how to implement a new procedure. They own it, so my level of scrutiny is reduced. When things go wrong, they know it's on all of us. At the same time, I try to continue to do some of the more menial work that comes to the team. I don't delegate addressing customer complaints and questions. I do everything my team members do. I say to them, "I am a team member, just like you." In the end, leading by example is a day-to-day thing. It's not like I say, "Oh, I haven't led by example this week!" It's just a day-to-day activity that I constantly do to make sure they see me in the role of an empowered leader. Then they feel more comfortable being empowered as a team."

As this leader suggests, role modeling can be a particularly effective lever to increase team empowerment, trust, and psychological safety, and you should attempt to lead by example as often as possible for role modeling to be its most potent.

The second behavior is *encouraging and allowing teams to participate in decision making*. One of the leaders we interviewed, a vice president of enterprise strategy at a large insurance company, is one of the best role models we found in terms of allowing team participation in decision-making. He said:

> If you are leading a team, or the most senior person present in a meeting, then consider the dynamics that create team empowerment. In many situations starting the discussion by stating what you think the solution is will result in those present agreeing with you because of your position power. I've also had situations where it has been necessary to coach other leaders to stop jumping in with a solution. That is not what team empowerment is about. Unless you let the team work together to find the solution, you lose the benefit of the team diversity and might as well not even have anyone at the meeting. The leader should ask probing questions to get their teams to think about things more, like, "Have you thought about it from this perspective?" If leaders just give

their viewpoint, it shuts the team down and does not empower the members. If the team creates the solution, they will have a sense of ownership, responsibility, and accountability for ensuring it is successful. What I know for sure is that the role of an empowered leader is *not* to have all the answers.

Thus, when you allow your team members to contribute their own thoughts and viewpoints to a discussion and participate in decision making, your team as a whole is more likely to be empowered and have higher levels of trust and psychological safety.

The third behavior is *providing effective coaching* for teams to become confident in their empowerment experiences.[43] A principal technical writer at a large technology-based company said:

> I have a small team of people who all do the same job I do. We've had trouble in the past with decisiveness. There would be good debate and discussion but no action. My manager was pressuring me to get my team to be more action oriented, so I started doing something small but powerful in our team meetings, which were mostly virtual. When we discussed different issues, I just started writing them down as decisions rather than discussion points. At first, some of the team members weren't sure we could make a decision. They said things like, "Shouldn't we check with so-and-so?" You have to understand, this team had a long history of a fear of failure because they had been mismanaged for years and taught to avoid risk. My strategy was a combination of forcing—well, strongly encouraging—them to make decisions and trying to convey the idea that taking risks isn't a bad thing.

Indeed, many team members simply need an encouraging leader to help them become confident in their own abilities or authority. By reinforcing empowered behaviors, you can increase overall team empowerment, trust, and psychological safety.

The fourth behavior is *sharing important and strategic information* with teams. One of our high-technology managers described sharing this type of information as a balancing act and said:

> Our tasks require a lot of interrelated pieces, and I'm basically the only one who has a system view of the whole thing. Sometimes when I give people responsibility for a piece, they lack the overview. I'll have to tell them that what they're doing is not going to work given my high-level overview perspective, so in that sense, I empower them by taking the time to explain why things would not work or why they would be great, why a decision would help

the greater good or not. I try to show them how what they are doing helps all the other teams. It's a balancing act—you take some of that burden away from the team when delegating, but they need to know enough for them to be motivated to suggest changes. At times, the balance can go the wrong way. I assume they know more than they actually do, and then things break down, so I have to correct that. Again, it's a real balancing act.

Although determining how much important and strategic information to share with teams is always a bit tenuous, finding a way to strike the right balance can result in great benefits to both you and your members in terms of team empowerment, trust, and psychological safety.

The final behavior is *displaying a high level of concern and caring* for teams. A tech manager from an insurance company with which we work talked about the many ways he ensures that his whole team knows he cares:

When projects go off the rails, it can be as simple as ordering in pizza and sitting with them late at night or on weekends, even if you're not hands-on keyboarding yourself. I see many leaders not doing this. In fact, it's the opposite. They post on social media that they're having an amazing time while their team tries to catch up on a project all night. Also, if a team has done a big release or overcome major challenges, you need to thank their other half—something as simple as, "Thank you from us for allowing Seth to come in on the weekend." You need to make the extra effort to thank your teams, especially as you may not be aware of what personal commitments they have had to rearrange or the impact that their dedication to the project may have on their family life. There have been times where due to challenges with a big release, it has been necessary to ask critical team members to give up a planned vacation. I hate to ask; however, there may be little choice. It is critical in these situations that the team members feel that you appreciate their sacrifice. Another example that comes to mind is that we had a team here locally do a big release that was critical to the global success of the organization. They put in significant extra effort over a period of months to make the project a success. I reached out to my boss's boss, who is a board member, to see if he would have lunch with my team in New York. I gave him my team members' bios in advance so he had insight into them as individuals and could ask them relevant questions. Actually, the funny thing is that those team members don't even know that I arranged it, but that's not really the point, is it?

TABLE 4.1. Empowering Leader Behaviors Targeted at a Team as a Whole

Empowering Leader Behaviors	Examples
1. Role model	Have your boss come to one your team meetings and provide examples of the ways in which you have displayed a high level of empowerment with him or her in the past. Have your boss talk about what worked (and what didn't).
2. Encourage and allow the team to participate in decision making	Give your team two or three decisions in the next meeting for which the members have complete discretion; guide them on their decision making, but ultimately accept their choices.
3. Provide effective coaching	With your team, dissect a decision or action that didn't go well for the team; use the time to developmentally coach the team and action plan for similar situations in the future.
4. Share important and strategic information	Use the beginning of every team meeting to share what is going on at higher levels of the organization. Make sure your team is not surprised by any upcoming events. Talk to your team about what impending changes mean for them.
5. Display a high level of concern and caring	Let your team choose an out-of-office activity they'd like to do (e.g., dinner, bowling night, spectator sporting event). Take the entire team out to the event they choose.

As this leader displayed, taking steps to genuinely show members that you care about your team's well-being is a crucial step in empowering teams. When combined with the other four behaviors, your team will have a much greater chance of experiencing high levels of team empowerment, trust, and psychological safety.

Table 4.1 provides practical examples of the five empowering leader behaviors.

Leveraging Your Company's Structures and Systems to Increase Team Empowerment, Trust, and Psychological Safety for Your Team as a Whole

In addition to the various leader coaching behaviors just discussed, the two organizational structural features associated with higher levels of team empowerment, trust, and psychological safety are *sociopolitical support* and *work design*. In this book, we refer to the latter as *team design* to distinguish the concept from individual work/job design (discussed in Chapter 3) and to focus it more squarely on the structural aspects of teams rather than work.[44] Just as with individual empowerment, you can use both of these features to enhance team empowerment, in addition to team trust and psychological safety. Regarding sociopolitical support, there are three main interventions you might take to enhance team perceptions of this form of support.

First, teams must operate in a *supportive organizational climate* that promotes team empowerment. Such a climate could include a great number of empowering leaders working together to make sure entire teams are comfortable taking risks and being proactive in their work. As a result, you should make sure you are encouraging all of the actions associated with teams displaying team empowerment. As mentioned in Chapter 3, the actions of a single leader are not enough to effectively promote a supportive organizational climate. Leaders need to collectively promote such a climate by integrating and coordinating their empowering team leader behaviors.

One of the leaders with whom we spoke stressed the importance of top leaders acting in ways that promote a supportive organizational climate:

> One of my other jobs at my company is that I am an employee sponsor for a charity. The company gives five days a year to volunteer at nonprofit organizations. It's truly one of our big cultural selling points. I am responsible for Habitat for Humanity. One of the things we have observed, and it's not surprising, is that right after a layoff, volunteerism plummets. People don't want to look like they have free time. I had been trying to get the larger organization to put out some statements of support for people continuing to do this even during layoffs or after. So, we had a senor vice president taking Q&A at a town hall meeting, and I asked him to state the company's support for people using their volunteer time after a layoff. Fortunately, he gave his own example of how he continued to volunteer after a layoff, in a way that suggested he role-modeled the behavior. He also said that "if you are getting a message from your manager that you shouldn't be doing this, let me know." So, I kind of saw that as major step toward making sure our team knew that it was supported by the larger organization.

As this anecdote shows, getting support from top leaders in an organization can be a particularly effective way to build a supportive organizational climate for team members, which is critical for building team empowerment, trust, and psychological safety.

Second, teams need to have a high level of *perceived organizational support*, or a recognition that an organization values and cares about its teams and has the members' best interests at heart. One insurance company executive said:

The most valuable asset for any organization is always going to be people. Organizations themselves don't care; it's people who care. So, we strive to emphasize that the employees are the company, and this is critical in any customer-facing organization or team. We do a lot of celebratory events at our site. Some team members came up with the idea to have a big holiday event in early December. We readily agreed that this would be a good idea, and a bunch of team members worked behind the scenes to make it happen. We also support Habitat for Humanity and the Kramden Institute, where our team members build housing and computers for those less fortunate. We allow our team members to use their work time to give back and encourage the managers and leaders to be involved. Beyond that, and to make it more personal, if we know that a particular team member worked significant hours last week, we make sure that someone else on the team reaches out to him or her to do something special or at least say thanks. We want to know how that person is doing, show some human touch. While we have some processes in place here in the company that help, it really comes down to the individual team members, managers, and leaders to make this successful. That really makes our entire team feel more appreciated, special, and supported.

Thus, as our insurance company executive emphasizes, it's the company's people who determine the level of perceived organizational support. To increase the support, you should reach out to team members and encourage them to do the same for others, which will in turn increase team empowerment, trust, and psychological safety.

Finally, you need to make sure that team members perceive that their organization has *a high level of trust* in the team. Our insurance executive commented,

Well, as a leader, I embody the organization. So organizational trust starts with me. I do several things to build trust. First, I always deal with integrity. I do not lie. I would rather say, "I cannot answer that," than lie. You have to strike a balance between insulating the team from crap that goes on but not so much that it becomes too insulated. I try to be visible with my team. I mean, how can you trust someone who is a nameless voice on the other end of the telephone? On the rare [he laughs] occasion that I do make a mistake, I acknowledge it. I say, "Let's be clear. I was wrong; you were right. We have more information now; let's move forward." I have had leaders throw me under the bus; that breaks trust and you never get it back. Sometimes they don't even realize what they've done, and that makes it worse! I always say, "Do not upward-manage me. Tell me the truth." Nothing frustrates me more than being misguided because it will come back to bite.

As this example illustrates, you should find ways to demonstrate to team members that both you and the organization have a high level of trust in their team to be successful. By first showing integrity in your own character and competence, you can help develop this sort of sociopolitical support among your teams and your company, which builds team empowerment, trust, and psychological safety.

In addition to sociopolitical support, team design is the other key structural feature that supports team empowerment. According to the work of Richard Hackman and Harvard's Ruth Wageman, there are six design "must-haves" for ensuring that members experience team empowerment, trust, and psychological safety and, consequently, high team performance: a clear, engaging direction; task interdependence; team rewards; team resources; authority to manage the work; and performance goals.[45] The book titled *If You Don't Know Where You're Going, You'll Probably End Up Somewhere Else*[46] sums up the essence of the first aspect—a *clear, engaging direction*—quite nicely. And although the title's sentiment is certainly true for individuals, it's even more important for entire teams because members often disagree on their team's direction, especially if a leader has not clearly communicated it. Therefore, you as a team leader need to ensure that all of your team members know where they are going and agree that the direction is engaging and meaningful. In fact, we would argue that this is the first job for any team leader. Note that this role does not, however, equate to your dictating or micromanaging a team's direction. Instead, your job is to help an empowered team arrive at its own internally driven sense of direction by being heavily involved in facilitating the process. And while reaching a clear, engaging direction is difficult for any team, it is a fundamental ingredient of a good, empowered team design that will help a team's members develop long-term commitment and persistence for reaching valued outcomes.

Our insurance executive provided some excellent ideas on how he created this clear, engaging direction:

> If you're giving direction, it should also be written. Talk alone often isn't sufficient. Some people are visual; some are auditory; some people miss stuff, so having the key points in written material is the anchor to which you can then talk. The balance of spoken and written content becomes even more critical when you have nonnative English speakers and/or other cultures; it needs to

be simple and straightforward. Some of the most mentally tiring meetings are where you have to stop every second sentence to allow what you've said to be translated for other listeners. Whether you are directing a single cohesive team or a team spread across geographies or cultures you don't need 100-slide PowerPoints; there needs to be a crispness to the message. Probably 90 percent of what you say may not be remembered, so communicating a clear, engaging direction needs to consider the audience and the key points they need to take away. I much prefer to be face-to-face with people in the room; it is a much easier dynamic to work with and see whether they are engaged. On the phone, it can easily become a monologue.

Setting a clear, engaging direction for a team often entails using different forms of communication. Consider your audience and their preferences, and then adjust your delivery accordingly, being sure to follow up and confirm that your message and your team's direction were clearly understood.

The second important aspect of team design is *task interdependence*, which we previously defined as the extent of communication, coordination, and integration required among team members to get their jobs done. Because interdependence is an important running theme throughout this book, we won't belabor it here. Suffice it to say that unless your team members have a real team task with which to work, there will not likely be a true sense of team empowerment, trust, or psychological safety.

The third important aspect of team design is *team rewards*, which we discuss more in the section on extrinsic team motivation. For now, we address the fourth critical element of team design, *team resources*, which includes the information, training, and basic materials teams require in order for members to get their jobs done. Team members obviously need the "stuff" required to get their tasks accomplished. An often overlooked but important organizational resource for team members is training on teaming. Often leaders expect their members to figure everything out when it comes to teams, which produces sometimes dire consequences for team performance. Teaming does not come naturally to everyone, especially those who have more individualistic values, so it is important that individuals get the training and development they need to be excellent team members.

Related to this point, one of the most valuable resources that teams possess is the breadth of knowledge, expertise, skills, experiences, and abilities that resides across its individual team members. Interestingly, however, teams do not always realize just what they have and, as a result, struggle to optimize their coordination efforts. A team's shared knowledge of who knows what" on the team is referred to as its *transactive memory system*.[47] Teams with stronger transactive memory systems are able to more efficiently and effectively coordinate their tasks by, for example, matching expertise with specific tasks and knowing who to call for help, and as a result, they demonstrate higher levels of performance.[48] Some relatively straightforward ways that you can facilitate stronger transactive memory systems include having team conversations that develop general familiarity among members (e.g., providing basic background information and discussing each member's other roles in the organization), directly communicating each member's relevant expertise (e.g., explaining why a member was chosen for the team), and discussing possible ways to maximize collaboration.[49] These steps not only foster member coordination early on but can also prompt members to think about future opportunities for cross-team learning as they navigate their other organizational roles.[50]

The fifth critical aspect of team design is *authority to manage the work*. In Chapter 3, we discussed the role of autonomy in creating effective work designs to enhance individual empowerment, differentiating between the structural feature of building autonomous working structures from the psychological experience produced by individual's actual perceptions of choice. The same is true for team design. An overall team needs the work systems, structures, and characteristics that enable its members to collectively have control over their work. Indeed, this is an essential ingredient for empowered teams. Without it, the inability to determine what tasks to carry out and how or when to do so will certainly sabotage any real sense of team empowerment, trust, and psychological safety.

The final must-have aspect of team design that Hackman and Wageman discussed is the existence of *team performance goals*. In Chapter 3, we highlighted the importance of setting SMART (specific, measurable, achievable, relevant, and time-bound) goals for individuals to boost their empowerment, and the same holds true for teams. The difference here, however, is that team goals must focus on collective performance, or what the team members hope to achieve by working together. Thus, you should spend considerable effort helping your teams develop a set of powerful team goals that help them energize and focus their overall team efforts. An important caveat here is that *team goals should be aligned with every team member's individual goals as closely as possible*. This is not always a simple endeavor, but misalignment between individuals' goals and their team's goals can have bad implications for the performance of both.

One of the managers with whom we work emphasized this point:

People should have about six to eight goals max. Two-thirds of them should align with project or corporate strategy goals, and the remaining one-third should be more personal goals. As a project manager, I need to know what those personal goals are. Since I don't have access to an HR system to see personal goals, I need to ask individuals and the team what they want to get personally out of the project in terms of goals. Also, the goals should flow from a project plan and charter. The more you anchor to the charter with goals, the better; otherwise, the charter is useless. While we may have team goals, not everyone on the team has the same individual goals. The "sprint" people get stretch goals, and the "marathon" people get different goals. The most important thing, though, is to anchor the goals to the common vision and ensure that they inspire, or at least interest, the individual and the team.

Clearly, aligning both individual and team goals is an important step to maximizing overall team effectiveness. Additionally, the evidence suggests that when you are confronting highly complex tasks, you should emphasize goals that center around learning more so than specific performance goals, at least initially.[51] Obviously, this is an especially important consideration in today's VUCA environment. As your team gains a more solid footing and builds the requisite skills, you can then shift to specific performance outcomes to pursue. As a leader, you can play a critical role in determining when it is appropriate to pivot from a learning goal to a performance goal emphasis. In some cases, teams may suffer from "analysis paralysis," in which case you may need to make an executive decision that pushes your team beyond deliberating different goal choices to implementing a specific goal pursuit.[52]

Beyond these six must-haves, Hackman and Wageman also argue that *team composition* is an important design feature of successful teams. Team composition encompasses the skill and demographic diversity of team members, team size, and the length of time the team has had stable membership. As we already noted in this chapter, one of the most important and distinctive advantages of teams in today's VUCA environment is that members often bring distinctive and complementary skills to the team's tasks. Indeed, there may be very little overlap between each member's knowledge, skills, abilities, and perspectives, which can propel a team to important synergies. By contrast, if team members are all alike, there is almost nothing to be gained from putting them together in the first place; that is, a single individual would likely be just as effective as an entire team. Yet the problem with a diverse team is that much of the evidence shows that it takes quite a bit longer for these teams to get down to business compared to teams whose members are all alike. If you lead a diverse team, you will need to spend a great deal of time on the front end trying to help members understand one another's perspectives and approaches to work. If this effort is successful, the payoff is great in that these teams almost always outperform homogeneous teams, particularly when outcomes such as innovation, creativity, and quality are most desired.[53]

We have already mentioned that team size can be problematic. In fact, once a team gets beyond six to eight members, it often stops being a real team (in terms of the definition we provided in Chapter 1). Very large teams are often more accurately referred to as a group or even a "team of teams."[54] Comprehensive reviews on empowerment are a little at odds with regard to how team size affects team empowerment. For example, one review found that larger teams had less team empowerment, meaning that team members tend to lose their sense of overall team empowerment if their teams grow too big.[55] This may not be surprising, as team empowerment entails shared perceptions of team aspects, such as meaningfulness and impact. Once a team grows beyond a certain size, the chances for team empowerment to be a truly shared experience drop off rather dramatically.

We mentioned that another comprehensive review, however, found that team empowerment and team performance were more strongly linked for larger, rather than smaller, teams.[56] Perhaps we can interpret these contradictory findings to mean that while smaller teams maximize the chance for team empowerment to be perceived, if you are forced to assemble a team that is a bit larger (say, ten to fifteen members), then it is imperative that you take all the steps outlined in this chapter to ensure a high level of team empowerment, which will help the team achieve optimal performance.

We won't comment too much on the last aspect of team design, the length of time the team has had stable membership, because this ideal is likely to be an unattainable luxury for most of today's teams. The truth remains, however, that the longer that teams can be kept intact, the more likely shared perceptions of team empowerment, trust, and psychological safety will be reached and maintained. We summarize the ways in which you can create empowering structures and systems for your teams in Table 4.2.

TABLE 4.2. Creating Empowering Organizational Structures and Systems Targeted at a Team as a Whole

Empowering Organizational Structures and Systems	Examples
1. Supportive organizational climate	Give your entire team a special project and "advertise" what the team is doing to the whole company. Be a sponsor and supporter of your team's objectives to the rest of the company. Make sure your team knows it has the company behind it.
2. Perceived organizational support	Make sure your entire team knows where to go in the organization if it has a problem or issue. Constantly reinforce the level of support the team has company-wide.
3. Organizational trust	Communicate constantly to your team that the overall company has trust and faith in it, and always make sure that those interacting with the team display trust.
4. Team design: Clear, engaging direction	From the very beginning, make sure your entire team knows what it is trying to accomplish and how it will get there; if the team loses it way, step back in. Use a team charter at the team's inception.
5. Team design: Interdependence	Make sure the task calls for real teamwork by assessing the level of interdependence. Reinforce the importance to team members of communicating and coordinating with one another to accomplish tasks.
6. Team design: Rewards	Is there something at stake for the team to succeed? Monetary team bonuses are great, but so are celebratory events like dinners, sporting events, or a special occasion with plaques and certificates.
7. Team design: Resources	Make sure the team has what it needs to succeed not just in terms of budget or materials but also training and development.
8. Team design: Authority to manage the work	Is the team designed in such a way that members can take the necessary autonomy and discretion when needed?
9. Team design: Performance goals	Make sure that at least some of the important goals are set for the team as a whole and that these team goals are aligned with individual goals.
10. Team composition: Skill and demographic diversity	Make sure the team is set up in a way that creates and supports diverse viewpoints and abilities.
11. Team composition: Team size	Try to keep teams no larger than about eight members. If team size gets too big, break the team down into subteams.
12. Team composition: Stable membership	This is a pipe dream for most of today's teams and leaders, but the evidence does show that team stability is linked to a host of positive outcomes.

An Oldie But a Goodie: Using Transformational Leadership to
Boost Team Empowerment, Trust, and Psychological Safety

In addition to the team coaching and team design factors already described, certain aspects of *transformational leadership*—leadership that encourages follower self-development and focuses on satisfying followers' needs[57]—are likely to be linked to whether team members experience true team empowerment, trust, and psychological safety. The basic idea behind transformational leadership is that leaders in organizations that are forced to grapple with competition and constantly changing business environments should behave in certain ways to motivate those around them to think about problems in new ways and effectively enact change. The 1980s and 1990s saw an explosion in an interest in transformational leadership, with such widely celebrated examples as Jack Welch with GE, Lou Gerstner of IBM, and Steve Jobs at Apple.

Although there is some controversy over what transformational leadership really means and debate as to the actual dimensions of transformational leadership,[58] four generally accepted dimensions are (1) *idealized influence*, or showing conviction and appealing to follower emotions, causing followers to identify with their leader; (2) *inspirational motivation*, or articulating a vision that is motivating and inspiring, challenging followers to pursue high standards, communicating optimism about goals, and providing meaning for followers' tasks; (3) *intellectual stimulation*, or challenging assumptions, taking risks, asking for followers' ideas, and encouraging creativity; and (4) *individualized consideration*, or paying attention to each follower's needs, acting as a mentor or coach and listening to concerns.[59]

Although there is evidence for the positive effects of transformational leadership on both individuals and teams,[60] some have effectively argued that two of the dimensions are more team focused (idealized influence and inspirational motivation), while the other two are more individual focused (intellectual stimulation and individualized consideration).[61] As a result, leaders who work to display idealized influence and inspirational motivation will be more likely to enhance team empowerment, trust, and psychological safety than leaders who display neither of these behaviors.

Regarding idealized influence, one of the managers with whom we worked in a large accounting firm said:

> The chief information officer who recruited me for my position in this firm, an Australian guy, definitely has charisma and personal power. When he

walked into a room, people noticed. He was also very good with the business in that we had very challenging projects and a lot of the team members were beaten down. He was the type of leader who would chat for ten or fifteen minutes, and the people just seemed instantly more engaged. He knew the right questions to ask. He also never tried to blame or scapegoat; he was really trying to help. As a result, our team performed exceptionally well and overcame all of the challenges associated with those projects.

Although followers might not describe every good leader as having this type of charisma, it is important to note that you should seek to cultivate a similarly effectual idealized influence with your team members without straying too far from your natural style.

One of our high-technology team leaders emphasized the importance of the other factor, inspirational motivation, and being able to inspire by storytelling:

One of our leaders was always the closer at our all-hands meetings. People connect through stories. In fact, one of our executives used to ask everyone in the company to be on the lookout for stories about amazing team members in the company. Once you found one, you could e-mail the executive's office, and he would end up calling the team member personally to thank him or her. You can't imagine how inspiring that was for the teams in our company. And, even lower down in the organization, our marketing department, for example, had all of these epic stories that they publish to motivate and galvanize teams. When I think of inspiration, I think of powerful stories.

Tips for Designing Extrinsic Motivation Systems for Your Team as a Whole

In this chapter, we have focused primarily on the role of intrinsic motivation for your team as a whole. Similar to Chapter 3, however, we cannot ignore the importance of extrinsic motivation for leading teams. And, unless you are an HR professional, you may not even realize that there is a whole science devoted to extrinsic motivation and how to best pay people! In fact, every year hundreds of academic and practitioner articles are published on compensation in such journals as *Journal of Compensation and Benefits* and *Compensation and Benefits Review*.

Along with a focus on how to pay individuals, there has also been a great deal of attention in the past twenty-five years focused on team-based reward and evaluation systems.[62] It is not our intention to rehash all of that here; rather, we focus on what the evidence suggests are the most crucial elements for enhancing performance management for entire teams. The results show that just as many companies ignore rewarding and evaluating individuals in team contexts for displaying teamwork behavior, *they also often fail to incentivize and evaluate overall team performance*. Unfortunately, despite the quarter-century of research emphasizing the importance and generally positive effects of some level of team-based rewards (we should qualify this by stating that a large majority of this research has been conducted in the laboratory or with students rather than in actual organizations),[63] most companies still use individual-based reward systems in complete opposition to the motivation of teamwork. Many of the participants in our executive education classes echo this sentiment, and even in our interviews and observations for this book, we couldn't find many examples of formal reward and recognition systems for teams as a whole.

Team-based rewards are often complex and difficult to implement; nevertheless, people tend to do what they get rewarded and evaluated for, and unless you build in some incentive for overall team performance, team members will simply not make teamwork a priority. But what makes them so complicated? Well, there is a long list of reasons why team rewards do not always produce the intended outcome of teamwork.[64]

For example, in Chapter 3, we discussed Levi Strauss's disastrous experience using a team-based reward system in its sewing plants in Tennessee and Texas. The main culprit for all of the hostility among team members appeared to be the almost immediate occurrence of slacking behavior. When employees were rewarded and evaluated only for team performance, completely neglecting individual performance, some team members quickly realized that they could allow other team members to complete the brunt of the work and still end up taking home a pretty decent salary. Thus, using team-based rewards exclusively often results in a team ending up with slackers who are no longer motivated to perform at a high level.

Levi Strauss, however, was in a quandary because there was absolutely no incentive for team members to exhibit teamwork in their former piece-rate pay system, which rewards individual members for the number of pairs of jeans they assemble during a specified time period. If an individual requested help from a fellow team member with a job-related issue, the latter team member probably quickly visualized a shrinking amount of pay at the end of the week. In addition, this issue is exacerbated in Western countries, where cultures emphasize that the individual, not groups or teams, is the most important unit of society.

So, again, the dilemma is that leaders and companies cannot use only individual-based reward systems and expect teamwork, but they also cannot use an exclusively team-based reward system because individuals lose their sense of individual accountability and become slackers, hurting overall team performance. So what else is there? Perhaps the answer lies in a combination of both individual- and team-based rewards. With a sort of hybrid reward system, you might be able to get the best of both worlds (incentivizing both individual and team performance) while at the same time minimizing the disadvantages of both (a lack of teamwork or social loafing). Indeed, some lab research has found that overall team performance can be improved by using hybrid rewards programs that balance individual and shared rewards.[65]

But do these programs work in the real world? To find out, Harvard's Ruth Wageman conducted a field experiment with Xerox copy repair technician teams.[66] She asked Xerox to incentivize separate sets of copy repair technician teams using three different methods tied directly to: team behavior and performance only, individual behavior and performance only, and a hybrid condition of both team and individual behavior and performance. Despite the intuitive appeal of a hybrid reward system for encouraging both individual performance and teamwork, Wageman found that these types of reward systems generated complete confusion among the technicians in their teams, motivating neither good individual nor team performance. She concluded, "Introducing some group-level rewards undermined technicians' sense of individual responsibility without providing strong enough collective motivation to fully develop the interdependent [team] process."[67] In the end, if people use their reward systems as signals for what behaviors they should exhibit (which they typically do), hybrid reward systems may leave many feeling hopelessly confused.

Therefore, despite the quarter-century of advice that sounds a lot like "if you want people to act like a team, you should pay them as a team," our suggestion to those considering using team-based rewards to incentivize teamwork is a perhaps surprising piece of advice: *Don't do it*. In fact, we cannot argue strongly enough how little in favor we are of team-based rewards.

However, let us clarify that by "team-based rewards," we mean specifically replacing a portion of an individual's base pay with some level of team-based incentive. It simply won't work.

Again, this notion is especially true in Western countries. In our own research, we examined why there appears to be a high level of resistance to team-based rewards in companies.[68] Using data from over 600 employees in a Fortune 50 insurance company, we found that one of the biggest culprits responsible for employee resistance to team-based rewards was, in fact, national culture. That is, employees resisted team-based reward systems more so if they also had highly individualistic cultural values in which the individual is more important than the collective. Related to this, we also found that many employees do not perceive team-based rewards to be fair; that is, they do not believe that rewarding teams as a whole is the right way to pay people based on their performance (we get the same comments from our MBA students about shared project grades!). This may be especially true for teams in which performance criteria are fuzzy or subjective (e.g., creatively responding to previously unknown challenges).

In addition, we found that employees in highly interdependent teams were actually more receptive to team-based rewards, which is consistent with our 3D Team Leadership approach that suggests focusing your leadership efforts more on teams as a whole when your members are working highly interdependently. Finally, employees were more receptive to team-based rewards when they were, probably not surprisingly, also highly committed to their teams and strongly preferred teamwork over individual work. In some of our original research on team empowerment, we also found that some level of team-based rewards was actually associated with higher levels of team empowerment.[69]

So, if we are not advocating for carving out a portion of an individual's pay and replacing it with a team reward component, what are we recommending you do to motivate and reward teamwork? Although we do advise leaving each individual team member's base pay alone, we do advocate for the power of *team bonuses*. Providing an incentive on top of an individual's base pay can have a powerful effect on motivating teamwork behavior without tinkering around with the individual component of pay.

That's just what a travel reservation company with which we worked did to incentivize teamwork. Using a balanced scorecard approach with various criteria that added up to 100 percent, the company developed four team-level metrics that they assessed every quarter: growth in the business (measured by market share; 30 percent of the total), profitability (measured by cost per travel booking; 25 percent of the total), process improvement (measured by decreases in cycle time for setting up travel reservation systems for customers; 20 percent of the total), and customer satisfaction (measured using surveys of actual customers; 25 percent of the total). Teams received performance-based bonuses on top of their regular pay for exceeding target goals set forth by the company every quarter based on these metrics. In true balanced score-card fashion, customer satisfaction and process improvement were negatively related to each other; that is, the less time the company spent setting up travel systems with a particular customer, the lower was that customer's satisfaction level. So, striking the right balance between the various dimensions of the scorecard was critical for overall team performance.

Sometimes that extra bonus does not have to be financial. One of our leaders in an insurance company said:

> When a particular team has worked really hard at nights and on weekends on a project, I tell the whole team to leave early on a Friday. I'll say something like, "I don't want to see any of you after lunch." We even had company-sponsored galas where we announce a winning team and the entire team and their families win a vacation, like a cruise. Instead of cash incentives, which can be tricky across countries because of different tax systems, we use a points system that can be redeemed for things in our company.

So if financial bonuses are not a possibility, you can look for other creative ways to implement meaningful team rewards beyond a simple cash bonus. The results of even these types of rewards can be strongly encouraging.

Beyond reward systems, performance management for teams as a whole can also involve adding a team-based component to company evaluation systems. Just as in Chapter 3, where we advocated for adding a teamwork component to each individual's performance evaluation, there is evidence demonstrating that providing evaluations for team entities can motivate the "I's" in the team to function more effectively as a unit.

Finally, there has been at least some evidence in support of using peer evaluations in support of encouraging teamwork.[70] One of the managers in a biotechnology company with whom we work talked about the importance of this feature in any evaluation system said, "When I go and assess individual performance, I'm looking at a 360 review. I ask everyone around them for feedback, very directly, as in, 'Is this person performing at a high level?' This is incredibly important in a team environment. You do not have the time to assess ten different people by yourself. You should be assessing them on how their peers evaluate them but also their customers." As we have previously mentioned in this book, feedback is an important factor in building empowered teams that also have high levels of trust and psychological safety, and peer evaluations can be insightful. After incorporating the tips we provided in Chapter 3 for making peer evaluations more valid and reliable, we encourage you to use them to your advantage in enhancing overall teamwork.

The last point we make about extrinsic motivation is a reminder from Chapter 3: many people are on more than one team, which will require you to be creative in terms of designing reward, recognition, and goal-setting programs for multiple teams simultaneously. Nonetheless, extrinsic motivation is an important factor that you can use to improve overall team performance.

In summary, we have discussed the importance of building a high level of team empowerment, trust, and psychological safety in order to maximize the overall team dimension in our model of 3D Team Leadership. When a team is operating highly interdependently, you should adopt a team focus with your leadership behaviors and actions. Regarding behaviors, we advise you to focus on three key actions: (1) displaying empowering leader behavior directed at teams by using the behaviors of role modeling, encouraging and allowing teams to participate in decision-making, providing team coaching, sharing important and strategic information, and displaying a high level of concern and caring for all team members; (2) creating empowering team structures and systems by focusing on enhancing sociopolitical support through creating a supportive organizational climate, ensuring a high level of perceived organizational support, promoting a high level of team trust, and building in important elements of team design, including a clear and engaging direction, task interdependence, team resources, authority to manage the work, team performance goals, and team composition; and (3) exhibiting the team-focused aspects of transformational leadership: idealized influence, inspirational motivation. We also warned against using team-based performance rewards that eat into an individual's take-home pay, instead adding a team-based bonus component on top of individual pay.

This is an ambitious list of things on which to focus when maximizing the team dimension of 3D Team Leadership. We wish we could tell you how to make this simple, but admittedly, it takes a lot of work. Suffice it to say that the evidence is strong in suggesting that the more you can successfully focus on all of these factors related to the team dimension of 3D Team Leadership, the better chance you'll have of maximizing the success of your teams. Of course, similar to our recommendations in Chapter 3, leaders should rely on sensemaking techniques like scanning the environment for cues, soliciting feedback from team members, and, when possible, drawing from their past experiences to determine which specific tool is lacking or needs more attention.

5   The Third Dimension: Subteams

IN THIS CHAPTER, WE INTRODUCE A NEW WRINKLE: SUB-
teams, which refers to two or more smaller subsets of members
nested within a larger team that work interdependently within and between
one another for the benefit of an overall team. We also have already referred to
the level of interdependence in this type of team as *multilayered* interdependence, which can be vastly more complex than the other types of interdependence discussed so far. For example, think of a software development team
that has subteam of coders (those who write computer code) and a subteam of
debuggers (those who look for errors in the code). Members often work interdependently with one another within each subteam: the coders coordinate
with one another to make sure members are not duplicating their efforts, and
the debuggers exchange information with one another on which aspects of the
code are problematic. These two subteams are also interdependent between
each other; that is, the debuggers have to provide information to the coders
about their errors, and the coders need to alert the debuggers for potential
trouble spots, as well as changes they are making to reduce errors, thereby
improving the overall code writing process.

Similar to the lessons in Chapter 3, many leaders have difficulty accepting
the notion that breaking down a team into smaller sets of members can deliver
value, and they have been indoctrinated from a very early age (think of under-
4 soccer leagues!) to believe it is flat-out wrong to focus on or encourage any
sort of arrangement that doesn't promote a "team as a whole" mind-set. To be

fair, there is a fine line between a "team that clicks" and a "team with cliques," especially when it comes to the idea of subteams. For example, as we noted in Chapter 2, team members often divide into factions based on non-work-related faultlines[1] like gender, race/ethnicity, age, or educational background (akin to cliques). Although they may appear similar in some ways, these factions rarely operate as effective subteams. Rather than wait for them to emerge on their own, you should work to *proactively create your own subteams* by making purposeful decisions about work flow based on relevant factors like previous knowledge, diversity in thinking, and functional expertise. When created and used properly, subteams represent an opportunity to generate all of the benefits of a traditional team, only multiplied by more units.

Beyond the opportunity to leverage mini-powerhouses under a single team umbrella, there is also another reason subteams have become necessary: many of today's teams and the scope of their tasks can be so large that they are unmanageable as a single, interdependent unit.[2] For example, aerospace teams that are involved in building next-generation aircraft can have teams that number in the thousands of members.[3] Granted, some of this is due to companies slapping a team label onto a group, but in many cases companies are legitimately hoping to generate interdependent work from upwards of fifty or more key stakeholders.

In *The Wisdom of Teams,* authors Katzenbach and Smith argue that very large teams would have members that struggle to interact constructively and, almost by necessity, break themselves down into smaller, more manageable subteams.[4] Again, this can be advantageous because subteams can lead to increased creativity and learning, which are imperative in today's VUCA environments.[5] A team of subteams can also have less overall team conformity (i.e., "groupidity") because subteam members have their own unique ideas and processes and are not as frequently subjected to overall team pressure. So it is imperative that you take steps to form subteams and devote an appropriate focus on these entities to ensure overall team success. Beyond evaluating team size, two other basic criteria can help you determine when subteams should dominate your focus.

The first is in ongoing teams that repeatedly face multiple and semi-unique tasks that require moderate or high levels of interdependence. In its most basic form, teams in this category can employ each subteam to perform distinct, team-like tasks and then combine their work at various points in a task cycle. When these arrangements become larger and more complex, they are sometimes referred to as a type of multiteam system (discussed in more detail in the next section). Importantly, for these arrangements to be effective, unique tasks should be reasonably independent to prevent unnecessary redundancies. However, subteams should also have the appropriate high-level strategic view to avoid surprises when outputs come together into a final product, service, solution, or idea.

The second situation when a subteam focus is appropriate occurs when a team follows a dynamic life cycle model and shifts into a period in which multiple interdependent tasks need to be completed at the same time. This is very different from and more complicated than the previous scenario. Leading an entity that switches between a group, a team, and a team of subteams not only requires leading each of the different entities at varying time points, but also demands that leaders be mindful of when teams are in transition (and sometimes proactively guiding the transition itself) and manage their shifts across the different foci. We provide some helpful road signs for recognizing and facilitating these transitions in Chapter 6. Our experience and work with companies suggests that a subteam focus is often the most difficult and unintuitive aspect to master. However, this also means that learning how and when to use subteams represents a tremendous opportunity to generate significant gains in your own team leadership.

A Brief Overview of Leading and Motivating Subteams (or How We Learned to Love Multiteam Systems)

A multiteam system, sometimes called a *team of teams*, is defined as "two or more teams that interface directly and interdependently in response to environmental contingencies toward the accomplishment of collective goals."[6] Compared to research on leading individuals in team contexts and teams as a whole, research on multiteam systems is in its relative infancy.[7] In fact, although the evidence is accumulating rapidly, much of this research has been conducted by a select few of our colleagues, namely Leslie DeChurch, Michelle Marks, John Mathieu, and Steve Zaccaro, within the past few years.[8] Note that the original definition was meant to apply to two or more entirely distinct teams, whereas we are applying the concept to one intact team with multiple subteams embedded within it. To be clear, the multiteam system folks will talk about a very large team consisting of a set of smaller, but still whole, intact teams within it.[9] To make sure the difference is clear and recognizing that multiteam systems are very large in size and scope, we refer to an overall team with several subteams within it as a multisubteam system. Although in relatively stable teaming environments this distinction is purely semantics, our treatment of leading subteams is very practical when considering that teams in dynamic environments might constantly morph from singular teams to more complex multisubteam systems over time.

Great leaders get the most out of their subteams by understanding the delicate balance of both the within- and the between-subteam dynamics that affect members' ability to perform at their best (said more plainly, they grasp the ins and outs of subteams). In essence, as a team leader, you'll need to realize that subteams cannot function well if their members are incapable of cooperating toward common subteam goals; in addition, each of the subteams themselves must also be on the same page with one another to ensure their work comes together in a way that contributes to the whole team's mission.[10] You're probably thinking, *Wait a minute! Do I basically have to do everything you described in the prior chapters, just with more teams! Isn't that exponentially more complex? What about my limited resources?*

We get it. Leading subteams is complex, to be sure, but ultimately it can be simpler and more effective than trying to lead a group of fifty or more employees as distinct individuals or getting them all on the same page as a single "team." Rest assured, however, that the 3D Team Leadership model still offers the most efficient and practical approach for getting the most out of subteams. Moreover, don't forget that the payoffs that come from effectively orchestrating a multisubteam system can be tremendous.

For many of the leaders with whom we have worked, the most challenging aspect of leading subteams is *managing the relationships between a set of subteams*, which represents only one of the multiple layers of interdependence. Before moving to the leader behaviors that can help master this part of the equation, we begin with a brief description of managing the within-subteam dynamics in each of your subteams, which builds on what you've already learned in Chapters 3 and 4. This should be straightforward, though no less important than the between-subteam leadership guidance.

The Most Important Things to Know about Leading
Each of the Subteams within an Overall Team

With a multisubteam system, a leader is basically responsible for managing multiple stand-alone teams that can each display any of the group- or team-like attributes discussed in Chapters 3 and 4, respectively. Accordingly, you need to either pay particularly close attention to the individuals within each subteam or the overall collective subteam, depending on their ideal interdependence. Let's quickly revisit the basics.

When a subteam's interdependence requirements are low, you should focus mostly on the individuals within that subteam. Specifically, you should be mindful to display the behaviors that focus on individual empowerment, which we discussed in Chapter 3. By contrast, when interdependence requirements within a subteam are higher, you should focus on promoting overall subteam empowerment, trust, and psychological safety. The specific behaviors we described in Chapter 4 include role modeling, encouraging teams to participate in decision making, providing coaching for teams to become confident in their empowerment experiences, sharing important strategic information with teams, and displaying a high level of concern and caring for teams.

Just as we stated in each of the two prior chapters, you need to constantly work to align the concurrent goals operating in your team. This, of course, becomes more complicated when subteams are added to the equation. To minimize confusion and maximize performance, try to create well-aligned goal structures—that is, overall team goals will clearly inform subteam goals, which will then clearly inform individual goals— that allow members to have a clear line of sight[11] for how they fit into the major strategic aims of the organization. Goal alignment is especially important when a team moves across different work arrangements throughout a life cycle, as incompatible goals at one point in a team's life cycle can spill over to create problems at a later point.

Finally, be aware that two or more subteams within the same overall team often face different interdependence requirements. Although subteams are typically employed when a team faces two or more distinct but moderately or highly interdependent tasks that require collaboration, there are times when a particular subteam is faced with relatively independent and routine work. Of course, you know by now that you will have to diagnose the best way different tasks should be carried out by each subteam in order to use the optimal leadership approach. We recognize how complicated this can be, particularly if there are numerous subteams within your overall team. Nevertheless, the fact remains that if a particular subteam's members are carrying out work that is highly interdependent, you should focus more on the subteam as a whole. If, by contrast, a particular subteam's members are working primarily independently (more like a group), then you can focus more on the individuals within that subteam. And if particular subteams morph from more group-like to team-like and back again, hang on! It could be a bumpy ride trying to keep up.

As an example, a software development team may at some point conduct a soft product launch with a small group of potential customers, which will then require some members to field routine service calls or e-mails (a task that can be done individually by a group-like entity) and another set of members to collaboratively fix issues in a hurried fashion (a potentially high interdependence task requiring a team-like entity). In this scenario, you would focus mostly on individuals in the first subteam, but focus primarily on the subteam as a whole for the second subteam, all while reiterating the overall team goals to both.

Navigating the Messiness of Multisubteam Systems through Leader Stretegizing and Coordinating

Although a team-of-subteams approach often sounds great on paper, it can easily devolve into nightmarish subteam-versus-subteam scenarios. This problem emerges because even well-meaning leaders can fail to manage the interdependence between each of the subteams, a layer of interdependence that is totally separate from within-subteam interdependence. In these cases, overall teams can fail even if their unique subteams appear to thrive. In fact, a great deal of evidence suggests that failure to manage the horizontal relationships and interdependencies between subteams is a key reason that these teams of subteams do not work.[12] Evidence-based approaches point to two key leadership behaviors that can remedy this issue: leader *strategizing* and leader *coordinating*.[13]

Strategizing efforts typically take place during a team's transition activities like planning, analysis, and goal setting. Coordinating behaviors usually occur during a team's work on action activities, which occur when members' interaction is focused on accomplishing goals, coordinating actions, and monitoring team progress.[14] As we noted in Chapter 4, interpersonally focused behaviors, like boosting motivation and managing conflict, are important across both transition and action activities.[15]

Because subteams reflect hybrid entities residing somewhere in between individuals and a team as a whole, both strategizing and coordinating leader behaviors should hit three points of impact: *within subteams*, or leader behavior directed at each of the subteams within an overall team; *between subteams*, or leader behavior directed at the interface between each of the subteams within a team as a whole; and *across subteams*, or leader behavior directed at the interface between an overall team composed of multiple subteams and its key stakeholders outside that team (e.g., other teams inside a company, teams outside a company, customers, clients).[16] This would entail a total of six sets of behaviors—strategizing and coordinating for within-, between-, and across-subteam interdependencies—which undoubtedly underscores the complexity inherent in multilayered interdependence.

Figure 5.1 shows the multiple layers of interdependencies in a multisubteam system: within-subteam interdependence, between-subteam interdependence, and across-subteam interdependence.

Best Practices for Subteam Strategizing

Leader strategizing in a multisubteam system refers to a leader's analysis of the system performance environment, a structuring of work, the defining of roles, prioritization of tasks, and planning and goal setting.[17] We next describe leader behaviors focused on strategizing within, between, and across a multisubteam system.

The leader-strategizing behaviors focused on each of the subteams within an overall team are gathering information about each subteam's performance environment and framing each subteam's task, setting objectives for each subteam, and planning how subteam members will work together within each subteam to accomplish their goals.[18] By way of demonstration, consider what a senior manager who led a team of more junior managers in a program management organization said about strategizing with her subteams:

> The first thing I did was teach each of my subteams how to use project scheduling software, pretty basic but important stuff. I also made it clear that each subteam needed to have three things—deliverables, durations, and dependencies; and, I asked each subteam to put these in writing. I explained that I needed to know their activities and how they would reach these. One of the project management tricks that I use is I work a lot with people in the planning stages to really get them to be crisp and clear with regard to what they

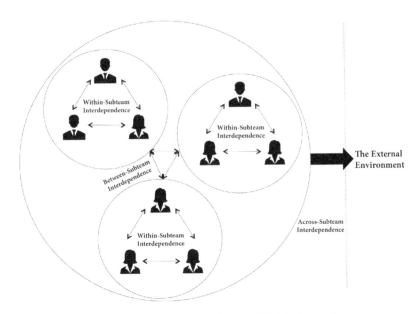

FIGURE 5.1. The Multilayered Interdependence of Multisubteam Systems

are planning to do. I've had problems in the past where I was a little too vague with strategizing, and six months or a year into the project, there would be confusion as to actually what was asked of them. So I learned that I needed to be crystal clear and also explain to them that other teams are going to be relying on them, so we need to set the right strategy and agree to it.

As this leader explains, working with each of the subteams within an overall team to generate a clear strategy can have major implications for the subteams' future progress and success, which of course will help determine the performance of an overall team as well.

Strategizing behaviors focused on the interface between subteams within an overall team as a whole (*between-subteam interdependence*) include gathering information about the multisubteam system's performance environment and framing the task, setting objectives for the multisubteam system, and planning how subteams will work together to reach multisubteam system goals.[19] A project manager at a large insurance company provided us with several key tools that he uses to lead his team's set of subteams:

I have a team of twelve people composed of four subteams of three members each. To strategize effectively with the subteams, I make sure that all twelve team members know what our business case is and that they have familiarized themselves with our team charter. I have had cases where team members don't read the charter, so they know now that I will ask questions. I always sit down with all of the team members and reinforce the overall view of what we're trying to do, the overall goal. In my opinion, the role of a 3D team leader is to have that initial conversation by posing questions. I've seen many leaders, for the sake of time, just give them the answers. The most important thing is to get the sub-teams to think as a whole first. I ask, "Who is the customer of our team? What is the benefit of what we're doing?" I make sure they have one or more shared goals, top-level goals. Assuming that the subteams basically have the same over-all purpose, I keep them together for strategizing. I wouldn't do this for each subteam separately. If it is a small team with a common purpose, you strategize together. If it is a large team with a common purpose, you would take the most senior person from each subteam and pull them together into a team and then, you do your deep dive with each of the subteams. The question I always ask is, "What is the benefit of having the members strategize together?"

Although this is only one example of how you might strategize between your subteams, the fact remains that you must find a way to guide the interactions and strategy of your multiple subteams in order to be successful.

Strategizing behaviors focused on the interface between a multisubteam system and its external environment (*across-subteam interdependence*) include gathering information about your multisubteam system's performance environment from outside the multisubteam system, helping to frame your multisubteam system's task to external stakeholders, and integrating your multisubteam system's plans with those of outside stakeholders.[20] We spoke about this topic with a senior project manager at a technology-based company. In our conversation, the manager emphasized the importance of constantly helping her team strategize across the multisubteam system:

The strategizing we have to do with external constituents is pretty compli-cated. The systems that we build are very expensive, so we have to commit early before making big investments. I personally do a lot of negotiations with our internal and external customers. With internal, I typically get a hand-shake agreement, but I verify in an e-mail to everyone also. I make sure all strategies and agreements are known, and I repeat them every month in our business reviews so that there is no misunderstanding within the overall team.

Clearly these types of strategizing behaviors can help subteams function effectively, as there is a need for all subteam members to understand what is expected of them from internal and external stakeholders. We next discuss leader coordinating, the other important leader behavior relevant to a multisubteam system.

Best Practices for Subteam Coordination

Leader coordinating in a multisubteam system refers to leader facilitation of the system work processes when members are actually doing the work. The coordinating behaviors that are focused on each of the subteams within an overall team (*within-subteam interdependence*) include managing the flow of information and coordinating the actions of the members within each subteam.[21] For example, a senior leader at a major insurance company discussed the importance of striking the right balance between empowering and micromanaging coordination processes within each subteam and said:

> I would give a big caveat and warning to every leader to avoid falling into the trap of micromanagement. We have a leader here who is a very bad micromanager, and some people on his team are going to quit. You can alienate the individuals in the team, but you are going to lose the creativity and the power of diversity that you're trying to tap. So I take a coaching approach with each of the subteams. Together, we create a project plan of what their tasks are, and I ask them to show me what the dependencies are between their subteam and the other subteams. I ask them, "What are the risks, and how will you mitigate them?" The key part of this role is that you will see gaps in their coordination plan. So then I say, "Have you thought about this or that?" It definitely takes more time initially, but it pays off in the end. They will own it and feel more buy-in and empowered.

Indeed, empowerment is a strong method for successfully coordinating subteams' work within a multisubteam system, though other management techniques abound as well.

The coordinating behaviors that are focused on the interface between the subteams within an overall team (*between-subteam interdependence*) include: managing the flow of information between subteams, coordinating the actions of subteams with one another, and prompting subteams to provide backup and display helpful behavior to other teams.[22] We spoke with a senior software engineer at a high-technology company about this, who said,

In our case, we did a few different things to try and improve coordination between the subteams. First, we created a separate team that we called a product owner team. What that team did was give us a top-level way to organize work across the subteams. And this architecture team was used to organize the flow of work to reduce interdependencies so that there would be less complex coordination needs. Second, the other thing we did was that we had a "scrum of scrums" [a term from the Agile project management approach referring to a meeting of the leaders of each subteam] in addition to each team doing a daily stand-up meeting. These meetings were used to bring up issues of lack of coordination across the subteams, and those discussions were facilitated by that.

Reinforcing this senior software engineer's suggestion that frequent meetings can help the members of each of the subteams understand one another's contexts and constraints, evidence also suggests that having at least a few members on each of the subteams with more generalized functional experience (as opposed to very narrow experience) can bridge these between-subteam gaps because it aids mutual understanding, particularly if a team leader provides big-picture information that improves multisubteam functioning.[23] By engaging in these and similar actions, you can greatly improve your coordination behaviors between subteams in a multisubteam system.

As we have noted, the lack of coordination between subteams is the biggest reason these teams of subteams fail.[24] Another evidence-based approach that can help to resolve this issue is to encourage subteam members to engage in between-subteam boundary spanning, which refers to a subteam's activities to create and maintain network connections with other subteams in an overall team to help accomplish team tasks.[25] The most important dimension of boundary spanning relevant for effective subteam functioning is task coordination, or aligning subteam activities with other subteams' efforts.[26] Boundary spanning between subteams can be carried out by designating a member of each subteam to formally take on this role (and this person should have more generalized functional experience) or rotating responsibilities among various subteam members. In any case, the key here is to make sure subteams are discussing and aligning the timing and sequencing of their between-subteam interdependent efforts when working on projects or tasks to maximize the potential for overall team synergy.[27]

The coordinating behaviors that are focused on the interface between a multisubteam system and its external environment (*across-subteam interdependence*) include managing the flow of information to and from external stakeholders and your multisubteam system and orchestrating the actions of your subteams with external stakeholders.[28] For example, a senior project manager at a high-technology organization emphasized the importance of coordinating time lines both internally and externally:

> I constantly have to make the subteams and our overall team aware of all of the interdependencies they have with our customers. If one of the subteams finishes its specific part of the project early, that's not always a good thing. Other subteams are doing things and ordering materials based on an agreed-on time line. So if the other subteams aren't aware that we have a subteam that finished early, they won't know to perform certain tasks or functions early also to line everything up. I have to provide reasons for why coordinating time lines with other constituents is important. I do this by explaining things from a broader perspective. Yes, your time is valuable, but we need to make sure we're coordinating in such a way that we're lining up milestones appropriately.

As is obvious from this example, the successful coordination of behaviors across a multisubteam system affects the overall success of the team and is an important part of managing subteams to which leaders must pay attention.

Table 5.1 summarizes and provides examples of the strategizing and coordinating behaviors focused within each of the subteams, between the subteams, and across the subteams' interface with their external environment.

What Else Can You Do to Maximize the Effectiveness of Your Subteams?

Beyond leader strategizing and coordinating, evidence supports several other critical leader behaviors that can maximize success in a multisubteam system. One especially critical step you can take in a complex system is to help members understand and balance the proximal goals (those more immediate or pressing) and distal goals (those in the longer term and therefore less immediate) in a goal hierarchy. By *goal hierarchy*, we mean "an interconnected network of collective goals, where the shortest term (proximal) goals are at the lowest levels of the hierarchy, longer-term (distal) goals are at higher levels, and superordinate distal goals that represent the multi-[sub]team system objectives are at the top of the hierarchy."[29] Subteams typically work independently toward lower-order goals; conversely, to achieve higher-order goals, multiple subteams have to coordinate their efforts by working interdependently. In some instances, subteams may face (or perceive) conflicting goals that must be first reconciled before they can fully commit to a pursuit.[30] You

TABLE 5.1. Empowering Leader Behaviors Targeted at the Subteams within an Overall Team

Subteam Leader Behaviors	Examples
1. Strategizing within each subteam	Help the members of each subteam understand their deliverables, durations, and dependencies.
2. Strategizing between subteams	Make sure each of the subteams understands how their tasks fit together for the benefit of the overall team.
3. Strategizing across subteams	Serve as a liaison between the overall team and outside stakeholders.
4. Coordinating within each subteam	Help the members of each subteam streamline their processes such that there is a high level of integration within each subteam.
5. Coordinating between subteams	Make sure that each of the subteams understands when and how to integrate and communicate the activities between each of the subteams.
6. Coordinating across subteams	Manage the interdependencies that exist between the overall team and external stakeholders.

play a critical role in this process. Seek out members, gather feedback, and provide clear communication that helps subteams and their members prioritize and integrate goals appropriately.[31] A manager at a large insurance company spoke to the complexity of trying to help his team prioritize the various layers of goals in his multisubteam system:

> There are two major goal priorities here. First, you've got your project goals for the whole system and then you have team goals for each of the subteams, which we call pods in our company. The overall project goals are delivered from on high; then it's my job to relay those goals down to the pods. For example, we had a reorganization and had to find efficiencies as a result of merging teams. One approach was to reduce the number of tools we use from 480 down to a standard suite of 60. We needed a transition plan of how to get down to that number. We did that at the top level with the whole multisubteam system. Then we cascaded the overall project goals down to the pods or subteams. From a subteam standpoint, I start with the requirements, and then we negotiate budget, scope, and time, and we use a triangle analogy here. We normally keep two sides of the triangle fixed and adjust the third one as needed. Then we push this down to the pods so that they can prioritize their activities. I also use the minimal viable product (or MVP) criterion, so that we work on the goals that get us this first and then we drill down. We

also prioritize based on risk, with the highest risk first. In this way, I work with them to understand what's more important and how they structure their projects.

Although structuring the various layers of goals within a multisubteam system is naturally complex, the process of aligning those goals is a crucial step to developing a well-functioning overall team.

When we discussed leading an overall team in Chapter 4, we introduced the concept of shared mental models to reflect a common understanding among team members regarding their expectations for collective behavior when a team is in action mode.[32] Shared mental models are especially vital in multisubteam systems.[33] In effect, they reduce the burden of complexity placed on team members by helping them anticipate and understand one another's actions, which in turn allows them to focus more intently on completing their most important tasks. Your efforts as a leader to help team members develop accurate and similar mental models can pay big dividends in preparing your team for the novel tasks that many of today's teams require.[34]

There are three main types of shared mental models that you should focus on when leading in a multisubsteam system. The first is a *task mental model*, which refers to shared understandings about task procedures, strategies, and information relating to how members should adapt task strategies in the face of changing circumstances.[35] To facilitate the development of a shared task mental model, you should take steps to ensure that all subteam members understand their tasks and how those tasks fit into the larger goals of the overall multisubteam system.

To achieve exactly this, a senior vice president of HR for a global consumer goods firm recounted:

> To make sure our team members were crystal clear on how they fit in, we typically relied heavily on visuals. In fact, we often used what we called a journey map to set the context. At the beginning of every meeting, we would use that journey map to show where we have been and where we need to go. Really it was a where-are-we-now kind of a thing. We reframed that as a way to set context every time we met. Since our multiteam system involved a merger of two companies, the only real confusion emerged around decision rights. People would say, "Hey, you don't have decision rights on this!" So we had to do two things: make sure we clarified boundaries and also make it clear who actually has those decision rights.

By using journey maps and clarifying decision-making boundaries, this senior vice president provided strong visual and verbal cues to help members place their specific tasks into the team's broader network of goals.

The second type of shared mental model is a *team mental model*, which refers to shared understandings about the capabilities of all team members, including task knowledge, abilities, skills, beliefs, attitudes, and preferences.[36] This type of mental model prepares members to play to one another's strengths and, inversely, compensate for one another's deficiencies when appropriate. Helping your team build a shared consensus of their respective strengths and weaknesses sometimes requires a delicate hand. Exemplifying this challenge, a technology manager at a large insurance company cautioned against the dangers of overtly and publicly discussing one another's weaknesses. He said:

> People get upset when you call them out publicly and suggest that they seek help. I would never do that. In fact, I did it differently by approaching people individually and saying things like, "I would like you to share your plan with Lynn and then come back to me," or I would then ask the person, "Do both of you agree with this plan?" If not, I would coach them on how they might take the initiative to shore things up. I also try to bring together people on the subteams with complementary skills to the greatest extent possible. Hopefully, they won't all share the same deficiencies that way.

As this manager points out, team mental models can be highly effective, but your role in developing them requires some forethought.

The third type of shared mental model is a *team interaction model*, which refers to a shared understanding about team members' task roles, their individual contributions, how they should interact with fellow team members when seeking or providing information and resources, and when they should step in to help a teammate who might be overloaded.[37] When there is a shared team interaction model, the subteams within an overall team are more likely to be able to effectively coordinate and integrate their efforts. Speaking to this point, the same technology manager said:

> You have to have a project charter for this, no question about it. The charter lays out the roles, and then you have an organizational chart. You also have a project plan that lays out which team member does what. You have responsibilities by role, and then you have responsibilities by each person's name. Projects will fail if you don't have this. It's funny, I asked a project manager

the other day for a project plan. He looked at me weirdly and said, "I think we have one. I'll have to check." And that's when I knew that team was in trouble. You have to have a contract so that roles and responsibilities are clear.

Therefore, a team interaction model reduces the potential for ambiguities and unproductive conflict within and across subteams, making the entire multi-subteam system more effective.

So, if shared mental models in multisubteam systems are so critical for success, what specific steps can you take to ensure they develop in your team? Evidence suggests two especially important practices. First, you should actively engage in *team-interaction training*, or teaching team members how to work together better as a team. Teamwork training can teach members how to approach, diagnose, and execute team actions when responding to unanticipated challenges. This can be done using formal training programs or giving informal feedback to both individual team members and entire subteams. Second, you can engage in *formal briefings*, typically structured as review sessions to provide feedback on task challenges (rather than teamwork issues) so that members will have a shared understanding of their subteam's probable obstacles and how to overcome them.[38]

A senior software engineer at a technology-based company indicated that he engages in this process informally once or twice a week: "We do this in our stand-up meetings weekly. We ask questions about progress on the specifics of the project, and we discuss who might have more work to do than time available in the sprint and then how the team can help out with staying on schedule. We say, 'How are you going to help, and what are the next set of obstacles we need to watch out for?' I think the teams found these sessions very helpful."

Another senior manager at a high-technology organization said that she spends a lot of time on team retrospectives, or what many refer to as after-action reviews. Describing these reviews, she said:

When I took over a particular team in my company, I realized pretty quickly that it had a bad name in terms of delivering on its projects. I understood immediately that I had to change the tone of this team. It reminded of that scene in the movie *Apollo 13* when mission control realizes the astronauts are in serious trouble. A reporter in the press conference says something like, "This is going to be a disaster." And the mission control director, played by Ed Harris says, "No, this is going to be our finest moment." I worked really hard to reframe the problems by attributing their difficulties to events they could not control. I really had to battle against a kind of learned helplessness in the team. Little by little, we started overcoming our obstacles. After we had reached many of our goals, I held a half-day session with the team going over all we had accomplished. I told them, "This team was forged in fire and we can do anything after this!" I even produced a slide deck that I shared with a lot of executives on how we turned things around. Now the company has a more formal survey for after-action reviews that captures all of this more succinctly.

A technology manager at a large insurance company also emphasized the importance of project reviews:

I definitely do this as part of project reviews, and the frequency depends on size of project. For example, a four-week project will be every day, but a twelve-month project will be weekly or biweekly. I want the project manager to come to see me to give me updates. In a multisubteam system, this could be the leader from each subteam. We talk about task challenges. If it's a smaller team, I will have more intimate knowledge of the project. If larger, I have to rely on other subteam leaders. We also do formal briefings where we sit in with customers on a monthly update. If the customer has a different perception, we need to solve that. Transparency will drive better behaviors.

The examples show that by actively training teams in teamwork and conducting team briefings on task challenges, you can develop the shared mental models that are so crucial for subteam (and overall multisubteam system) success. However, as discussed in previous chapters, extrinsic motivation can also play a critical role in the success of a team's subteams. We turn to this topic next.

What Types of Extrinsic Motivation Are Critical for Subteams?

In Chapters 3 and 4, we focused primarily on intrinsic motivation for individuals in team contexts and teams as a whole, respectively; in this chapter, we have also addressed the critical role of intrinsic motivation for subteams within an overall team. Yet similar to the previous two chapters, we cannot ignore the importance of extrinsic motivation in the leadership of subteams.

We have already discussed the fact that many companies today still ask their employees to exhibit teamwork behavior while simultaneously being evaluated on and rewarded by predominantly individual-based systems—essentially asking for one type of behavior but rewarding just the opposite. Employees thus see teamwork as a sham and then go about their own individual business to obtain high performance ratings and rewards. Still worse, they may actively compete against their own teammates in an attempt to look better in the eyes of a team leader.

In prior chapters, we suggested that companies that rely on teaming should use individual-based rewards alongside evaluation systems that incentivize and recognize individuals to exhibit teamwork. As part of this program, we also encouraged the use of team bonuses (but not at the expense of individual-based pay) to focus team members' attention on achieving their team goals as well as their individual goals. Finally, we stressed the importance of aligning individual and team systems to avoid member confusion and frustration.

The same key underlying tenets hold true when dealing with subteams, although there are some wrinkles that deserve mention. Importantly, we do not want to create any unnecessary confusion by layering on yet another level to the evaluation and reward system to promote subteam teamwork and collaboration. We have already mentioned how quickly this could spiral out of control as employees struggle to understand and achieve individual, subteam, team, unit, division, and organizational goals!

Despite the fact that some who study multiteam systems more generally argue for "multitier and multifaceted compensation systems" to align motivation across individuals, teams, and an overall unit,[39] we do not go so far in our recommendation. Our rationale is rooted in the fact that we are adapting the multiteam concept from its original, large-scale use down to a level that instead reflects multiple subteams within an overall intact team (a multisubteam system). Thus, because members in each of the subteams are still a part of one integrated overall team, we believe a better alternative is to *use goal setting, not money, to motivate team members to focus on their subteam's success.* After all, the whole point behind a multisubteam system is to orchestrate (and eventually coordinate) the activities of various subteams within an overall team. Relying too heavily on financial incentives for subteam-specific objectives will likely create an overly complex and confusing compensation system and, moreover, cause team members to lose sight of the overall team goals. So, to be clear, we encourage leaders to set clear SMART goals for specific subteams (that fit within an appropriate goal hierarchy) while keeping the bulk of financial rewards based on individual performance-based rewards combined with team bonuses. Importantly, including some evaluation of each member's within and across subteam teamwork behaviors can help these varying elements feel more aligned.

Regarding the importance of using goal setting for subteams within an overall team, a manager in an insurance company said:

> Usually there is an overall team goal. But, subteams have different—but congruent—goals, as well. You sometimes have to remind them that if you hit your subteam goal but you don't hit the overall goal, you will have failed. They'll get credit for their individual bit, but they won't get credit for the overall team goal. We try to break down silos by having goals at the top and subteam goals. My only frustration is that we have all of these goals, but sometimes we don't discuss them when we're assessing performance at the end of the year. Well, some managers do it better than others. I make sure to meet at least monthly with my subteam members, and I ask them how they're tracking on their goals. The next month, all we talk about is personal development. The next month it's back to goals, and the next it's personal development again. As a manager, you have a responsibility to help coach and support your team members in meeting their goals and personal development. If you have not discussed their goals or personal development with them, especially if all your discussions were just around project progress and timelines, then you've failed in one of the key responsibilities of a manager.

As this leader noted, following up with subteams about progression in completing their goals is another essential tactic for enabling them to be successful. Though basic, don't forget to acknowledge and debrief after subteam goal accomplishment and shortcomings. And as we said in the prior chapter, don't rush rigid performance goals on a subteam when they are tackling an especially complex problem. Start with ambitious learning goals; then move toward specific performance goals once they have a better grasp of their situation.[40]

In terms of rewards and recognition to ensure that team members accomplish both their individual and team goals, a senior engineering manager at a high-technology company said:

> I wanted to figure out a way to make sure that team members writing code for me did the little things beyond simply the code itself. So I applied scouting

rules to code writing. For example, I would say to them, "The scouts would say that it's not enough to clean up your campsite when you leave; you need to make it better than before you got there." I even had pins made up to recognize people for making something better. Team members could nominate someone on their team or even another team and reward them for making things better for someone else. My team members in Bangalore really liked that because the recognition came from fellow team members. In the United States, we had some frustration because a manager might nominate someone and say, "Tim worked really hard; he's so deserving of this." And we had to reply, "Working hard and doing well is not enough for this. It has to be something more." We had to come up with a Wiki page that stated why we were calling it a scouting award and how you get one.

This example illustrates that you can employ more creative means to recognize and reward team members for completing individual and team goals rather than simply rely on financial incentives. We suggest that you find similar means of extrinsically motivating your team members so as to avoid the confusion of adding on another competing level (i.e., subteam) to evaluation and reward systems.

Best Practices for Avoiding the Dangers of Subteam Faultlines and Fractures in Multisubteam Systems

Unfortunately, the omission of subteam financial incentives will not entirely eliminate the tendency for team members to focus more intently on pursuing their shorter-term subteam goals over the broader team goals. Many years of social psychology research have shown a very natural tendency for people to quickly identify with their immediate groups (sometimes called in-groups) and begin competing with people that they perceive to be members of other groups (sometimes referred to as out-groups).[41]

This happens all the time in our MBA and executive education classes. As an example, we often randomly break a class of students up into teams and engage the teams in a simulation or class exercise designed to teach them some important lesson about teamwork. Even if many of the students are strangers to one another, it always amazes us how quickly they bond with their new randomly assigned teammates and begin displaying very competitive attitudes and behaviors toward other teams. Within fifteen minutes, the students on a particular team will be competing strongly against the other teams as if they have known their own team members for an extended period of time, obviously viewing their own members as insiders and members of other teams as outsiders. Unfortunately, this subgrouping effect is not exactly what we want in today's organizations in which cooperation and collaboration are of paramount importance.

We have seen in our classroom exercises that a danger of breaking up members of a single overall team to complete unique tasks is that they exhibit *less between-team cooperation and collaboration*. This tendency does not always manifest in combative us-versus-them interactions (although we have seen it happen), but rather more innocuously through subteam members communicating more frequently with only their fellow subteam members over others in the overall team.[42] Although this might be fine or even beneficial when members are working interdependently within their own subteams, it can hinder their ability to later integrate their work into the overall team's objectives. Fortunately, evidence points to several best practices for reducing subteam-versus-subteam dynamics.[43]

One of the most basic steps for ensuring functional subteaming is to assign each subteam a clear and specific purpose. This step will help subteams see that they are not competing with one another, but rather have an important and complementary role in the overall team's success. Moreover, explaining why each subteam's purpose will require everyone's contributions ensures that members don't view their subteam as a safety net for reluctant or self-serving individual members. Of course, you also need to be mindful that individuals with preexisting relationships, shared department affiliations, or other non-task-related commonalities may naturally band together as a way to deal with the anxiety they feel working in a VUCA environment, particularly when a team is just forming. Although these subteams may be initially useful for general divisions of labor (sharing common tasks across members), they might also prevent meaningful collaboration for more interdependent and complex team tasks later. Again, you should actively form subteams based on task-relevant characteristics, such as areas of expertise and functional backgrounds.

One leader with whom we worked in a large financial institution said:

> One thing I know about subteams is that they tend to form on their own whether you like it or not. I find that people who are the most alike, not just in terms of things like age or gender, but also in terms of interests, perspectives,

and ways of thinking about things, are the ones most likely to group together into these subteams. So, even though that probably makes them feel comfortable, as in birds of a feather, it does nothing to help overall team success because you want people who are different working together in smaller subteams for the benefit of the overall team. That's how you get creativity and innovation in teams, from the diversity of the members. So, I try not to let my team members form these subteams on their own. I purposefully—and I do this right from the beginning—create formal subteams based on task-relevant experience. And I give them assignments that help the overall team; I don't let them focus on putting their subteam ahead of their overall team. They need to see a connection between what they're doing and how it benefits their team. And, again, I do this very early on because if enough time passes, it will be too late to ungroup the subteams. I guess, in a way, this might seem heavy-handed, but most of my team members thanked me for working with people they might not have naturally gravitated to. I've led some pretty successful teams, so I think it paid off.

Another best practice for minimizing subteam fracturing is rotating members of the team to different subteams when feasible. Doing so reinforces overall team commitment by exposing the maximum number of team members to one another, and it also increases transactive memory (recall from Chapter 4 that this refers to the team's knowledge of who knows what in a team).[44] Rotating members could also have the side benefit of cross-training,[45] which ensures that more accurate and shared mental models form among team members.[46] Moreover, cross-training can help soften the blow of team member turnover, which is likely an inevitable event in today's VUCA environment. Perhaps not surprisingly, rotating team members among subteams can have costs, namely, temporarily disrupting healthy within-subteam dynamics. Nevertheless, the advantages can far outweigh the negatives.[47]

Speaking about the benefits of this practice, a technology manager at a large insurance company said:

> I intentionally move members across the subteams. I put a coder into a product support role. They hate it, so a side benefit is that they become better coders! If you do not rotate across tasks, you will be blindsided by things you can't foresee. I focus on getting people early in their careers to move across the various functions, which has several benefits. First, people think they know what they want to do (I want to be a coder!), but often they don't know

what they really want until they do it. Second, it's much easier to move people around earlier in their career because more senior folks have a lot of business expertise so they don't want to switch (and the company doesn't want them to either!). Finally, we're finding that younger employees today will just switch jobs when they don't feel challenged, so moving them around means that they will feel that they have mini-career shifts to keep things interesting.

An additional approach for minimizing threats associated with subteams is to increase the number of subteams with an overall team, which in effect makes each subteam smaller. Teams with a greater number of subteams will have less threat to their overall team identity.[48] Speaking to this point, the highest level of threat to overall collective team identification—or the extent to which team members emotionally identify with and are invested in their overall team— occurs when a team has two prominent subteams, which would most likely lead to a team's fracturing along subteam lines in a classic faultline situation.

We have seen this pattern emerge repeatedly in our own work with companies. At a global aluminum producer, for example, our findings showed that the lowest level of team performance occurred when teams consisted of about half of the members from one country and half from another. This resulted in a lot of communication and coordination within the same-country subteams, but very little between those country-specific subteams due to this unhealthy faultline.

Similarly, in a team leadership study we conducted across three organizations,[49] we found that in some teams leaders formed very high-quality relationships (recall the LMX concept from Chapter 3) with about half the members and very low relationships with the other half. Those teams fractured along this leader treatment differential, resulting in very low levels of overall team coordination and performance. The lesson here is clear: increasing the number of subteams (especially if you are in danger of having only two) can decrease the occurrence of faultlines and thereby contribute to overall team identity and performance. An important, if not obvious, caveat is that your overall team must be large enough to warrant more subteams.

Finally, there is increasing evidence that collective team identification is especially important for promoting learning and performance in teams with multiple subteams. For example, one study showed that when team members from multidisciplinary subteams did not collectively identify with their overall team, a great amount of diversity actually had a *negative* impact on both team learning and performance. In contrast, when members of the multidisciplinary subteams were able to form a collective sense of overall team identification, the opposite occurred and increasing diversity actually had a *positive* effect on team learning and performance.[50] Clearly, you should strive to create a sense of collective team identification to keep the subteams within your overall team from fracturing apart.

How do you go about creating this collective team identity? The best way is "by creating the right mix of task and goal interdependence among team members, by showing support and recognizing the team, by allowing teams to develop a shared history together rather than changing membership frequently, and by increasing contact among team members."[51] Of course, we have already discussed that the chances of your keeping team members together for indefinite periods of time are becoming increasingly difficult, which means that the challenges of creating overall team identification are also increasing. That said, you could be creative in building a strong collective identity.

One of the project managers with whom we worked in large technology-based company said it really comes down to two things: symbolic gestures and small but meaningful rewards, and the country in which the team members live and work. She said:

> We had a team that was a spread out around the world. There were some members on the East Coast, some on the West Coast, and others in Bangalore, India. In California, they really wanted team T-shirts with project logos. When we didn't give these, they complained. In Pennsylvania, they laughed when we handed out T-shirts. What they really wanted were gift cards when the team succeeded. In Bangalore, they really wanted certificates, not a monetary gift or a T-shirt. They wanted something they could put up on their wall. But what was interesting there is that they did not want the project manager to present them with their certificates. They wanted them sent from the United States directly to the vice president there, and then the vice president would present them with their certificates. It meant something to them in terms of status. And it's even the littlest things. Like we used to send champagne and cake to each site when a team reached an important milestone. People in the United States loved that. But in Bangalore, we found out that they weren't even allowed to have food in their conference rooms! They much preferred to get together with their team members for a dinner out. So we had to find very creative ways to create team identity, but it had to differ from site to site, even within the United States.

As this example illustrates, both geography and symbolic gestures can have a strong impact on the team's collective sense of identity. Interestingly, and thankfully, you can gather information from your various subteam members to find out what works best quite easily (and economically).

In this chapter, we have provided practical advice and tips for leading the subteams within an overall team (or what we referred to as a multisubteam system). Even though some of the lessons from Chapter 3 (leadings the "I's" in teams) and Chapter 4 (leading a team as a whole) can be applied to leading subteams, it should be clear by now that leading a multisubteam system is exponentially more difficult than leading the "I's" or a team as a whole. And as we hope is clear by now, a team of subteams exhibits multilayered interdependence, which is much more complex than even the high levels of interdependence characterizing real teams. The fact remains, however, that subteams are sometimes the best way to accomplish today's VUCA-type tasks. Thus, you will have no choice but to figure out to embrace the complexity of this relatively new form of teaming. By applying the principles from this chapter, combined with a little practice, feedback, and an open mind, we are confident that you can master the complex challenge of leading a set of subteams within an overall team.

6 Putting It All Together: Knowing When to Focus on What in Your Team

THE PREVIOUS THREE CHAPTERS DESCRIBED HOW YOU could navigate each of the three dimensions in our 3D Team Leadership model. Here's a quick rundown of the basics. Chapter 3 outlined the actions and behaviors associated with leading individuals in a team. Individual-focused leadership, we argued, is most effective when teams are operating more like groups completing tasks with a relatively low level of interdependence. Chapter 4 shifted to the behaviors you can use to lead your team as a whole (as a single collective entity). In contrast to individual-focused leadership, team-focused leadership is optimal when success depends on higher levels of interdependence. Chapter 5 introduced subteam-focused leadership. Drawing from a multisubteam system perspective, we explained how focusing on subteams can be particularly useful when your team's ultimate performance can be achieved with a multilayered interdependence arrangement. Multilayered arrangements, we argued, work best when your teams are relatively large and face unique tasks concurrently that can be later integrated together.

In this chapter, we provide *an integrative view of the 3D Team Leadership model* so that you can start immediately applying these lessons in complex environments. Let's start with a bit of good news: If you've reached this point in the book, you already know the most fundamental principle. To determine which team leadership dimension you should focus on at any given time, you need to understand what level of interdependence among team members is required to optimize success. Pretty straightforward, right?

Well, as many great team scholars before us have already implied, "straightforward" and "teams" are rarely used in the same breath.[1] The first question we typically get from prospective team leaders goes something like this: "How exactly do I know what level of interdependence is right for my team at any given time?" Although most leaders grasp the fundamental concept that the ideal level of coordination between members—and hence their interdependence—will increase as tasks become more complex, they still struggle to confidently determine the specific thresholds that should guide their focus across each dimension. This makes sense, and as we noted in Chapter 2, what appears complex to one team may feel rather routine to another depending on myriad factors. And as we have reiterated throughout this book, another particularly important wrinkle in many of today's teams is that they are not static entities—they face varying levels of interdependence as they progress through different stages of their life cycle and, consequently, they need to be shape-shifters to succeed. One day they may need to operate like a real team, the next day a group, and another day a full-fledged multi-subteam system.

Determining the Right Level of Interdependence for Your Team: Art, Science, or Just Plain Guessing?

In Chapter 2, we provided a surface-level primer of how you might go about identifying your team's optimal level of interdependence. In short, we argued that you can determine the relative complexity facing your team by relying on a combination of your own expertise and experiences, monitoring and/or benchmarking your team's functioning, and encouraging and seeking feedback from your team members. In Chapter 3, we told you that getting rich feedback was a benefit of building high-quality relationships with your team members. Nested within these suggestions, we also noted that you will have to be mindful of your team's composition: who the members on your team are, their areas of expertise, as well as their previously shared experiences together as a team when assessing the ideal arrangement. Specifically, we acknowledged that a team with a high degree of expertise might view a task as rather simple, whereas a team full of newcomers may instead view it as highly complex. Similarly, we reasoned that teams that have operated together for an extended amount of time, and especially if they see the same or similar tasks repeatedly, might begin to see a once complex task as fairly routine. In this sense, what's past may become prologue. This, of course, is consistent with the episodic nature of teams discussed in Chapter 4.

We stick by this advice, but we also acknowledge that it may feel overly general to you—especially if you are just starting out or are dealing with a completely new situation. The good news, however, is that we can offer some more specific guidance to help inform your decision making. As a rule of thumb, it takes time to get to know your team's capability in terms of the individuals on it and the team as a whole, so you will be unlikely to get things perfect from the start. That's okay. The most successful 3D Team Leaders we know tell us the art of using our model lies in balancing your *proactive* intentions with *reactive* good sense. In other words, your initial focus might be based on your most educated guess, but you may then start to pick up clues that suggest things need tweaking. When that happens, you have to be willing and able to change course.

In Chapters 3, 4, and 5, we discussed the importance of aligning your focus with your team's optimal interdependence level using several firsthand accounts. Embedded within these chapters were also stories about what happens when the focus is not on point. We encourage you to pay attention to these failures just as much as you do the success stories. If you can learn to quickly detect signals indicating that you are not focusing on the right dimension, you can switch your focus before things get even worse. In fact, these kinds of mistakes can lead to harmful efficacy-performance spirals, which essentially means that a failure at one point can hurt a team's confidence, which leads to the likelihood of even more subsequent failures that reduce confidence even more, and so on.[2] Importantly, negative spirals tend to get stronger and harder to correct over time, so it is imperative that you respond quickly after identifying a mismatch between your focus and the team's optimal level of interdependence. When this happens, we encourage you to engage in active experimentation among your team members and, in some cases, redefine success and failure to help your team get things righted again.

Another exercise to help you diagnose a suboptimal focus is to think in explicit terms about what high or low levels of interdependence mean for a team and what it might look like if that were mismatched with the specific task a team was given: high actual interdependence when it should be low, or low actual interdependence when it should be high. Essentially, raising a team's level of interdependence should not just be viewed as increasing members' level of collaboration, nor should we assume that increased collaboration is always a good thing. That's an overly rosy picture of interdependence. Interdependence in many ways also reflects a team's burden. Classic research, for instance, viewed task interdependence as reflecting the minimum number of connections among members to complete a task and a factor that reflected requirements for coordination, communication, and collaboration to properly function.[3]

When you push your team members to work together interdependently for a simple task, you are in effect asking them to make their task harder than it needs to be.[4] This is sort of like the three-legged race in the classic children's field day event when two people tie one of their legs together, then race other conjoined teams: it may seem neat at first, but it really would be much simpler to untie everyone and just see who is the fastest. Of course, if we asked those same kids to each pick up a couch and move it across a room, then they might welcome the opportunity to work together—even if it means having to do a little extra communication and coordination.

When teams are working or are being pushed to work in a highly interdependent fashion on tasks that are better suited for a more independent, individual-focused arrangement, they may demonstrate several symptoms you can use as clues to adjust your focus. Some common signs to look for include feelings and expressions of wasted time, frustration, withdrawal, excessive free-riding, and noticeably slower production compared to other teams doing similar tasks. Because team members are usually juggling multiple roles in their jobs, they may assume that the work will get done regardless of their involvement, so they are better suited to invest their psychological and physical energy toward their other teams where they can make a clearer contribution. We should note here that some team members simply enjoy working together, even if it isn't necessary. These situations are harder to diagnose for leaders because, unless there is a clear comparison point, happy team members may often be confused with productive team members. To fight against these situations, closely monitor your team's productivity and continue to set aggressive goals that push your team to look out for the most effective ways possible to complete their work.

By contrast, teams whose members are working in a low interdependence arrangement (more group-like) when they should be working in a higher interdependence arrangement often demonstrate a different set of symptoms. Specifically, we caution leaders to be on the lookout for excessively quick meetings or a constant push to cancel regular meetings, very low levels of task conflict and discussion regarding complex issues, vague or ambiguous reports of past interactions with other members (e.g., "Yeah, Bill and I have been thinking about that and plan to meet next week . . ."), and incoherent or hodgepodge products for key milestones. As noted in Chapters 4 and 5, one of the key ways you can intervene in these circumstances is to hold regular briefings and planning meetings to help your team strategize and outline more interdependent coordination.

Lauren, a senior manager who oversees several teams in a major advertising agency, described to us how she deals with these situations:

> My teams are always trying to be creative and think of the next edge we can use to impress our clients. It used to be just coordinating between print, web, and social media, but now we're expanding into even more novel media. Sometimes I've got a team that has a lot of prior knowledge of a particular client and product space that guides our initial work, but on other teams, I get a green crew that starts out in the proverbial wilderness. Both have great unique potential in our business, but it always takes time for me to figure out what I'm working with. As a general rule, I almost always start out focusing on the entire team. I like to think big, so to me, everything is going to be a highly collaborative process that goes beyond any one individual. I communicate this openly. Most of the time, we can quickly generate a list of ideas and start vetting our team's next steps.
>
> Unfortunately, sometimes our projects don't quite flow like that at first. I usually figure this out because my team members are fidgety in our meetings and the team discussions feel forced. We just don't click, I guess. After a little probing, usually through side conversations with my team members, I see I missed the mark. When this happens, I try to pivot quickly to an individual focus and structure some of our initial tasks in a way that permits less interdependent work. For example, maybe we'll each do some upfront research or prepare an independent idea sheet before our next meeting. Rather than just switching my focus out of the blue, I am upfront about why I'm changing course. I say things like, "Hey guys, I think I rushed the team thing on this one. Let's take some time for each of us to get up to speed so we can build momentum heading into the nitty-gritty parts of the campaign." Of course, I always try to focus my efforts on one-on-one coaching to make sure I'm getting all I can from them during these times.

Next, we move beyond just figuring out what level of interdependence is appropriate to discuss teams that move, either predictably or unpredictably, across different levels of optimal interdependence.

Tips for Shifting Your Focus to Maximize Team Performance in Dynamic Settings

Many teams today move through frequent changes in the type of tasks and challenges they face. Some are relatively simple, and others are massively complex. We have observed several common problems in these environments. The first is that some teams fail to realize that work and team design issues are dynamic, ongoing concerns that should be constantly reevaluated.[5] As a result, these teams never shift their interdependence arrangements regardless of what task they are facing; they end up continuing to act like a group even when their tasks become more complex and require more interdependence (or vice versa). A second, albeit very much related, problem we see in dynamic environments is that leaders themselves are either unable or unwilling to shift their focus onto the most appropriate dimension of a team. This, of course, goes against the main crux of 3D Team Leadership. The third problem is that teams do shift into different arrangements (groups, teams, subteams), but not in an optimal manner. For example, even when facing a complex task that should require high levels of interdependence, some members will decide to work independently on smaller parts of a task before piecing together the sum of the parts near the project deadline. Often this is done because members don't want to coordinate schedules, feel uncomfortable working together, or simply don't feel that the rewards for accomplishing team goals outweigh or are compatible with their own individual goals. Teams in this condition typically produce an unfocused set of ideas rather than viable, coherent solutions.

Great leaders navigate these obstacles by understanding what their team's current task requirements are (e.g., low, high, or multilayered interdependence), determining how an entity should operate (e.g., group, team, multisubteam system), and then focusing their leadership efforts on the correct entity. The remainder of this chapter is designed to help you master each of these aspects. We'll start with a classic example of 3D Team Leadership in action.

3D Team Leadership in a Historical Example: The Race to the South Pole

Over 100 years ago, Norwegian polar explorer Roald Amundsen was leading a team of fellow Scandinavians in a race to the South Pole. His competitor was Robert Falcon Scott, an English Navy captain who had been disgraced for making a costly mistake during British war games in 1907. While Scott was seeking repair to his reputation and eventual legacy as a military hero, Amundsen was fulfilling his lifelong dream of reaching the South Pole before any other human. Actually, this part is not entirely true—Amundsen spent most of his life preparing for the same assault on the North Pole, but his dream was interrupted by reports that an American, Frederick Cook, had beaten him to the punch shortly before he was to depart for a North Pole expedition.

Turning his attention to the exact opposite end of the earth, on December 14, 1911, Amundsen and four of his team members were successful in reaching the South Pole well before Scott's team. However, in no small feat, Scott's team also made it on January 17, 1912, a little over a month after Amundsen. Despite both teams' relative success in reaching the desolate and foreboding destination, their fates took very different turns on the return journey. Amundsen's team arrived safely back to base camp on January 25, 1912. Scott's team never made it back: two members committed suicide and three others (Scott included) died of starvation after a series of disastrous mishaps. For those interested in learning more about Amundsen and Scott's fascinating race, we highly recommend Roland Huntford's *The Last Place on Earth,*[6] which was made into a television miniseries. Jim Collins provides another account in his book *Great by Choice.*[7]

So, what does a race to the South Pole have to do with leading teams in today's business context? A lot, actually. Namely, the South Pole metaphorically (and in actuality) represented a true VUCA environment. Even though most of today's leaders are not facing negative 40 degree Fahrenheit temperatures (which is, incidentally, also negative 40 degrees Celsius), dragging sleds for up to 12 hours a day at altitudes reaching 10,000 feet, or battling scurvy and starvation, you are nonetheless *leading teams into the unknown.* Furthermore, multiple accounts of Amundsen's and Scott's respective performances in the race support the tenets of our 3D Team Leadership model.

Amundsen, for example, put aside a command-and-control style of leadership for a more open, consensus-building style to create a cohesive, dedicated, and high-performing team. More than that, at varying times during his journey, Amundsen switched his focus across each of the three dimensions in his team. For instance, at one critical juncture, he faced a major challenge to his leadership by his second-in-command, Hjalmar Johansen, stemming from a disagreement over when the team should have embarked on their assault on the South Pole. Interestingly, Johansen had a legitimate gripe: Amundsen's poorly timed decision caused his team to get caught in a white-out blizzard. After barely escaping death during their return to base camp, Johansen accused Amundsen of caring more about "polar glory" than the lives of his men. Seeing his team on the verge of fracturing (recall the faultline concept) and knowing that everyone on his team would need to work together to survive, Amundsen called his entire team together for a meeting. He first addressed his team as a whole and attempted to rebuild the damaged cohesion lost in the debacle of their ill-fated early run.

Next, because many of his team's upcoming challenges would have to be conquered by smaller subsets of members (e.g., a subteam might be tasked with exploring unknown territory, while another might be assigned to test boots, sleds, or other tools needed to reach the South Pole), Amundsen shifted his focus to subteams. Specifically, to remedy potentially harmful faultlines that emerged from previous experiences (Johansen, in particular, was unwilling to reintegrate into the team), he created new subteam arrangements that would give the team a better chance for success. This was not easy given several members' reluctance to change (including Johansen, of course, who was put on a separate subteam that was not going to the Pole and was led by a relatively inexperienced team member).

Finally, at the very end of the team meeting, he told his team members that he wanted to speak to each one privately. He took the time necessary to coach and mentor all team members one-on-one, even Johansen, in order to ensure that each member's individual needs were being met. In doing so, Amundsen leveraged the power of the "I's" in his team.

In contrast to Admundsen, Scott serves as a foil to our 3D Team Leadership model and a cautionary tale for how *not* to lead teams effectively. Rather than a leader who empowered his team, Scott, wrote author Roland Huntford, was an "insecure, unhappy, emotional disciplinarian" whose "instincts were to evade responsibility and shift the blame."[8] Moreover, perhaps in part due to his rigid disciplinarian approach, he failed to embrace all three dimensions of his team. For example, he pitted various members of his team against one another rather than viewing his team as a whole dimension as something he should manage and support. The historical account also gives no indication that he gave any thought to the composition of his subteams, and when he was challenged about the suitability of a particular member for a subteam assignment, he essentially shut any objections down. Moreover, he did a very poor job of managing the "I's" in his team; for example, after promising one team member, Teddy Evans, that he would be on the subteam that would make the final charge to South Pole, he changed his mind at the last minute without any adequate explanation (lucky for Teddy, as it turns out, because he made it back alive while the members of the polar party didn't). Failing to recognize the three critical dimensions important for effective team leadership and mismanaging the dimensions he did recognize, we believe, played a critical factor in the team's tragic outcomes. Although many business teams do not end up in such tragic circumstances (thankfully), we've spoken with numerous potential leaders who display similar behavior toward their team.

What makes Amundsen's team leadership skills all the more impressive is that there weren't any road maps for team leadership in the form of books, articles, consultants, or seminars in the early 1900s. He was a natural 3D team leader. Unfortunately, 3D Team Leadership does not come as naturally to most of us as it did for Amundsen. It requires that we question our preconceived notions about teams; it mandates that we forgo a need for complete control; most important, it demands that we embrace flexibility. Rest assured, the 3D Team Leadership model is supported by more than just accounts from a century-old race. Today's great team leaders use 3D Team Leadership principles in all cultures and organization types. In contrast to the subzero temperatures that made Amundsen's leadership so critical, our fieldwork suggests that 3D Team Leadership is also imperative in much, much hotter contexts, literally: fire and rescue crew teams.

Trial by Fire: 3D Team Leadership in Action Teams

Fire and rescue teams represent a fascinating and challenging environment to study. Moreover, they represent an ideal context for examining 3D Team Leadership. They are action teams working in truly VUCA environments; they complete a wide variety of tasks in very short order; and they shift frequently from individual-, team-, and subteam-focused work.

We conducted a large-scale examination of these teams in which we extensively observed, interviewed, and surveyed multiple stakeholders—crew members, crew leaders (captains), and organizational executives (department chiefs)—from ninety fire crews across multiple fire departments in the United States. The sample consisted of large and small municipalities, urban and rural environments, unionized and nonunionized employees, and several other factors that permitted us to test the robustness of 3D Team Leadership principles in different contexts.

One of the first things we sought to confirm was whether the leaders in our sample displayed behaviors consistent with prior leadership studies. Research originally conducted decades ago at The Ohio State University argued that leaders focus on two main things: getting tasks done and building relationships with people. Task-focused behaviors, formally referred to as "initiating structure," reflect the extent to which leaders define and organize their own and followers' roles, push for goal accomplishment, and create well-defined patterns and channels of communication. In short, this is the "getting things done" behavior. Person-focused behaviors, originally coined "consideration," reflect the extent to which leaders display concern and respect for employees, have employees' welfare in mind, and show appreciation and support.[9] In sum, this is the "building effective relationships" behavior.

Since this original work, literally thousands of additional studies on leadership have attempted to uncover "what leaders really do." And despite the many models and approaches that have emanated from this research and the hundreds of different leadership behaviors described, the conclusion drawn from the Ohio State studies remains the same: *leaders focus on tasks* and/or *people* (we do acknowledge that some work suggests a third category, change-oriented or transformational leadership, which we included in Chapter 4).[10] Moreover, when leaders exhibit these behaviors effectively, employees perform better and are more satisfied with their jobs.[11] However, these relationships are a bit more nuanced. For attitudes like job satisfaction and motivation, consideration is more important. For actual task performance outcomes like productivity, initiating structure is more so.

As we expected, our results were consistent with this pattern. Leaders used both types of behaviors, and, not surprisingly, each type of behavior was associated with different outcomes to varying degrees. The next test, and frankly the one that matters the most here, is whether leaders really targeted their behavior toward the three different entities in their teams: the individuals, their team as a whole, and subteams within their overall team. Indeed, we found that crew members made distinct assessments of six types of leader

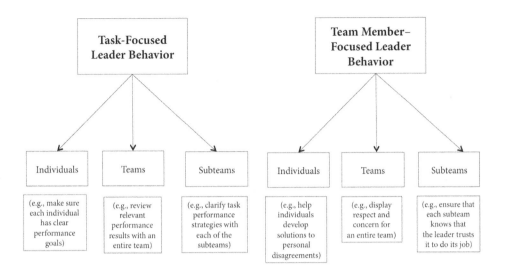

FIGURE 6.1. Task-Focused and Team Member–Focused Leader Behaviors Aimed at the Three Dimensions of the 3D Team Leadership Model

behaviors: a focus on tasks and a focus on relationships with team members, multiplied by the three dimensions underlying our 3D Team Leadership approach. Moreover, we found that whether each type of leader behavior was effective depended on the level of interdependence, matching the basic tenets of 3D Team Leadership. Obviously, we view this alone as a game changer, but there's more. Leaders who demonstrated more "switching behaviors" (i.e., when they shifted their focus from individuals, their team as a whole, and the subteams within their overall team) had higher-performing teams compared to those who demonstrated less, which is not surprising given the wide variety of tasks that fire and rescue teams face daily. Figure 6.1 depicts the six leader behaviors along with representative examples of each.

In sum, our study of fire and rescue crews provides clear support for the 3D Team Leadership model in ongoing teams with changing interdependence requirements. We next describe how our 3D Team Leadership model works in another commonly used type of team: project teams.

Using 3D Team Leadership in Project Teams:
A Software Project Development Team Example

Most project teams follow some sort of life cycle, and various life cycle approaches come and go. They also vary wildly across industries. In some environments, for example, project teams follow sequential, lockstep *waterfall*-type models that place tremendous emphasis on getting things exactly right in one stage (or milestone) before moving on to another. In other industries, recent trends point to more flexible, *Agile*-type models that can permit many iterations within and across traditional project milestones. For example, in the software industry, the "DevOps" approach develops and operates software at the same time, not in discrete steps.[12] To make these approaches work, many companies that use these models, including Google and Facebook, require their developers to write and change code while operations personnel deploy it, all while millions of users around the world simultaneously log in and use the software. Some companies even use a hybrid of both Agile and waterfall-type models.[13] The point here is not to emphasize one project management model over another; we are agnostic to specific choices, especially since every project is different. Rather, it is to understand how your team approaches its work and determine what level of interdependence is required at any given point in its project life cycle. From there, you can appropriately determine which dimension gives you the most bang for your buck.

We kicked off the book by describing the many team roles that Anna, a senior vice president at a large technology firm, was juggling. One of her close colleagues, Tom, is a senior engineering manager whose primary team leadership responsibility is to manage new product development teams specializing in sophisticated software products for a variety of clients. Tom's company adopts their project model from Agile (again there are many types) that emphasizes scrums, which typically take the form of daily stand-up meetings focused mainly on project progress and updates, and sprint teams, which work on short, focused projects for usually one or two weeks at a time. For the uninitiated in Agile terminology, note that words like *scrum* and *sprint* were borrowed from rugby, which provides a nice parallel to some project teams' style of advancing teamwork. One of the sprint teams Tom leads affectionately refers to itself as "Team Elite." Team Elite has seven members: Asha and Gautam, more junior software developers located in Bengaluru, India; Josh and Steve, two senior software developers located in Sydney, Australia; Millie, who is serving as the product owner located in Dublin, Ireland; and Emma and Dan, the stakeholder representatives located in Raleigh, North Carolina, who work most directly with the client.

Leading the Individuals in a Team

In certain time periods in the Agile life cycle, Tom's team members work relatively independently from one another. For example, at the beginning of the Agile life cycle, Tom works with his team to identify the business opportunity, which involves bigger-picture issues and market concerns. Regarding this early stage, Tom says:

> For this project, we really aren't working in a very team-like fashion. We're still a team, don't get me wrong, it's just that I really don't have my team members working too closely together on tasks at the outset. I can gather most of the data here myself, and a lot of this information is so big picture that the team members can provide some input, but not necessarily a lot. This is also the point at which I look at different strategies that might be employed for the project, and a lot of times I don't pick one and stick with it; I leave open several possibilities that might work. Once I've done my market homework and I've identified several potential strategies, I take all of this information and conduct a feasibility analysis to find out if it makes sense to even move forward on a project. Sometimes this phase can take a week or less, but more and more I'm finding that it's taking much longer due to the complexity of our projects and the demands our users and clients are placing on us. So during this time, I'm gathering a lot of information from the market, our product owner, and our clients, and the team members are helping me with some of this, but a lot of this comes out of my one-on-one meetings with members, not meeting with the entire team. That does not mean, however, that my team members are standing by waiting for me. Even in this phase, members are doing at least some initial work even though we don't have all the answers in the beginning. So, they're still plenty busy and they're usually on other teams as well.

What Tom is describing here is exactly what we mean by a team that is in a low team interdependence phase. Tom does have a team with seven members he knows he's going to use moving forward with the project. But, he doesn't need his whole team working interdependently at this point in the team's life cycle to get the goals of this phase accomplished. He can rely on team members' primarily individual contributions of their knowledge and skills. Based on the relatively low level of team interdependence at this phase, Tom would be wise to focus most of his attention on motivating, and using team design principles, for the "I's" in his team, as they are the most important dimension in the 3D Team Leadership framework at this point (recall the lessons for leading the "I's" in team contexts in Chapter 3). Tom needs to find ways to maximize the experiences of empowerment for the individuals within his team, including the four dimensions of choice, impact, competence, and meaning.

We found Tom to be a natural 3D team leader (we actually nicknamed him "Amundsen"). As he describes:

> The first thing I do is walk the talk [what we called *role modeling and leading by example* in Chapter 3]. When I want to accomplish something that I think is important and that the company thinks is important, I don't always ask my boss for permission. I just do it. And I think by behaving in an empowered way myself and talking about my actions with my team members, it kind of sets things up for them to feel comfortable about being more empowered themselves.

> The second thing I do is to encourage all of my team members to speak up and be involved in decision making [what we called *encouraging and allowing individuals to participate in decision making* in Chapter 3]. Even when people are quiet—and some of my team members are classic introverts, so they won't necessarily jump in and offer their opinions and information right away—I will find some time after a meeting to follow up with them one-on-one to get their input. I try to do this within a few days. It's really important to me that they feel heard, involved and that they know I value their input. That's a big part of empowerment for me.

> The third thing I make sure I do is coach [what we called *providing effective coaching* in Chapter 3]. Since the members of Team Elite are in four different countries and time zones, this consumes most of my time when empowering them. I have frequent one-on-ones and check-ins to make sure we are on the same page. But I try not to use these short meetings to make them feel like I'm spying on them or trying to control what they do. That would be empowerment in reverse! What I try to do is help them build up their skill sets and make them feel comfortable and confident about how they fit into the big picture and how much they are helping us get to where we want to be. The advice I would give to any team leader who wants to empower his or her team members is to err on the side of too much coaching. Anything less, and

people are going to feel like you are not developing them and that you don't care about them. And, sadly, they probably won't stay in the company very long, especially these days.

The fourth thing I make sure to do is make them feel as though they are insiders to the extent I can. What I mean by that is that I keep them updated, and I share as much important information with them as I can, unless of course it's something highly confidential [what we called *sharing important and strategic information* in Chapter 3]. Providing information is a form of sharing power, at least in my opinion, because I know a lot of leaders who just won't share anything. They keep everything to themselves, and then their team members get surprised when they hear something that their boss definitely should have been the one to tell them. These people are power hungry, and they just hoard information. And then they wonder why their team members don't feel empowered!

The last thing I do as a team leader should be a simple one, but I see a lot of my peers struggle with it, and that is just make sure your team members know you have their best interests at heart [what we called *displaying a high level of concern and caring* in Chapter 3]. And you don't have to be somebody's best friend to show you care. I mean, I am friends with some of my colleagues at work, including some of my team members, but showing that you care does not have to mean being someone's buddy. It can be as simple as remembering that their daughter had a soccer game or that they had a big presentation to the higher-ups the week before. I see other team leaders struggle with this because they don't like people that much. I mean, I'm a people person, so I'm lucky, I love this part of my job. But, I guess there are some people who just have to work at it a bit harder.

In addition to the five behaviors of empowering leaders that Tom displays in this phase of the Agile life cycle, Chapter 3 also described two main ways that leaders go about creating empowering structures and systems. First, leaders to need to ensure that there is a high level of sociopolitical support by (1) creating a supportive organizational climate, or making sure individuals feel comfortable taking risks and being proactive in their jobs; (2) ensuring that each individual team member knows she has the support of their organization as a whole, or that the company has her back; and (3) making sure that all members of the team know that the company trusts them to do their jobs. Commenting on these, Tom said,

Well, these are less about me and more about making sure my team members know our company has their best interests in mind. It's one thing if my people get that I care about them and will back them up and encourage them to take risks, but what if I leave or get called out to another project? What then? They better know that the company they've made such huge sacrifices for actually gives a damn about their well-being. I have to do some level of communicating and interfacing with other organizational leaders to make sure this is happening. I can't just do it by myself.

Also in Chapter 3, we discussed the importance of building high-quality relationships to ensure that individual team members feel empowered. We also acknowledged that the accumulating evidence suggests that leaders might be well served to build relationships of varying quality with their team members based on how critical those team members are for team performance. The rule of thumb is that leaders should strive to build high-quality relationships with all individual team members, but if they cannot (due to limited time or resources), then they should make sure there is a climate of fairness in their team, which will likely lower the potentially negative reactions to leaders who build high-quality relationships with only some of their members.[14] Different relationship quality here should apply more to work-related, rather than interpersonal, factors like assigning certain jobs of varying importance and visibility, as all team members will value being treated with dignity and respect.

Regarding this topic, Tom commented:

> Because most of our Agile teams are pretty small, I think I do a good job of relationship management with all of the team members. It still takes a lot of work, especially when a team has members in different countries, and the way I go about building a relationship can depend on what country the person is from. Usually there is a hub of the project, and often the people in the hub are in the same location. If a team member is not in the hub, it's easy for him or her to feel left out and not very empowered. But I look at it as a pay now or pay later type of thing. If you invest the time up front and do the hard work initially, it's going to pay off big time down the road because it's really hard to repair a relationship once it's gotten off track. You'll spend much more time doing this compared to what you would have spent up front doing it right initially. But if you don't and you end up neglecting your team members, you're going to pay exponentially higher costs later because you'll be doing a whole lot of damage control and trying to rebuild the lost trust.

Finally, in Chapter 3 we discussed how leaders could use extrinsic rewards (remember that empowerment is the gold standard for intrinsic motivation) to motivate the "I's" in team contexts. Tom's company allows for spot bonuses to reward individuals for behaving in ways that benefit the team. He said,

> In our company, we are allowed to give spot bonuses to those individual team members who are doing things that really help their team. We can do this without getting any high-level approval. At the end of the day, there has to be something in it for the individual team members to want to make sacrifices and work hard for the team. I do realize there are cultural differences at play here, but most people do need a little incentive now and again to really go the extra mile for the team. I think our spot bonuses work pretty well for that.

Leading the Subteams within a Team

During other phases of the Agile life cycle, team members split up into subteams to get their work done. For example, Tom suggests that the next logical phase is to get initial support and funding for the project; working with stakeholders and Millie, the product owner, to initially model the scope of the system; modeling an initial architecture for the system; and estimating the costs of the project. Tom describes it this way:

> This is where the different members on the team can kind of group together in smaller subteams based on their skill sets to get various aspects of this phase done. For example, in Team Elite, Millie and I are pretty much focused on getting support and funding for the project. We might ask some of the members to help occasionally with this, but funding is my baby, and I'm pretty good at convincing folks about the support we need. Emma and Dan usually manage the stakeholders because they are on our team specifically for this task. They work very closely with the product owners, usually in person if they can but sometimes via video- or audioconferencing. My developers, in this case Asha and Gautam in India and Josh and Steve in Australia, are mainly in charge of putting together the initial architecture for the system. They're not writing a bunch of code at this point, but they're working mostly on the architectural strategy. So, we basically have three subteams working pretty much simultaneously doing different tasks. My challenge is that I have to focus my energy on leading each of these subteams, but I also have to make sure I'm coordinating between the subteams as well because the overall team won't work unless the subteams are coordinating what they do.

To help Tom and other leaders overcome the challenges inherent in leading subteams, in Chapter 5 we discussed the leader behaviors and actions designed to target the subteam dimension. The approaches discussed there are best suited to leading in this phase of the Agile life cycle because this stage has multilayered interdependence within it. Recall that we discussed two sets of leader behaviors in Chapter 5—strategizing and coordinating—and three potential points of impact of these behaviors—within, between, and across subteams. Tom describes his approach this way:

> In this phase, we take the potential strategies we developed in the last phase, and we start to drill down on the most promising strategy for accomplishing the project. I have to make sure I'm building and communicating the strategy for three different targets: each of the subteams separately, the interface between all of the subteams, and the interface between the whole team and the company, the product owners, and the clients. It's a juggling act to be sure, but there's really no other way to approach it in our Agile environment. We need to be nimble but also coordinated in our efforts.

Tom's strategizing behavior, which consists of gathering information about the performance environment, framing his team's task, helping his team set objectives, and planning how his team members will work together to accomplish goals, has to be done with three different targets in mind:

> Again, even though I do work separately with each of the subteams within my team, I constantly have to make sure that my subteams are collaborating in line with my whole team's strategy. So I move back and forth between strategizing with each of the subteams and the whole team to make sure we have alignment. Because we are using Agile, I have to make sure that each of the subteams is constantly interfacing with stakeholders, including inside our company and outside with clients. It's not like the days when we used a waterfall model and we did all of the development upfront with very little client interaction. We would just build and build and build and then release. But with Agile, it's an iterative process with a lot of customer interaction.

With this level of complexity, the other most important leader behavior in a multisubteam environment is coordinating: managing the flow of information and orchestrating the actions of members to make sure they are integrated and aligned. Just like strategizing, coordination also has to occur with three targets: each of the subteams, the interface between the subteams, and the interface between the entire team of subteams and the external environment. Tom says:

It's similar to the strategizing I have to do, because I have to make sure I'm paying attention to all three aspects when I am coordinating. And it gets exponentially more difficult every time I step up a level. For example, I can work pretty easily on coordinating within each of the subteams, and since they are empowered, I don't have to do a lot of hand holding here. It gets a little bit more difficult to coordinate between the subteams because each subteam is really doing a different set of tasks. I mean, they're different but they are still related. So I need to have frequent check-ins to make sure we're on the same page. We can do some of this with the scrum meetings. The most difficult coordination I do is make sure all the subteam efforts are coordinated and aligned with corporate goals and customer expectations.

The other important aspect of leadership for maximizing multisubteam system performance, which we discussed in Chapter 5, is to make sure all members of a team have a shared mental model for how to behave and work together. Tom said:

> Fortunately for us, we have an Agile model kind of guiding our actions, so in a way, the Agile framework is the shared mental model. That said, individuals are still individuals, and they can interpret things differently. We also have five members located outside the United States, so Agile does not always create a perfectly shared model despite the apparent clarity around a specific approach. Things like "quality" or "deadlines" don't necessarily mean the same things in different countries. We have to make sure each of the team members fully understands how we are planning to work together and how best to prioritize. Sometimes it takes a little extra coaching to get there with a global team.

For extrinsic motivation in a multiteam system, Tom followed our advice from Chapter 5 and does not use financial incentives:

> We just found trying to do another layer of compensation—beyond individual and team—was just too much. We thought that people would get confused, and we knew HR wouldn't like it. And in many cases, subteam work is usually very fluid and may not always last long enough to warrant its own system. So, I try to focus on goal setting as the primary driver for our subteams to perform well. They already have their individual and team incentives, so I think goal setting works as a nice complement here.

Leading the Team as a Whole

In still other phases of the Agile life cycle, tasks call for highly interdependent teamwork, when members work together as a real team. Tom describes typical activities in this stage as collaborating closely with stakeholders, implementing functionality in priority order, analyzing and designing, ensuring quality, regularly delivering working solutions, and testing. Tom says,

> In a phase like this, we start to really work together as a high-performing team. We need all hands on deck to work interdependently at this point. This is where the word *sprint* in *sprint team* becomes really important. All seven members of the team meet daily in a scrum. I'm also coordinating with other teams, so I typically have a meeting every week with the team leads from those teams, which we call a *scrum of scrums*. It gets pretty complicated.

Tom's description here perfectly exemplifies a high team interdependence phase. Tom needs a real team at this point in his team's life cycle to get the goals of this phase accomplished. He needs to rely on all of his team members to collectively contribute their knowledge and skills. During this stage, Tom should focus most of his attention on motivating and using team design factors for his entire team, as this is currently the most important dimension in the 3D Team Leadership model (recall our discussion of leading a team as a whole in Chapter 4). Tom needs to find ways to maximize the experiences of empowerment for Team Elite as a whole, including the four dimensions of autonomy, impact, potency, and meaning. Beyond empowerment, the members must also experience team trust and psychological safety to motivate his whole team.

In Chapter 4, we discussed the leader behaviors that are best suited for enhancing team empowerment, trust, and psychological safety. Our discussion focused on three behaviors: displaying empowering leader behavior directed at teams (team coaching), creating empowered team structures and systems (team design), and exhibiting team-focused attributes of transformational leadership. Regarding the first, Tom said:

> I typically make a subtle—well, maybe it's not so subtle—shift in how I behave toward the team in terms of empowerment. In the earliest phases, I focus on allowing individuals to participate in decision making; I provide one-on-one coaching; I make each team member feel like an insider by sharing information; and I make sure each individual team member knows that I care about

him or her. Then, in the next phases, I started emphasizing more attention to the subteams and how they coordinate with one another and the customers. But when we are in this type of phase and we are working as a real team, I still do these same behaviors, but I just make the team the focus of them. For example, I will ask the entire team for its input; I will provide lots and lots of team coaching; I share information with the whole team; and I make sure the whole team knows I have its back.

It's important to remember here that a focus on an entire team is not mutually exclusive with a focus on a team's individuals or subteams. As Tom says,

> It's not really an either-or thing. It's a matter of degree. I still provide some coaching, feedback, and leadership for individuals. I mean, realistically, how could you not? My team is made up of individuals! But when the work calls for us to really work together as a team, I just start emphasizing the overall team much more so than the subteams and the individuals in our team. I don't forget they exist, but I just don't focus on them as much.

Tom's advice here about changing your primary focus but still acknowledging the existence of the other two dimensions is critical to 3D Team Leadership. After all, at some level, you will always have three foci to attend to when leading teams, and you should never completely ignore any of the three; it's just not realistic. For example, individuals on a team are rarely all in the exact same place in terms of their understanding of the project and comfort level in contributing; subteams are constantly drifting toward perilous faultlines; and a team's collective identification as a strong entity can ebb and flow for any number of reasons. The utility of the 3D Team Leadership model is that it provides guidance for when to give more attention to one dimension than the other two, and it tells you which of your team's many needs is the most important to satisfy first.

Besides the empowering leader behaviors described in Chapter 4, we also discussed the importance of having a well-designed team, which is also a team leader's job. We identified six team design factors in our "must-haves" list for effective teams: a clear, engaging direction; task interdependence; team rewards; team resources; authority to manage the work; and team performance goals. Tom believes that Team Elite is a well-designed team:

> We make sure all of these things are in place. It's my job as a team leader to make sure we have that engaging direction. If we don't have it, we'll flounder. I've seen teams lose their way pretty quickly without direction. I don't dictate

the direction, but I am ultimately accountable for making sure it's understood and that it fits with our overall company goals. Team interdependence is pretty much already built in when we hit this type of phase. This kind of complicated software development can't be done without everyone working closely together, particularly in an Agile environment. As far as team rewards, we do use team bonuses when we complete our projects on time and if customers are satisfied. We collect a lot of data on customer and user satisfaction, and we use those data to determine what the team gets. These bonuses, combined with the spot awards for individual team members who contribute to the team, generally mean that we have good team players on our teams. Availability of resources kind of goes without saying, and we certainly know the power of goal setting in our company. We use team goals all the time. We set goals for individuals, subteams, and my overall team, and we make sure they are aligned across all of those levels.

We also mention another element of team design here: the size of a team. Tom said, "For my Agile teams, I don't want them to get any bigger than nine or ten members. Anything larger than that and we find that the coordination challenges get too great, especially when members are in different countries." We concur with Tom's assessment here, and not just for Agile teams. We have already discussed that the evidence on team size suggests that the costs and problems of larger teams outweigh any potential advantages more members can bring to the team. In fact, we mentioned one study that found that as teams grow larger in size, members experience less and less team empowerment.[15] All in all, it's optimal to keep teams somewhere in that sweet spot of five to eight members. If a leader gets stuck with an overly large team, creating subteams (more Team Elites) may reduce some of the problems associated with large teams. Of course, leading in a multilayered interdependence context (a necessity for subteams) also introduces its own set of challenges, so leaders must be thoughtful in how they choose to leverage larger teams.

The final leadership attribute of leading entire teams that we discussed in Chapter 4 was the two team-focused behaviors associated with transformational leadership: idealized influence and inspirational motivation. Idealized influence refers to the charisma and persuasiveness that leaders bring to their teams.[16] Tom said,

Well, I'm not sure if my team would call me the most charismatic of leaders. But I don't think charisma means you have to light up a room every time you walk into one. But you better be able to persuade your team members effectively because sometimes all of them don't report directly to me, or they're actually on four or five teams with several team leaders. So I need to use my influence skills to make sure they're motivated and engaged.

Inspirational motivation refers to leaders who use strong visions to help motivate their teams. Regarding this aspect, Tom said,

> Oh, I definitely use a vision statement with my teams. I mean, we have a company vision too, but I still outline one for my teams as well. I try to keep it short and meaningful. We've all seen a lot of bad visions out there, the ones that go on for pages. I just want my team members to remember what we're here for and not to lose sight of the big picture and where we're going." Thus, Tom uses both idealized influence and inspirational motivation to effectively lead his real teams.

In many project life cycle models like Agile, teams can shift in different directions when it comes to task interdependence. For example, Tom must also manage shifts from higher levels of team interdependence to more moderate or low levels. He recounted:

> So when my team moves from higher to more moderate levels of interdependence, this represents another shift in focus for my team and, as a result, for me as a team leader. The intense teamwork, the daily scrums, the weekly scrum of scums are winding down, so I shift back into basically what I did as a leader in earlier phases, and I focus more on the subteams, both individually and how they connect with one another. My team members expect this shift as a normal part of Agile, so it doesn't come as a surprise to them.

Teams also often shift all the way down to low task interdependence. Relaying this experience, Tom says, "I shift my focus again to an emphasis on the individuals in my team. I do a lot of one-on-one mentoring again, trying to create some learning opportunities based on the cycle the team members just went through. And, of course, the cycle then repeats itself in Team Elite or the other teams that the members are a part of."

Tom's examples of leading Team Elite display exactly what many leaders face in today's VUCA business environment: dynamic team, with varying levels of team interdependence throughout a team's life cycle. As Tom shows, team leaders must know the level of team interdependence their teams have at any given point in time, be that in a project life cycle model or something else, for leaders to guide and manage their teams effectively.

Given Tom's natural inclination toward 3D Team Leadership, we wanted to find out more about how he puts the whole 3D Team Leadership model in motion. Specifically, we asked Tom to explain how he manages the shifts of focusing on the individuals, his team as a whole, and the subteams within his overall team. He explained:

> Fortunately the project life cycle model we follow, which comes from Agile, kind of dictates the ebb and flows of my focus. I know when we get to a certain part of the life cycle that I need to start emphasizing a different dimension of the team. For example, in making a subtle shift between subteams and the overall team, I typically use a sprint planning meeting to first debrief all of the subteam activities completed during a sprint, and then I start to emphasize the whole team or the individuals in the team if that's what the life cycle called for by reminding them of overall team goals, making sure the all of the team members are communicating and coordinating with one another, and explicitly laying out expectations for how the entire team is going to produce the next set of deliverables. But again, it's not like I completely stop focusing on individuals or subteams at this point; they are still integral parts of my team and help my team succeed. It's just that I start changing the way I interact with my team—both tactically and symbolically—to get members focused on the ways in which they are supposed to work together. I guess I nudge them; I don't bulldoze them. Following a model makes things more predictable. I mean, that's why we use Agile so much.

It's fortunate for Tom that using a model helps to guide his behavior so that he knows—and his team expects—that these shifts in his behavior and focus are imminent. But what about teams that don't follow a predictable life cycle? Again, we live in a world in which we can't always predict which element of a team—the individuals, a team as a whole, or the subteams within an overall team—should be emphasized. In response to this question, Tom said:

> I've worked in previous companies and roles where we didn't follow a project life cycle, so it was never determined in advance which dimension of a team should get most of my attention. I found that I could still shift my behavior among the three dimensions when necessary, but the difference was that I had to do a little bit more coaching with my team to help the members anticipate when the shifts were going to occur. Again, in Agile, they pretty much know when they're going to happen, so they're automatically more receptive to my changes in behavior. But in more unpredictable environments, I've had team

members sometimes say I'm being inauthentic because I was changing focus in unpredictable ways. I took that feedback hard because I knew I was focusing on the right things at the right time, but what I didn't realize was that these shifts were confusing my team members. I remember one guy saying, "I don't know if you want us to focus on the team thing or the individual thing or something else!" He was pretty heated about it. That's when I had to start laying the groundwork for my shifts a bit earlier than I do now using our Agile process. Your team members don't like surprises, and I don't like them much myself!. So I started sending cues and communicated much better so that my team members were ready for the changes I had to make.

We also asked Tom about how he handles being overloaded by the demands of attending to the three dimensions of 3D Team Leadership. In Chapter 1, we drew from established psychology research to argue that leaders cannot be all things to their teams at all times. There just aren't enough hours in the day (or shots of espresso) that would allow complete and total focus on everything the team needs. We asked Tom about this, and he said:

I do get overloaded from time to time. Things are changing in our industry and our company every day, and I have to stay up with all of the changes and help my team deal with them, too. I do things to keep myself from burning out. One, I delegate and empower, plain and simple. There are certain tasks, including leadership tasks, that I can hand off to my team members. This allows me to focus on the things I'm supposed to be focused on, and it also develops leadership skills in my team members so that they will eventually go on to lead their own teams. So whether I'm focused on individuals, teams, or subteams, I can get my team members, usually the highly motivated and ambitious ones, to take on some responsibilities that I then don't have to deal with.

The other thing I have to remember is that when I get stressed out or overwhelmed, I sharpen my focus and narrow my attention to the one dimension that is the most important at a given point in time. It is important to remember that you never lose sight of the other two dimensions when you are focusing primarily on one. For example, just because I'm emphasizing my overall team at some point does not mean that the individuals or the subteams disappear or are not relevant. They are always there and always important. It's just that you have to learn how to really drill down on the one dimension of teams that is critical. When I have more time and am not as stressed, I will make sure to provide at least some attention to the two dimensions that are not as critical. For example, if I'm focused mainly on my whole team but I find that I have some extra time, I will do one-on-one check-ins with individual team members to make sure they are on track or do some developmental coaching. I know this might sound kind of complicated, but after awhile it becomes second nature. It's like my basketball coach in high school seemed to always know when to yell at us and when to be kinder and supportive. Over time, you just get a sense of when to do what. My teams have been pretty successful, so I must be doing something right!

To summarize this chapter, we took each of the critical lessons from the previous chapters and put them all together using examples and explanations of how our 3D Team Leadership model works in the real world. First, we used a life-and-death historical example of Roald Amundsen to show how a true 3D team leader was able to accomplish something no one else at that time had been able to do: reach the South Pole. We then shared our own research with one type of action team, firefighters, who also risk their lives to make sure that the rest of us are safe and sound in a dangerous world. Our work with firefighters provided compelling evidence that leaders who shift their focus depending on the optimal level of team interdependence enjoyed the most successful teams. Just like Amundsen and Scott's experience, doing the right things at the right time makes all the difference. We ended the chapter with Tom, who turned out to be a natural 3D team leader in the software development industry. Tom knew when and how to change his focus when his team needed him to, and he exhibited all of the best attributes of a leader who could really switch when the time was right.

We believe these three examples show how leaders can diagnose their team's level of interdependence and, importantly, make adjustments when there is a mismatch between how the team chooses to do their work and how they should do their work. Likewise, each example indicates the importance of leaders adjusting their leadership focus, actions, and behaviors to match the appropriate interdependence of their team at any given time. By applying these concepts to your own teams, you can realize the full potential of the 3D Team Leadership approach and see meaningful increases in individual, subteam, team, and overall company performance.

7 3D Team Leadership across Cultures

UP TO THIS POINT IN THE BOOK, WE HAVE PRESENTED our 3D Team Leadership model without much regard for cultural differences; moreover, we have admittedly described its design and practice using mostly Western examples. Yet our work and that of others overwhelmingly suggest that an increasingly important part of operating in VUCA environments is leading teams across cultures. Cross-cultural issues in teams emerge for many reasons: leaders from one country are assigned to a location (and team) in another country (expatriates), members on a team come from different cultural backgrounds (a global team), and members of a team are spread across the globe (a global virtual team, discussed in the next chapter). In these cases, leaders face the additional challenge of energizing and directing their team's members often without a uniformly held set of norms, rules, and implicitly expected leadership behaviors.[1]

The most successful leaders not only understand the basic principles of 3D Team Leadership, but also recognize what the key cultural differences are between the countries around the world and are flexible and adaptable enough to alter their behavior and approaches when moving across cultures. Although a complete discussion of all of the potential cultural differences that can affect a team is outside the scope of this book, this chapter does describe several of the most common cultural distinctions and challenges that face today's team leaders based on our and others' work with global teams. We start by questioning the fundamental assumption that the concept of teams has a common meaning all over the world.

A Team Is a Team Is a Team, No Matter Where You Are in the World, Right?

We have worked with teams in dozens of countries on five continents. Teams are, in fact, a big deal in every single one of them. Yet this experience has also taught (and frequently retaught) us an important lesson: the word *team* itself has varying connotations in different countries.

As an example, consider our work with a chip manufacturer in Manila in the Philippines.[2] On our first morning in the facility, we observed a team meeting for the self-named Be Cool team. Besides switching very easily between Tagalog, the first language spoken by about a third of the population of the Philippines and the second language spoken by many others, and English, which is also widely spoken, the other phenomenon we noticed early on was that team members were calling one another family names like *father, mother, uncle, auntie, brother,* and *sister.* Very naively, one of us leaned over to our host and asked whether the company had hired an entire extended family to join the Be Cool team. Our host laughed heartily. "Of course not," he replied. "That is how a lot of members identify their roles on teams here in the Philippines. There is always a father, a mother, sisters, brothers, and so on. It is a way for team members to know their place in their team and their responsibilities. Teams are families here." Not surprisingly, our experiences with U.S.-based teams are rarely this colloquial!

Further illustrating this point, cross-cultural teaming experts Cristina Gibson and Mary Zellmer-Bruhn have identified different metaphors used around the world in reference to the concept of team, including family, military, sports, and community.[3] Consistent with our experience, they found that teams in the Philippines commonly discussed their team roles using community and family terms. Perhaps not surprising, they found that teams in the United States described their roles in sports terms more frequently than community or family.

Why does this matter? Our Filipino host at the company told an enlightening story of one U.S. manager who had been assigned to lead two teams of Filipinos in the plant. In team meetings, the American manager often used phrases like "crossing the goal line," "winning at all costs," and "playing the

assigned position on the team" during team meetings in an attempt to motivate his Filipino team members. Such language emphasized that a team's
members should have a competitive and assertive approach. But this outlook
was inconsistent with their natural disposition toward teams as families and
communities, so this leader did more to befuddle than motivate his teams
toward superior performance. A better approach would have been to direct
the teams in ways that appealed to their familial tendency toward being supportive and nurturing.[4] In part due to this issue, the U.S. manager had to
spend months retraining to adapt to the style of teaming in the Philippines.
The training and commitment to improvement ultimately paid off, and the
leader ended up with happier, more closely knit, and more successful teams.

An important caveat here is that understanding team metaphors and general tendencies in a particular culture is merely a starting point for thinking
about potential differences between your leadership approach and your team's
expectations. For instance, Gibson and Zellmer-Bruhn also noted that team
metaphors are somewhat dependent on other factors beyond just the home
country, including characteristics of a particular company. So how exactly
can you drill down to the best possible understanding? To be sure, there is
no substitute for actually getting to know your team on a personal level, as
understanding potential differences will help you keep an open mind and
avoid making dangerous assumptions. Yet there is also evidence that understanding a team's underlying cultural values can help you more precisely hone
in on your team's preferences and expectations. We dive deeper into this issue
below with an eye toward further honing your 3D Team Leadership potential
globally.

Maximizing Global Team Success by Understanding Cultural Value Frameworks

Researchers have spent several decades attempting to create frameworks and
taxonomies that can help explain how countries are different on various values (e.g., beliefs in what is right or wrong, good and bad). Although about a
half-dozen frameworks describe various sets of major cultural value dimensions, we briefly highlight two of the more prevalent and evidence-based sets
that have emerged over the past several decades. We also note that although
there are varying frameworks, they tend to coalesce around five to six major
dimensions that are common across almost all of the models.[5]

Probably the most widely known framework is that of Dutch researcher Geert Hofstede, who worked with IBM to develop an original set of four major cultural dimensions addressing important work-related questions: "Do people prefer to work primarily alone (individualism) or in groups/teams (collectivism)?", "How important are status and hierarchy in terms of getting things done in organizations (power distance)?", "How much tolerance do people have for ambiguity in their work (uncertainty avoidance)?", and "Do people put more emphasis on assertiveness, achievement, and competition (quantity of life or masculinity) or taking care of others and societal welfare (quality of life or femininity)?"[6] We doubt that anyone majoring in business or getting an MBA in the last three decades emerged without at least hearing something about Hofstede's cultural value framework.

In later years, Hofstede introduced two more cultural value dimensions to his framework. The first, Confucian dynamism (long-term versus short-term orientation), deals with people's values regarding respect for tradition, a focus on the past, and respect for social obligations versus adaptation of traditions to a modern context, a focus on the future, and more limited respect for social obligations. The second, indulgence versus restraint, refers to whether people in a society are relatively free to gratify basic and natural human drives connected to enjoying life and having fun or instead suppress gratifying needs and regulate life using strict social norms. Although the Confucian dynamism and indulgence-versus-restraint dimensions certainly provide useful insight into how individuals may think about problems, a majority of the research to date has considered only the original four dimensions. Accordingly, we will focus most of our attention on the originals later in the chapter.

A second framework of cultural dimensions that has drawn significant attention was developed as part of the Global Leadership and Organizational Behavior Effectiveness program (known more commonly as GLOBE), which was originally led by the late Bob House from the Wharton Business School. Building on the work of Hofstede and several other cross-cultural frameworks, the 170 researchers on the GLOBE team worked over ten years to collect and analyze data from over 17,000 managers in sixty-two countries in the telecommunications, food, and banking industries. This research resulted in nine cultural dimensions; two paralleled Hofstede's power distance and uncertainty avoidance dimensions, but others offered a finer grained view of culture. For example, GLOBE researchers broke Hofstede's

individualism-collectivism dimension down into two dimensions that differentiate between the target of collectivism (large institutions or smaller families): *institutional collectivism*, or the degree to which organizational and institutional practices encourage and reward the collective distribution of resources and collective action, and *in-group collectivism*, or the degree to which individuals express pride, loyalty, and cohesiveness in their companies and families.[7]

The GLOBE team took a similar approach to understanding quantity of life (masculinity) and quality of life (femininity), breaking the dimension down into four elements: (1) performance orientation, or the degree to which a society encourages and rewards performance improvement and success; (2) assertiveness, or the degree to which a society encourages people to be assertive, confrontational, and aggressive in dealing with others; (3) humane orientation, or the degree to which a society encourages and rewards people for being fair, altruistic, generous, caring, and kind to others; and (4) gender egalitarianism, or the degree to which a society minimizes gender inequality.

Finally, the GLOBE team identified future orientation, or the extent to which a society engages in future-oriented behaviors like delaying gratification, planning, and investing in the future. This dimension corresponds closely with Hofstede's fifth and sixth dimensions, Confucian dynamism and indulgence versus restraint. Next, we describe how individualism-collectivism, power distance, uncertainty avoidance, and masculinity-femininity affect the use of our 3D Team Leadership model.

Importantly, we should caution that cultural values refer to higher-level properties displayed by a country or society that, on average, are reflected in the individuals native to that particular society; individuals within a society can still vary meaningfully on the importance they place on each value, of course.[8] Increasing across-country immigration also means that just because someone resides in a particular country does not mean she or he espouses all of the cultural values embedded in that country. Thus, leaders should use cultural frameworks only as a starting point, not a definitive guide for how team members from different countries should be treated (we return to this point when we discuss cultural stereotyping later in the chapter).

Individualism versus Collectivism: The Most Important Cultural Value for Understanding the Applicability of 3D Team Leadership

The cultural value that appears in all major cross-cultural frameworks and has received the most attention is individualism versus collectivism. Not surprisingly, this is also the cultural value that has the strongest link with teamwork.[9] After all, the major benefit of teams is that they generate value through collective processes and outcomes beyond what individuals can produce, right?

The United States, Canada, Great Britain, and Australia score relatively high on individualism, meaning that the primary emphasis in these societies is on the individual rather than on the family or groups to which individuals belong. Broadly speaking, organizations in these countries focus on personal achievement, individually based rewards and recognition, and the value of being different. In fact, in an interview we did for *Bloomberg BusinessWeek*, "Why American B-School Students Can't Stand Teamwork," we talked about the role of cultural individualism as one reason that our MBA students often groan when we announce team projects in our classes. The oft-heard complaint is, "Why should someone else's performance or goals affect my grade?" or, "I want to make an A on the project, but not everyone on the team does, so I end up doing all the work to get an A." We hear similar sentiments in many Western organizations.[10]

In large contrast, high collectivism countries like Japan, Malaysia, Thailand, and many Arab and African nations place primary emphasis on the groups to which individuals belong. In these countries, people tend to focus on collective achievement, team-based or equally shared rewards and recognition, and conformity. In fact, one Japanese proverb reads, "The nail that sticks out will be pounded down" (in phonetic Japanese, *deru kui wa utareru*). Although this saying may not always reflect day-to-day reality at work, it does show that, in general, there are greater pressures to conform in Japan compared to countries like the United States. These pressures in turn can influence how people expect and prefer to be motivated and rewarded in teams. For example, studies have shown that there is much less slacking behavior in collectivistic versus individualistic societies, as collectivists do not want to let their fellow team members down.[11]

Not surprisingly, differences on the individualism-versus-collectivism dimension can have profound implications for how the 3D Team Leadership model is applied. The most obvious impact is that leaders in one country may need to be constantly mindful of a specific dimension more so than leaders in another country. For example, if you are leading in individualistic contexts, as in many Western countries, you will need to be constantly mindful of the "I's" in your team because, on average, team members in these contexts will desire individually based rewards, feedback, and motivation or coaching. Moreover, the formal performance management systems in these countries still, by and large, emphasize individual contributions more so than collective outputs. By contrast, if you are leading in a more collectivist country, you will need to continually focus at least some of your efforts on teams as a whole to satisfy members' expectations for team-based rewards, feedback, and motivation or coaching.

Supporting this premise, our findings at a Fortune 50 insurance company showed that employees who scored higher on collectivism were much more likely than their individualistic counterparts to accept team-based rewards.[12] Similarly, we discovered that team members will be more strongly motivated by an emphasis on individual empowerment in individualistic countries, whereas an emphasis on team empowerment is generally more effective in collectivist countries.[13] Importantly, however, both individual and team empowerment can significantly predict performance across countries to some degree.

This, of course, does not mean that a focus on individuals or a team as a whole is always the dominant focus of a leader's efforts. Rather, the cultural context informs a baseline area of focus that leaders will maintain throughout a team's life cycle. Also, recall that we already discussed that the primary reasons to focus on different elements of your team are to help teams make sense of their team environment and, related, to make sure they are working in the most optimal interdependence arrangement. To the latter point, we noted that pushing teams to work in a highly interdependent fashion could, in some cases, make tasks more complicated than they need to be (i.e., simple or routine tasks). Understanding your team's shared values can help you more finely tune your focus with these aims in mind. For instance, when you have a team with members scoring high on individualism, you should invest extra efforts into making sure they transition appropriately when moving from a simple to complex task requiring more interdependence because you will know this might go against their underlying tendencies. In essence, you know in advance that you'll have to do more to help them make sense of the change (collectivists, by contrast, will embrace the transition more naturally). From an inverse perspective, you may have to be more explicit about leveraging sub-teams or individual-based work when your team approaches things with a baseline collectivist approach. Let's work through an example.

Hudson, a manager at a global tech firm, leads a team of U.S.-based employees tasked with developing a new sales software program for several high-profile clients. This is a temporary project team, and because of this arrangement, the team members will remain on a standard individual-based compensation plan. Although each team member has a relatively high degree of expertise regarding some function relevant to the new software program (e.g., sales experience, software programming), they must work interdependently as an entire team to develop a quality product. Obviously this presents a dilemma for Hudson: if he focuses too heavily on individuals, especially those who traditionally expect to compete for rewards, such as salespeople, teamwork will suffer, but if he focuses too much on his team as a whole, his team members might lose interest because they are not explicitly rewarded for team performance.

Hudson understands the challenge and considers two approaches. The first is to find the time and energy to focus intensely on both the individuals *and* the team as a whole at the same time (the "power through" approach). The second is to focus primarily on his team as a whole and secondarily on the individuals in his team.

The first option is perilous for two main reasons. It assumes that Hudson actually has the personal resources, such as time and energy, to maintain an intense focus on both dimensions. And even if Hudson does have the resources now, uncertainties in upcoming demands from his other job duties may compromise them later. Moreover, intensely focusing on two dimensions at the same time can potentially send mixed signals and confuse members. As we noted earlier, *if you're focused on everything, you're actually not focused on anything.*

The second option, however, gives Hudson more leeway in how he uses his resources and protects him from unexpected demands that may arise later. This is ideal for him because he is already working at near capacity—that's how he got promoted to this leadership role in the first place! In addition, this approach sends a more coherent message to his team members: we as individuals matter and can benefit from working together, but the team as a whole is more important. Hudson wisely chooses this approach.

When interacting with his team, Hudson focuses intensely on empowering his team as a whole, constantly reiterates his team's goals, and provides recognition and feedback based on his overall team's outputs. Furthermore, he actively encourages his team to work interdependently and to avoid taking suboptimal divide-and-conquer approaches that some members may feel tempted to pursue. However, Hudson is also mindful to reserve a relatively smaller part of his time to meet with all individuals on his team and help them understand how working for the overall team goal can help them individually. In this case, in particular, he works to align individual and team interests by highlighting the gains in visibility and reputation (both are key predictors of future opportunities for members) that each member can expect if the team performs optimally.

In addition to the amount of emphasis placed on the "I's" in a team (more focus on this in an individualistic country) versus a team as a whole (more focus on this in a collectivistic country), the individualism-collectivism dimension also has implications for the task-versus-people focus that we described in Chapter 6. Recall that we noted that the bulk of leadership research suggests that leaders do two things: they get things done and build relationships with people. Because people in collectivistic societies place a great deal of importance on relationships when doing business, 3D team leaders would be wise to focus a bit more of their time and attention on building and preserving relationships. People higher in collectivism want to know their colleagues before getting down to business, and much of how things get done is based on strong relationships. In contrast, in individualistic countries team members will be more task focused and less concerned about relationships, as they typically view relationships more instrumentally and as more replaceable than do collectivists. Our advice is to be mindful of the task-versus-people elements of leadership based on your team's cultural composition: you should never completely abandon one for the other, but you can find utility in prioritizing between the two.

Finally, the individualism-collectivism dimension can also have an effect on how team members view and relate to their subteams. In collectivistic countries, members make strong distinctions between in-groups—members to whom one feels a strong sense of loyalty and obligation—and out-groups—members to whom one does not feel a strong connection and, at worse, has a certain level of animosity toward—whereas these distinctions are less common in individualistic countries. A potential problem could occur when leading an overall team composed of subteams in highly collectivistic countries, as team members could consider their own subteam as a type of in-group and the other subteams as out-groups. This would be especially true if the members of each subteam are located in the same office, as this represents an even stronger distinction of in-group versus out-group. Although this is not always a strong concern in individualistic countries, team leaders in collectivistic countries should take steps to reduce in-group–versus–out-group distinctions, perhaps by moving members from one subteam to another from time to time or engaging in very clear steps that reinforce one overall team identity and team goals.

High versus Low Power-Distance: How Status and Hierarchy Affect 3D Team Leadership

In addition to individualism-collectivism, the cultural value of *power distance*–or the extent to which people in a country place an emphasis on status and hierarchy in organizations—has also received a lot of attention. In countries high in power distance, like Japan, India, Malaysia, and Brazil, strong emphasis is placed on respecting each person's level, status, or position in organizations. Employees are reluctant to question their supervisors because they do not want to imply that their supervisor did not do an effective job of communicating expectations. Employees are also highly unlikely to challenge their bosses' directives or decisions because the expectation in these countries is that the boss knows best.

In contrast, low power distance cultures like the United States, the Netherlands, Israel, and the Scandinavian countries place much less importance on a person's title in company hierarchies. In these countries, a higher-level position does not equate to knowledge or having all the answers. Thus, employees feel more comfortable speaking up and offering their own ideas in the presence of supervisors. They take initiative when they feel that it is appropriate, and they even challenge their bosses if they believe they have a better answer or approach.

When we were working with a biotechnology company with locations in Argentina, Belgium, Finland, and the United States, we noticed an interesting subtlety in our European visit that highlighted the impact of power distance on work-related behavior. At the plant in Jämsänkoski, Finland, when we asked what we should do for lunch, the staff gave us directions to the employee

favorable response from team members who may otherwise have been skeptical or afraid to buy-in.

Finally, you would be wise to pay close attention to local employment laws in the countries in which you operate. Some aspects of team empowerment, such as incentives for team performance, might run contrary to labor union contracts or other local laws. We found this to be true in Finland when we asked about the possibility of using team-based pay. The response was, "The unions would never allow that!"

By using the four-step process we have set out, you can more easily implement an empowerment program in a high power distance culture. And although each country varies in how it responds to such changes, you can partner with HR professionals and other knowledgeable professionals to help craft an empowerment program that is best suited to each country's culture. With these things in mind, we now turn to the third cultural dimension in Hofstede's framework, uncertainty avoidance.

High versus Low Uncertainty Avoidance: How Tolerance for Ambiguity Can Affect 3D Team Leadership

In addition to the values related to teamwork and status among organizations, people can be categorized by the extent to which they tolerate ambiguity in their daily working lives, which is reflected in the cultural value of uncertainty avoidance. People in countries that are high in uncertainty avoidance, like Japan, Singapore, Spain, and Switzerland, generally strive to reduce ambiguity and unpredictability in the workplace through policies, laws, procedures, and structures. For example, the concept of lifelong employment in Japan was designed for just this purpose. "Lifelong" employees typically stay with one company their entire working lives, which serves to minimize uncertainty by standardizing one's career path in a company; however, only about 40 percent of Japanese workers still have this privilege today, as part-time work in Japan has increased substantially in the past few decades due to continuously uneven economic performance. The many well-known laws and rules characterizing Singaporean society serve the same purpose. In short, strict laws produce normalized behavior and routinized norms.

Countries that score lower on uncertainty avoidance, like New Zealand, Jamaica, and the Scandinavian countries, have fewer rules and greater ambiguity. In these countries, you are likely to find more opportunism and openness to risk taking in business ventures. One need only set foot in Jamaica or many other Caribbean countries to get a clear sense of what it means to have less reliance on the precise rules and enforcement mechanisms that are designed to minimize uncertainty. As your first taxi driver will likely tell you, street signs are merely a suggestion.

Although the implications of uncertainty avoidance on 3D Team Leadership might be less obvious than those of individualism-collectivism and power distance, the extent to which team members are able to tolerate and handle ambiguity will still have an impact. For example, the level of tolerance for risk taking will likely vary widely between high and low uncertainty avoidance countries. Being willing to take some risks is imperative for teaming in a complex environment, but this does not mean teams should be reckless in their pursuits. As a leader, you should monitor the current decision-making practices of your teams to ensure everyone is on the same page regarding acceptable and unacceptable risks.

In addition, team member reactions to empowerment might be tricky and somewhat counterintuitive in high and low uncertainty avoidance countries. For example, members in high uncertainty avoidance countries might resist taking on more authority and responsibility because it would introduce more ambiguity into their working lives compared to when a leader made all team decisions. Yet this might also work in reverse: giving team members more authority over their work might increase their own sense of personal control and, in effect, decrease the level of uncertainty and ambiguity. You must therefore tread this ground carefully when determining the exact impact of uncertainty avoidance on your team members' receptivity to empowerment. When teams with high uncertainty avoidance values face especially novel tasks, they can benefit from being told explicitly that multiple solutions may achieve positive outcomes and that company leaders do not know the "right" answer. This framing may help the team members feel safe in pursuing novel ideas with their full force.

Quantity versus Quality of Life: How
Values of Achievement versus Cooperation
Affect 3D Team Leadership

The final cultural dimension we discuss in relation to 3D Team Leadership is quantity of life (sometimes referred to as "masculinity") versus quality of life (or "femininity"). In countries that exhibit higher quantity of life values, such as Italy, Japan, South Korea, and Venezuela, there is greater emphasis on assertiveness, achievement, material wealth, and gender inequality. By contrast, countries that place more emphasis on quality of life, like Belgium, the Netherlands, Portugal, and the Scandinavian countries, tend to emphasize societal welfare, interpersonal sensitivity, taking care of others, and friendly cooperation.

The cultural dimension of quantity versus quality of life will likely have the strongest impact on a 3D team leader's methods of motivating team members. For example, in higher quantity of life countries, you will be more likely to motivate team members if you focus on setting up competitive atmospheres, using financial incentives such as individual and team bonuses, and offering perks like coveted work areas, a prestigious parking space, or other significant performance-based recognitions.

By contrast, in higher quality of life countries, using financial incentives to motivate team members could actually backfire. This interesting result is a product of these countries' typically higher than average tax systems. Giving someone a pay raise could have the unintended consequence of pushing the person into a higher tax bracket and thus resulting in a net loss of income. Motivators in high quality of life countries include increased vacation time, volunteer opportunities, and flexible scheduling—things that contribute to a higher quality of life inside and outside the workplace.

The other implication that quantity versus quality of life has for 3D team leaders is that team members in high quality of life cultures place more importance on the value of building strong and meaningful relationships. As a result, we encourage you to spend more time on relationship-oriented activities (e.g., discussing personal matters, sharing meals) when dealing with team members in higher quality of life countries. In contrast, higher quantity of life countries put less emphasis on relationships and much more emphasis on getting things done and performance. Thus, you would be wise to focus more of your efforts on task-based activities (e.g., helping team members reach their goals, facilitating task accomplishment) in these countries.

Table 7.1 provides some practical tips for using the 3D Team Leadership model in different countries.

Where Can I Find Information on the Values of the Countries in Which I Am Working?

Because your specific application of the 3D Team Leadership model depends in part on culture, you clearly need to know the values of each dimension for the countries in which you lead. Fortunately, Hofstede and the GLOBE team provided numerical scores and rankings for countries' various cultural value dimensions. However, Hofstede's original database provides country rankings based on data collected between 1967 and 1969 and again between 1971 and 1973, meaning that many management researchers and leaders are using data that are fifty years old to learn how cultural values should inform their leadership decisions today. Although the GLOBE project used data collected in the early 1990s to create their scores, one only needs to take a look at the major cultural shifts that have happened since this time (e.g., the changes to the Soviet Union, the shift to more free market capitalism in China, the Arab Spring) to realize that these original scores may be outdated and not very useful.[18]

To remedy this problem, along with colleagues and cross-cultural experts Vas Taras and Piers Steel, we set out to explore the mismatch between these original scores and the actual cultural conditions of countries today. Luckily for us, researchers have been conducting thousands of studies using Hofstede's cultural value dimensions since the original publication of his book in 1980, and most of these studies measured countries' cultural values using relatively similar survey measures that are comparable over time. We embarked on a massive search for all of the studies we could find that assessed Hofstede's four original cultural values from 1980 to the present day. Using these data, we were able to calculate new cultural value score rankings separately for the 1980s, 1990s, and 2000s.[19]

There are several trends that should be of interest to team leaders all over the world.[20] First, despite the fact that many companies use individual factors such as intelligence and personality testing to hire and promote their employees, our analysis showed that cultural values were stronger predictors of some important employee outcomes, including how committed people are to their companies, how much employees identify with their companies, whether

TABLE 7.1. Using the 3D Team Leadership Model in Different Countries

Cultural Values	Implications for Using 3D Team Leadership
High individualism	Emphasize recognizing and rewarding individuals in team contexts and individual-based empowerment (i.e., the "I's" in the team).
High collectivism	Focus more on emphasizing the subteams and the overall team (including focusing on team rather than individual empowerment).
High power distance	Empower more slowly and carefully. Make sure that team leaders retain more power and authority, especially at the beginning of an empowerment process.
Low power distance	Feel free to build ambitious empowerment programs for individuals and teams.
High uncertainty avoidance	Provide more structure and feedback, and carefully monitor the willingness of team members to take risks.
Low uncertainty avoidance	Generally the more empowerment the better, as teams will likely embrace ambiguity and feel freer to take more ambitious risks.
High quantity of life	Focus on setting up competitive team atmospheres. Use financial incentives such as individual and team bonuses, and offer perks such as coveted work spaces, prestigious parking, or recognition based on performance.
High quality of life	Focus on team building and making sure all team members are treated well and have access to high quality of life motivators such as time off, volunteer opportunities, and comfortable work environments.

employees are good organizational citizens, the extent to which people prefer to work in teams, and whether employees seek feedback. For example, you can tell a lot more about how much someone prefers to work on a team from his or her collectivism scores compared to a personality test. Interestingly, the reverse was true for other employee outcomes, such as job performance, absenteeism, and turnover. Nevertheless, the fact remains that employees' cultural values matter.

Second, we found that how strongly an employee's cultural values can predict his or her attitudes and behaviors depended on the level of cultural tightness versus looseness in any given country. Cross-cultural expert Michele Gelfand and her colleagues defined *cultural tightness-looseness* as "the strength of social norms and the degree of sanctioning within societies."[21] What this means is that in countries that are culturally tighter, societal institutions enforce a relatively narrow degree of socialization by putting more constraints, monitoring, and sanctioning in place that allow for a very small amount of variance in people's behavior. In countries that are culturally looser, there are relatively lower levels of constraint, monitoring, and sanctioning, thereby allowing for a wider band of acceptable behaviors. In short, we found that you can be more confident that cultural values will predict people's attitudes and behavior in culturally tighter societies, such as Pakistan, Malaysia, India, or Singapore, relative to culturally looser countries, such as the United States, Israel, Hungary, or Ukraine.[22]

Third, because we were able to separate the cultural value scores by decade, we could identify cultural shifts that were occurring over time. There is a heated debate going on in the management field regarding this topic. On one side, cultural change deniers argue that the idea that cultures around the world are becoming more alike is simply a myth.[23] Hofstede himself argued that cultural change moves at glacial speed, and that his country scores from the 1960s and 1970s would be applicable until at least 2100.[24] On the other hand, people like *New York Times* columnist Tom Friedman argue that rapid advancements in communication and information technology, such as the Internet, as well as the rise in global business ("the world is flat"), have made cultural change a far quicker process.[25]

Who is right? Our decade-by-decade analysis shows that the world is actually flattening (though it is not nearly completely flat), supporting Friedman's assertions.[26] In general, countries are transitioning to states of higher individualism and lower power distance, uncertainty avoidance, and quantity of life. In other words, countries are converging toward more Western, or "modernized," cultural values.[27] This is not necessarily a smooth transition, though, as some are actively pushing back against Westernization in their countries. One example is the tension being experienced between the rapidly growing group of information technology workers in Bengaluru, India (known there as "techies"), who are bringing more Westernized values, and the established residents embodying more traditional Indian values.[28]

Although national cultures appear to be converging quicker than Hofstede originally suspected, they are hardly so fluid that we should ignore country differences altogether. Indeed, our work suggests that we are still a long way from a monoculture approach to doing business and leading teams worldwide. Our point here is that you are still likely to see more commonality across cultures than you might initially expect.

Finally, we are able to highlight which cultures have undergone the most significant shifts over the past forty years. With regard to the United States, the biggest shift occurred on the individualism-collectivism dimension. Hofstede's original data has the United States pegged as the most individualistic nation in the world, which is not surprising given the importance of individual achievement and recognition in the country. However, our data from the 2000s note that the United States has significantly decreased its emphasis on individualism over the past several decades. Although the United States is still squarely in the individualism camp, such a shift is possibly a reflection of the increased importance of teaming in U.S. schools and organizations over the past few decades.

The winner of the "most changed" award goes to South Korea. In Hofstede's data, South Korea had one of the lowest individualism scores in the world, which is consistent with most of Southeast Asia's emphasis on collectivism and group harmony. However, our analysis of the data for the 2000s shows that South Korea has exactly the same individualism-collectivism score as the United States for the same time period. According to Hofstede, South Korea also originally had one of the higher uncertainty avoidance scores, but our analysis shows that there has been a shift over time toward a relatively low uncertainty avoidance score. In addition, the country has significantly moved toward valuing quantity of life over quality of life (we did not have enough data to assess differences on power distance). We speculate these shifts are likely due to the rapid economic development experienced over the past several decades.

Although we cannot make any comparisons regarding China because it was not included in Hofstede's original data, related data show that China has undergone massive cultural change in a relatively short amount of time. Indeed, likely due to China's rapid economic development over the past thirty years, we are in the midst of one of the fastest and most fundamental shifts in national culture in the history of the world.[29] In fact, a study of three generations of Chinese managers showed that younger managers are more individualistic and less oriented toward the long term.[30] These shifts in individualism are also reflected in our data for just about every country in Asia.

Although it is widely recognized that shifts in capitalism are associated with corresponding changes in individualism levels, what is less discussed is the societal impact of shifts from collectivism to individualism. Several well-publicized incidents in China have reflected the surprise and occasional derision at the erosion of collectivistic values among today's Chinese.[31] For example, crackdowns on expensive gift giving notwithstanding, overt signs of material wealth are increasingly prevalent in China, from the occasional tricked-out Ferraris and Lamborghinis to ubiquitous smartphones. Such individualistic expressions of wealth were unheard of in China in previous decades. The Chinese have even coined a (not so complimentary) term for those who are now "suddenly rich"—*tuhao*, or "nouveau riche," and the even more derogatory *baofahu*, or "breakout household."

Social commentary aside, we used to joke with our executive education classes that you don't see many employee-of-the-month awards in Japan or China. We can still say this (for the most part) about Japan, but it's no longer true in China. In Chapter 3, we briefly discussed how employee-of-the-month awards and team leaders' recognition of individual team members can have spillover effects; that is, individual recognition leads to higher performance of the recipient's fellow team members and the recipient's overall team.[32] What is interesting about our investigation is that although the phenomenon was rooted largely in Western principles and theory, the results were supported in a Chinese setting. To us, this underscores the sizable shifts in the Chinese culture from relatively collectivistic to more individualistic.[33] Instead of being met with shame or embarrassment, as would be expected in highly collectivistic societies, individual recognition benefited the recipient as well as his or her surrounding teammates. These findings support our core arguments in Chapter 3 that there are, in fact, "I's" in teams—even in countries where you'd least expect to find them.

Changes in cultural values can call into question many of the assumptions most of us had even just several years ago about how to lead. That's why we reemphasize that 3D team leaders should access the most recent cultural value scores when designing their performance management systems for teams in different countries.

Doesn't Cultural Stereotyping Lead to Making False Assumptions about Team Members?

With all of the discussion about cultural value dimensions, country profiles, and the resulting appropriate leadership behaviors, there is an obvious question: *Are we running the dangerous risk of cultural stereotyping in our global teams?* Once again, just because a person was born and raised in Argentina or China or France, does that automatically mean that the person embodies all of the cultural values typical of people from that country? Or, alternatively, is there enough variation in the cultural values within a country that we should be cautious in imposing a country's generalized set of values on any particular individual? As we have alluded to in our prior arguments, the answer is an emphatic, "Maybe. Maybe not."

These questions remind us of the same phenomenon that still occurs when many companies use personality tests, such as the Myers-Briggs, to help leaders and team members understand one another better. Millions of people have taken the Myers-Briggs, which categorizes people on four dimensions: extraversion-introversion, thinking-feeling, sensing-intuition, and judgment-perception. Test takers then receive feedback that places them into one of sixteen types based on a combination of the four dimensions. A common objection we hear is that people feel as though they are unfairly "put in a box" or "stereotyped" after they get their results.[34]

We suspect members would have similar concerns about leaders using their cultural values scores on a survey instrument to make assumptions about teamwork styles. For example, you might be hesitant to ask those who score high on individualism to engage in a great deal of teamwork behavior, fearing that an individualist's potential resistance to teamwork will lead to lower commitment and satisfaction, as some of our own previous work has shown.[35] The evidence regarding within-country variation of cultural values legitimizes these very real fears and concerns. Again, a great deal of research shows that there can be as much (or more) within-country variance on cultural values as between-country variance.[36]

In addition, our own research shows that defining cultural values by country may not be the best container for considering and evaluating such dimensions.[37] For example, if country essentially equates to culture, then you would expect to see a high similarity on values within each country and great differences on values between countries. We found exactly the opposite when creating our up-to-date versions of Hofstede's dimensions: about 80 percent of the variance in Hofstede's original cultural values resides within countries (meaning that less than 20 percent resides between countries), confirming that country itself is often a poor unit designation for considering culture.

To explore potential alternatives, we pitted country against seventeen other demographic and environmental characteristics to determine if they were better containers of culture than country. Our results showed that the demographic characteristics of occupation, socioeconomic status, education level, and generation, in addition to the environmental characteristics of economic freedom, extent of globalization, long-term unemployment, wealth distribution inequality, corruption, crime rate, and share of employment in agriculture, were all better containers of culture than country. Indeed, country was only the fifteenth best container of culture out of seventeen possibilities.

That means that if you put people from a variety of countries who share the same occupation in a room together, they are much more likely to have a common set of values compared to a room full of people from the same country but who have different occupations. So, there is a definite and real danger in assuming that each individual from a specific country actually holds the dominant cultural values of that country.

In addition to these results, cultural paradoxes also reinforce the problems associated with cultural stereotypes.[38] Cultural paradoxes refer to the notion that people in various countries often behave inconsistently with the country's dominant cultural values when situations significantly change. For example, as cross-cultural experts Joyce Osland and Allan Bird point out, Americans are highly individualistic, yet they have the highest rates of charitable giving in the world and volunteer for numerous community projects and emergencies. If the Japanese are high in uncertainty avoidance and Americans low, why do the Japanese incorporate ambiguous terms into their short business contracts, while Americans painstakingly spell out every possible contingency? Also in the United States, autocratic behavior is often tolerated in CEOs, even though America is generally characterized as egalitarian and low in power distance.[39]

How can these apparent contradictions be explained? There are many possibilities, but Osland and Bird suggest that the major causes appear to be things like cultural assumption traps, misinterpretations due to lack of cross-cultural experience, an either-or approach to understanding cultures rather than a "shades of gray" approach, and a lack of recognition and understanding of the many cultural paradoxes that exist in each country. Once a less simplistic approach to culture is applied, many of these seemingly intractable paradoxes can be explained.

As an example of cultural complexity, consider how leader-follower relationships compare across the United States and China. In the United States, workers rely on their individual relationships with their leaders primarily for professional support and individual feedback, which is consistent with the country's individualistic culture. Our research, however, suggests that in China, which still has strong elements of collectivism despite recent upticks in individualism, individual leader-employee relationships can mean even more than in the United States.[40] Why? One explanation is that compared to the United States, transitional economies like China lack the bureaucratic structures needed to make employees feel safe (e.g., supervisors can fire and promote employees at will without regard for formalized rules or fairness). Chinese employees therefore strive to develop deep, closely held personal relationships—referred to as *guanxi*—to protect their professional and personal well-being.

Indeed, the Chinese reliance on *guanxi* has caught many expatriate leaders off guard and caused numerous struggles in building effective teams. Many U.S.-based leaders, for instance, are reluctant to accept birthday or holiday gifts from employees or oblige any offers for help outside work from employees (likely viewing them cautiously as bribes). Consequently, Chinese employees sometimes view a leader's nonacceptance as a sign that the leader may not fully value the employee (and, hence, will not protect him or her). Concepts like *guanxi* are not unique to China; for example, *jeitinho* in Brazil, *blat* in Russia, and *wasta* in Arab countries convey similar sentiments. Thus, although some cultures may value collectivist approaches, this does not necessarily mean that leaders can avoid building individual personal relationships up front without consequence.

As a result of all of the above information, we strongly advise against using cultural values as the sole and final determinant of your leadership behavior in specific countries. Rather, we advise that country score information be used as a baseline, or first best guess, when trying to figure out how people's cultural values might influence their reactions to and behaviors in teams. Relying on local experts, engaging in your own sensemaking, and making adjustments based on team member feedback are all imperative.

Some of our own work on transformational leadership exemplifies this point. First, using employees from China and the United States, we confirmed that Chinese employees, on average, scored higher in power distance than their U.S. counterparts (like the country-level studies have indicated). Second, and more interesting, we found that *individuals scoring higher in power distance reacted less positively toward transformational leaders, regardless of their country of origin.* The explanation is that a transformational leader's focus on challenging followers to find their own ways of doing things is less compatible with members that feel a strong desire for explicit direction and leader control (i.e., high power distance).[41] Thus, an inexperienced leader might assume that all Chinese team members would react negatively toward transformational leaders and, correspondingly, that all American team members would react positively toward transformational leaders, which would likely be a critical oversimplification. At the conclusion of our original article describing these findings, we gave the following advice to team leaders: "The age-old 'When in Rome . . .' advice (i.e., lead individuals according to their country-level culture) perhaps should be modified to 'When in Rome, get to know Romans as individuals' (i.e., lead individuals differently, depending on their individual cultural value orientations)."

In sum, there is nothing wrong with arming yourself with knowledge of other countries before trying to use 3D Team Leadership in them, especially if you have no prior familiarity. Indeed, this practice remains an essential first step in developing your global team leadership effectiveness. However, doing so alone is not enough. You must also take the time to get to know your team members' unique value preferences to determine the best leadership approaches for your specific teams.

Best Practices for Leading Culturally Diverse Teams

Although the logic we have set out so far obviously applies when you move across cultures (e.g., moving from the United States to China to lead a team of Chinese employees), we have not yet fully addressed what happens when you are taking on a team that is *culturally diverse*. This increasingly common circumstance differs from the situation in the preceding section because you are now guiding a team composed of members from different countries who will likely bring varied cultural values to your team.[42] Standing by our adage to "get to know Romans as individuals", we suggest taking a few additional, evidence-backed steps when leading these types of teams.

A large-scale examination of how cultural diversity affects team processes and performance showed that cultural diversity has a kind of double-edged sword effect.[43] Perhaps not surprisingly, the results show that members in more culturally diverse teams have more conflict between one another and feel less socially integrated (i.e., members are less attracted to their team, less satisfied with other team members, and have less social interaction between members). This aligns with a great deal of evidence demonstrating that increased diversity in general can hinder teams' adoption of effective team processes, which subsequently hurts team performance. Interestingly, however, evidence also suggests that increased cultural diversity can lead to increased team creativity and more satisfied members. Your challenge as a leader, obviously, is to minimize the negatives while maximizing the positives of cultural diversity.

Evidence shows that culturally diverse teams seem to struggle the most when they (1) are performing tasks that are more, rather than less, complex (indicative of most of today's teams); (2) have members who work more face-to-face rather than virtually; (3) are larger rather than smaller (another reason to keep teams small if possible); and (4) a bit counterintuitively, have members who work together more often.

With many of the characteristics we have noted often out of your control, how can you overcome them to maximize the processes and performance of culturally diverse teams. Our work suggests that you need to spend a great deal of time, especially initially, focusing on the "I's" in your teams. Doing so will allow you to understand the unique needs, concerns, and motivators of each of the members on your team, which will help you to create the type of team climate necessary for effective team processes and performance to occur. However, this understanding can come from an in-depth knowledge of each member gained over time in one-on-one meetings and interactions. Note that this deviates from our recommendation that the level of interdependence always dictates your focus. Here we are saying that even if a culturally diverse team has a high level of interdependence early in its life cycle, you must still devote a portion of your time to the "I's" in your team because understanding the unique demands, challenges, and needs of each team member will go a long way toward getting a diverse team off on the right foot. In other words, culturally diverse teams represent an important exception to our "interdependence drives everything" in terms of your focus.

In addition to paying attention to the "I's" in your team, you should also focus on your team as a whole in culturally diverse teams. In particular, you need to create a unified team identity, which can be an extremely tenuous task in these teams.[44] Without a strong shared identity, you will likely forgo the important synergies residing in your team. Interestingly, our work with global communities of practice in a Fortune 100 company suggests this may be especially difficult when your teams have a roughly even split of members along nationality lines[45]—for example, five French and five Brazilian members in a team of ten. To combat this challenge, leaders can offset the potential downsides of incongruent cultural beliefs between two groups by building a "third culture".[46]

There are several other evidence-based steps you can take to build a strong team identity. First, it might be helpful to assess the team's cultural distance, or how far apart the members of the team are with regard to their cultural values. You could employ the GlobeSmart tool we mentioned earlier in this chapter to map your team's overall pattern of cultural value differences rather than relying on country of origin as a proxy. This guide would give you some indication as to how much work will be required to move your team toward a unified identity in the face of cultural value differences.

In addition to cultural values, some evidence suggests that a team whose members have previous work experience in a country other than their birth country can promote creativity and innovation, particularly if the cultural distance between a team member's home country and the country in which the person has work experience is moderate. For example, if the two countries involved are the United States and Canada, the relatively small cultural distance might not provide sufficient novelty to stimulate creative processes or the ability to implement creative outcomes. Conversely, if the two countries are the United States and Japan, the relatively high cultural distance could mean that a team member might not be able to generate anything novel or creative due to the stress and lack of adaptation to the new culture.[47] As a result, you can expect to draw on the creativity and breakthrough thinking of a culturally diverse team, particularly one in which a team's members have had a fair amount of previous international experiences. The caveat here is that when members are very different from a cultural perspective, you have your work cut out for you to ensure there is enough effective communication and collaboration to make these differences work for the good of the team, not against it.

For example, one key component necessary for building a unified team identity is psychological safety, defined in Chapter 4 as the extent to which a team's members feel safe for interpersonal risk taking. Vastly different cultural values among team members can make people feel uncomfortable in sharing their unique ideas and taking risks. To foster psychological safety, team leaders should be consistently accessible, ask for team members' input, and encourage team members to discuss their own mistakes in a constructive manner. Another way to build psychological safety and, in turn, enhance the building of a unified team identity is by using a team contract or charter, which should answer the following questions: What is the team's purpose? What are the team's vision, mission, goals, tasks?

What is the role of each member? How will team members work together? What is the meaning of important team elements such as deadlines, quality, and trustworthiness? Importantly, although even seemingly straightforward task attributes, like deadlines and quality, are critical everywhere, they may have different technical meanings or connotations in different countries.

What Characteristics Should a Successful Global 3D Team Leader Possess?

We now briefly discuss the specific attributes that can assist you in motivating and managing globally diverse teams. The most important attribute is a high level of cultural intelligence (CQ). An individual with high CQ "teases out of a person's or group's behavior those features that would be true of all people and all groups, those peculiar to this person or this group, and those that are neither universal nor idiosyncratic."[48] In other words, a person high in CQ has the ability to spot patterns and trends when appropriate but can also discern the unique aspects of cultures and individuals. Note that this is not the same thing as cultural sensitivity (e.g., a person could have a high CQ but still be insensitive), which is obviously still needed.

CQ has three components, all of them important when operating in cultures outside one's home country: *cognitive* (i.e., the head), *emotional/motivational* (i.e., the heart), and *physical* (i.e., the feet). The cognitive aspect refers to your ability to notice clues to a culture's shared understandings and make accurate inferences. Building your cognitive repertoire could start by using the latest up-to-date cultural values scores we discussed earlier as a means to get a head start on increasing your cross-cultural knowledge. This should also help you to perceive the nuances of a foreign culture and make sense of cultural patterns and trends. The emotional or motivational component refers to your ability to make mistakes in a foreign culture without getting frustrated and to persevere even in unfamiliar territory. As many have probably experienced, when you are in a country with which you are unfamiliar, it is easy to let even small mishaps and mistakes lead to frustration, especially when culture shock sets in; however, those high in CQ regulate their emotions in the face of this potential frustration. The physical component refers to the ability to adopt habits, customs, and mannerisms characteristic of a given culture. In other words, you are able to alter your behavior like using proper handshakes and keeping an appropriate distance from others to make them comfortable in a novel environment.

Fortunately, evidence suggests that a significant amount of CQ can be developed and learned over time.[49] Cross-cultural experts Christopher Earley and Elaine Mosakowski provide a six-step approach for increasing your CQ.[50] We describe each step below using Melanie (a leader in a high-tech firm with whom we worked) and her experiences in a corporate training program as an example.

Step 1: Examine CQ strengths and developmental needs using a survey instrument. We recommend that you conduct a CQ self-assessment and, perhaps more important, ask your leader, peers, and team members to evaluate you as well. Recounting her experience with taking the CQ survey, Melanie said, "Because I had already worked in three countries in the previous ten years, I rated myself pretty highly on all three dimensions of CQ, so I was a little shocked when I received my 360-degree feedback ratings and most of the raters had me very low on the emotional/motivational dimension, but pretty good on the cognitive and behavioral ones." Reading from an actual feedback form, she shared an example of one of the comments: "She tends to cut me off when I'm speaking to her in English. I guess it's because my language skills aren't that great, and English is not my first language, and so she finishes my sentences for me a lot of the times. I feel like that's disrespectful because often she doesn't even get what I'm saying. And, she sighs heavily like I'm wasting her time." As is common in many 360-degree feedback experiences, Melanie had no idea she was showing impatience and irritability when speaking with her associates in the countries in which she worked. Even though she understood the cultural differences and managed to incorporate that knowledge into displaying culturally appropriate behaviors, she was less able to manage her emotional frustration when dealing with others who were not like her.

Step 2: Find training opportunities focusing on developmental needs. For example, if you are low on physical CQ, you can take an acting class to better understand how to increase behavioral flexibility and adaptability. Melanie described her training and development activities as follows:

> After I received this feedback, I found a workshop on active listening. It had great content but also allowed you to practice in the class with other participants, and they get to rate you on a scale of 1 to 10 on how much they felt understood. It seemed a little hokey at first because they ask you to do things like paraphrase what the other person is saying before you offer your own

thoughts and, of course, never interrupt while the person is talking. That's a hard one for me because I'm a real extravert and Type A. But after practicing it a few times, it started to feel natural and I got increasingly good understanding ratings throughout the practice sessions. The second thing I did was make sure to take time out for myself when I was working in a different country. Before, I would just spend all my hours working and not any time relaxing. I do yoga when I'm at home, so I started to find yoga studios when I traveled, too, or if I couldn't find one, I would do some of the poses in my hotel room using an app on my phone. That really helps me get some calmness and deal with other people in a more patient way.

Step 3: Apply lessons learned from the training by practicing what you learned. Melanie started to slowly apply what she had learned from the CQ class when she was working with people from different countries in the home office. She said:

> I started practicing the lessons in small ways, I didn't try to tackle everything at once. It's funny, when people see that you are a good listener, they trust you more and you learn so much. By slowing things down a little bit and really listening carefully to what they were saying and keeping my impatience in check—which is an ongoing battle, believe me—I think I was able to make the changes more naturally. I didn't want to come across as inauthentic, and I think I would have if I just dove right in and tried all of the CQ and active listening techniques all at once.

Step 4: Organize personal resources to support the new approaches developed in training. This is important as you try to make sure you get adequate support and information about the effect your training and development are having on others around you. Melanie said:

> I enlisted the help of a peer of mine who is often in meetings that I am leading and even ones where I am just a member. I told him the things I had learned and just asked him to keep an eye out to see where I might be doing well or not so well. It's a good thing I picked a person who was brutally honest, because he did point out a few times where my behavior just seemed a little "forced," or at least that's the way he put it. So, I got a chance to make adjustments along the way.

Step 5: Enter the new cultural setting you need to master. After practicing in the home office with foreign nationals who were also located there and getting feedback from her peer, Melanie embarked on an extended assignment in another country. She said, "What was interesting about the training was I could apply it whether I was actually working in one of the overseas sites myself or when I was leading global team meetings from a distance. CQ is not just about face-to-face interaction, I also found it very helpful in my virtual team interactions."

Step 6: Reevaluate newly developed skills and how effective they have been in the new setting. This would be an excellent time to use multirater feedback and conversations with colleagues. Melanie indicated that she conducted another 360-degree CQ feedback assessment one year after she did the first one, and she was rated much higher on the emotional/motivational dimension of CQ.

We would add a Step 7 here: *Have fun!* Try not to take yourself too seriously, and don't be afraid of making mistakes or looking foolish. It's for this reason that one of us speaks much better French after a couple of glasses of good French Bordeaux. You are just not as afraid to make mistakes and trip over the language! Melanie agreed and said, "I think after the training, I also learned to lighten up a little bit more. Before when I would make a mistake, I would get down on myself. I'm a real perfectionist. But I've learned to laugh things off more when I make a cultural faux pas. It's not easy, but I try to have a little fun with it."

Evidence suggests a few other attributes that would help leaders use the 3D Team Leadership model effectively across cultures.[51] Openness to experience, which refers to the degree to which a person has a broad range of interests and is fascinated by novelty, is one of the traits contained within what is known as the Big Five (the other four traits are conscientiousness, agreeableness, emotional stability, and extraversion; in total the Big Five captures the majority of one's overall personality). Those higher in openness tend to be creative, curious, and artistic. In a new cultural context, high levels of openness would likely be associated with a 3D team leader who was flexible enough to thrive in unfamiliar territory and adapt his or her approach in different cultural contexts. Personality traits like openness to experience are less malleable than some other leader attributes, including CQ, but they are not entirely stable over one's lifetime.[52] Moreover, even just being aware of your natural tendencies (personality traits) can help you see opportunities for improvement.

To this end, and irrespective of your personality, a vital aspect of using 3D Team Leadership globally is your willingness and ability to be flexible and adaptable. In a global setting, adaptability and flexibility would be specifically applied to such areas as facility with language, being able to mimic behavior in different social situations, and having the behavioral repertoire to adapt in different cultures.

Resilience in the face of stress is another important factor. Leaders in global contexts are bombarded with competing priorities, novel environments, and frustration produced by infrastructure differences like traffic, technology, access to daily necessities, language barriers, and housing issues. Such demands create tremendous stress on top of the various work-related issues and concerns. A leader's ability to tolerate and bounce back from stress is invaluable.

Finally, integrity is also a pillar of 3D Team Leadership in all instances, but plays a major starring role when you enter a new culture. To clearly demonstrate integrity in new and unfamiliar contexts, you should behave ethically at all times, be loyal to your organization's values and strategy, exhibit honesty, and be trustworthy. Of course, these are critical elements for doing business worldwide, although the forms may differ from country to country.

Although this list is not exhaustive, the question must be asked: Are effective global 3D team leaders born or made? The answer is: yes! Effective 3D Team Leadership in global contexts is part personality (e.g., openness to experience, stress-coping ability), part skill (e.g., CQ, adaptability/flexibility), and part values (e.g., integrity). Since a few of these are innate and change only modestly over time, some leaders may have a natural head start in acquiring the full repertoire needed to be an effective cross-cultural 3D team leader. Yet many of these are skills that can be developed over time, meaning that most prospective leaders can work their way toward being highly successful global 3D team leaders. After conducting an honest assessment of the attributes that are more difficult to develop, you will need to build your teams in such a way that they can compensate for those attributes that you as a leader lack. A team with a complementary set of characteristics will help ensure success in novel environments.

In summary, we have explained when and how leaders should adapt various parts of the 3D Team Leadership model when leading team members from different countries. The lessons in this chapter can be used when you are asked to asked to move to a new country to lead a team of host country nationals or when you are asked to lead a team that is globally diverse[53] (regardless of where you are physically located). We have also warned you not to make cultural assumptions using country stereotypes. Country-level information about culture is a good place to start; however, we stand by our advice to "get to know Romans as individuals" to maximize your team's performance. We have noted the importance of CQ and pointed out that it can be developed over time and that it is not something innate that some possess and others do not. The qualities of openness, patience, listening, and empathy can also go a long way to helping you become a true global 3D team leader.

8   3D Team Leadership in Virtual Teams

I N CHAPTER 7, WE PROVIDED AN OVERVIEW OF TYPICAL
cultural issues that can be challenging for leaders in global contexts,
as well as some practical advice that you can apply to mitigate potential problems. Although cross-cultural issues can be present in various settings, we
primarily examined them through the lens of individuals who are charged
with leading a team composed of members whose cultures are outside their
own—for example, an individual from the United States leading a team of
Brazilians in Brazil or a diverse team of members with different nationalities situated in the United States. In this chapter, we extend this discussion
to *global virtual teams*, which feature a globally diverse and geographically
dispersed set of members. Ideally, virtual teams allow organizations to leverage boots-on-the-ground views from all over the world and get collaboration
from the best employees regardless of their location. Yet virtual teams introduce several additional and unique challenges beyond the cultural consider-
ations described in the previous chapter that leaders must overcome.[1]

Our experience helping organizations understand and leverage virtual
teams began in the late 1990s, light years ago in terms of technology. But even
as we have witnessed remarkable advances in the options team members have
for communicating worldwide, virtual teams still face several common obstacles that limit their effectiveness.[2] To start, virtual team members are typically
less familiar with one another than traditional face-to-face team members;
they may have never actually met in person or, at best, met only once or twice.

In addition, leaders and team members do not meet that often, which places a premium on each encounter. These challenges create serious relationship-based pressures for leaders even before the task-related challenges begin.

Another painfully straightforward issue that continues to plague virtual teams is time zone differences. Most companies we worked with originally initiated audio- or videoconference calls during working hours at headquarters and over time observed that team members in the other locations were resentful for having to be on calls at all hours of the night and early morning.[3] In response, many companies now rotate meeting times to be fairer to the people in their far-flung affiliates (Anna in Chapter 1 followed this process). Nonetheless, even such good-faith gestures sometimes fail to eliminate feelings of inconvenience and unfairness.[4]

Finally, our experience reveals that virtual teams are notorious for failing to work in a true interdependent fashion, regardless of the approach called for by the task. For instance, in part due to scheduling challenges like time zone differences, a lack of rich communication and deep personal relationships, and varying work cultures, virtual team members often find it simpler just to break overall team tasks down into individual or same-location subteam assignments. Then, right before their next scheduled meeting, members or subteams will hastily compile their work into a single (and often incoherent) final output. Unfortunately, and as we have noted before, low and moderate levels of interdependence prohibit teams from optimally performing many critical tasks and defeat the purpose of creating a virtual team altogether.

Our takeaway here is twofold. First, virtual teams are messy.[5] Second, leadership is vital for helping virtual teams overcome this messiness and achieve their true potential.[6] To better understand what employees want and expect from leaders in virtual teams, we interviewed dozens of virtual team members in high-tech companies and asked the following question: *What characteristics make for a prototypical, high-performing virtual team leader?* Some responses were:

- Be proactive, organized, and able to make trade-offs (time, cost, scope).
- Have the skill to select the right mix of people.
- Be flexible, understand different cultures, and overcome language barriers and misunderstandings.
- Meet deadlines, set expectations for team members, conduct resource

and budget planning, and develop new talent, all of which require special skills in influencing without power, listening, relationship building, delegation, and control.

- Motivate others, maintain a positive attitude, and resolve conflicts fairly.
- Build a special relationship with each member, share rewards and credit with team members, and engage in small acts of kindness with team members.
- Be realistic about time lines, make priorities clear to everyone, and have a high level of technical expertise.
- Be able to identify strong leads in host countries, and get the right skill set on the team.
- Work with stakeholders and keep them informed (relationship management).
- Be a good knowledge-sharing role model.

If you've ever worked on a virtual team, you've probably either heard or said many of these things yourself. In isolation, each expectation may seem quite reasonable, but when viewed together, the list may seem overwhelming. And keep in mind that it might actually be even worse; the expectations we listed are only a very small slice of what team members actually reported! We won't deny it: being a virtual team leader is difficult. However, it isn't impossible. Applying the principles of 3D Team Leadership, in conjunction with empowering individuals, your team as a whole, and the subteams within your overall team can help you get the most out of your virtual teams—all while preserving your sanity (at least, most of it).

We'll start with a discussion of some basic issues to keep in mind when building a virtual team, then move toward some actionable steps for leading each of the three dimensions effectively in virtual contexts.

Best Practices for Building a World-Class Virtual Team

In many cases, you might have at least some choice in selecting the members of your virtual team (if you do not have this power, breathe easy; we'll discuss some ways to overcome selection deficiencies later in this chapter). As always, prospective team members should be evaluated on their relevant knowledge, skills, and abilities to determine whether they have the raw tools to make a meaningful contribution to the team's mission. Beyond these prerequisite factors, you can also evaluate several other criteria that may help you stave off unwanted problems of virtual teaming.

To be certain, many of the lessons regarding cultural values that we presented in Chapter 7 are also applicable to global virtual teams. However, there is at least one very big point of divergence when considering global *virtual* teams. As we noted in Chapter 7, individuals who score higher on collectivism are typically better suited for working in teams because they often place a premium on team concerns. In virtual teams, however, this relationship is not so straightforward; in fact, the evidence suggests that people scoring higher in individualism actually have more confidence in their ability to succeed in a virtual team.[7] Why is this the case? The most plausible explanation, in our view, is that members scoring higher in individualism can better manage the significant in-between periods void of team interactions that commonly occur when members are spread out across the world. Those higher in collectivism might miss the close, interpersonal connections that are more easily developed and reinforced face-to-face.

Of course, this does not necessarily mean individualists should be selected over collectivists without deeper consideration. Rather, we are suggesting that you take action in preparing your collectivist-leaning employees for the upcoming challenges and realities of virtual teaming. Beyond evaluating the basic value of individualism-collectivism, several other attributes may predict an individual's ability to thrive in a virtual team environment.[8] Our work with numerous companies suggests the following:

- comfortable working with large amounts of ambiguity
- capable of getting work done without a lot of direction
- proactive in anticipating challenges and tackling them head-on
- highly effective communicators, particularly when using relatively lean communication tools (tools with less information-carrying capacity, such as messaging, e-mail, and social media)
- High cultural intelligence, specifically being sensitive to and responding appropriately to cultural differences
- highly energetic so that they can keep up with the demands of fast-paced work and long hours required to work virtually in a VUCA environment

Although selecting individuals who can handle and thrive in virtual teams is important, a related concern is the overall composition of your virtual team. Two important elements of virtual team composition are skill and demographic diversity. Skill diversity is often a moot point in virtual teams because these teams are typically built to be cross-functional, but demographic diversity (other than country of origin) may be more of a challenge. Although some demographic variables (e.g., gender, race/ethnicity, age) can act as a proxy for the unique views within a team that can promote novel or holistic thinking, some research suggests that diversity on these attributes can also lead to unhealthy team processes and lower performance in some instances.[9] Rather than attempting to reduce demographic diversity—which is unethical and often illegal—we recommend embracing diversity as an opportunity and working to help members overcome short-term, surface-level issues (we discuss several techniques later in this chapter).

Team size is also an important consideration. Evidence suggests that team diversity can be easier to leverage in smaller teams,[10] with the optimal virtual team consisting of about five to seven members. However, many teams in practice are likely to be larger due to the complexity of their projects. When teams become overly large, we encourage you to create core or parallel teams of smaller size (recall the discussion about multisubteam systems in Chapter 5) in order to take advantage of the cohesion and commitment typical of smaller teams. Finally, although VUCA environments tend to create inevitable membership changes in virtual teams, you should try to keep membership as stable as possible (again, we realize this is not likely).

Once a virtual team is created, you need to know how to (virtually) lead each of the three dimensions in our 3D Team Leadership model.

Best Practices for Leading the "I's" in Global Virtual Teams

Leading individuals in virtual teams can feel unnatural for many of us. In some cases, each member has a day-to-day boss at his or her current location (distinct from the actual virtual team leader), and you may feel as if you are overstepping your bounds when trying to develop one-on-one relationships and offer feedback from afar. In the same vein, because leaders and members sometimes do not know one another well or even at all, you might experience significant discomfort and awkwardness in your individual interactions with team members. Some leaders, for instance, are overly timid and fail to engage at all. Others write off the personal aspect of the relationship altogether and instead focus solely on tasks, which leaves team members feeling underappreciated and unclear about how their own goals fit into the team's goals. These are all massive mistakes.

The best virtual team leaders we have worked with find a way to connect with individual team members. Indeed, evidence shows that leaders who focus more on building relationships, compared to those who are more task focused, are viewed more positively (i.e., as more intelligent, creative, and original) by virtual team members.[11] This is not to say that a task focus is not warranted; rather, it suggests that ignoring individual relationships can compromise your ability to motivate team members.

One of the most basic steps to demonstrate a focus on individuals is to make a routine of conducting regular check-ins—a quick e-mail, phone call, or even text message—with each individual member to reduce feelings of distance and disconnectedness that members of virtual teams commonly experience.[12] Although seemingly small, this relatively simple step can help establish the personal rapport with individual members that is often overlooked when technology-based communication is the main form of interaction. Moreover, establishing rapport initially can make more substantive conversations in the future, such as setting expectations, establishing training interventions, or delivering critical feedback, feel more natural. Evidence also suggests that frequent communication, along with generally positive leader-member relationships, fosters more team innovation because members are more willing to contribute their voice to the team's decision-making efforts.[13]

Making contact with individual team members is especially critical at the beginning of a virtual team's life cycle. During this time, you should not only express a general interest in individual members' backgrounds and concerns, but also communicate realistic expectations about what is required of them in their virtual team. Importantly, individual expectations should be similar in content across members, though you should also acknowledge members' unique cultural values when delivering your message.

Establishing similar expectations for individuals is critical for two reasons. First, mismatched expectations from different members can generally lead to motivational problems, dissatisfaction, and lower individual performance on a team.[14] Second, constructing similar expectations can help build shared norms and reinforce a team's charter, which typically answers the questions of *who* (their roles), *what* (the vision, mission, goals, and tasks), *when* (the frequency of meeting, adherence to deadlines), *where* (in face-to-face versus electronic meetings), and *why* (the team's purpose). Adherence to a charter can improve a number of individual outcomes such as trust, willingness to be a part of the team, and individual performance.[15]

Another way to emphasize the individuals in a virtual team is to invest time and resources toward training, developing, and coaching specific members who demonstrate deficiencies. In fact, although virtual teams are more prevalent today than ever before, many employees still do not have a great deal of experience working virtually, especially cross-culturally. To reduce problems associated with experience gaps, you can facilitate training interventions[16] on topics like intercultural sensitivity,[17] teamwork,[18] and technology use.[19]

As is always the case, the suggestion to conduct more training deserves a more nuanced discussion. To better inform this discussion, we worked with a large U.S.-based travel reservation company with operations in over fifty countries to investigate the effectiveness of an online virtual team training intervention—specifically, Team Tools Interactive by LightSpeed Learning. The travel company had each individual team member work through a series of sixteen training modules (four modules per quarter in a calendar year), with the hope that their skill proficiency (as assessed by a series of end-of-module tests) would improve team customer service ratings. The results were not straightforward.

To our (and, most important, the company's) dismay, we found that no matter how high the level of team training proficiency—how well the team members actually learned the skills—there was absolutely no effect on customer service. Just imagine the collective groan from the people who had spent thousands of dollars getting the licenses for this training when they discovered that it made absolutely no difference for the most important thing that this company cared about: its customers! Digging a little deeper into this result, we identified three "it depends" factors that influenced whether the training has a positive impact on customers. First, the training was more effective when teams had high levels of technology support; when support levels were low, training proficiency actually negatively affected customer service. This drives home a simple though often overlooked aspect of virtual teams: organizations must provide team members with the right set of tools to get their work done and adequate training to use the correct set of tools effectively. Without these baseline requirements, many team training interventions are worthless.

Second, the training was more effective when teams had longer-tenured team leaders. Although today's VUCA environments make it mostly impossible to keep leaders and teams paired for extended periods of time, a potentially more fruitful approach for improving training outcomes is to hone the leadership qualities that are typically seen in longer-tenured individuals. In particular, we posit that long-tenured leaders have had the opportunity to reduce members' uncertainty about what is expected (consistent with our previous recommendation to proactively establish expectations for individuals) and, related, foster environments of trust among team members. Both factors, we reason, are critical for helping members feel confident that displaying the skills they learned in the training program will be appreciated and helpful for the team.

Supporting this position, the training was also more effective when the teams had high levels of trust. In these teams, training proficiency positively affected customer service ratings; the opposite was true for low-trust teams. In this sense, members need to believe that their fellow colleagues can be counted on before they will exhibit any meaningful behavioral changes. A key lesson here for virtual team leaders is that they must spend time building up trust (see Chapter 4) before asking members to invest a great deal of time and effort toward learning new ways to interact and operate.

Finally, as we alluded to in the introduction to this chapter (and our section in Chapter 2 on shared leadership), *a single person often cannot be the sole source of leadership for a virtual team*.[20] Based on our experience working with many companies using virtual teams, leaders who think they can fulfill all of the core leadership roles are setting themselves up for failure. Obviously, leaders with control issues and those who rely on micromanagement need not apply to be virtual team leaders. So where does this leave us?

If you are leading a virtual team, you need to ensure that you provide team members with appropriate leadership skill-building activities. Following the advice we gave in Chapter 3 on empowering individual team members is a good place to start, particularly when it comes to the autonomy dimension.[21] You need to delegate leadership activities to the various members on your virtual team and then rotate responsibilities among members.[22] This will strengthen you as a leader because you will then have more time to focus on the leadership responsibilities that are most appropriate for a virtual team leader, such as obtaining resources for the team, removing obstacles to the team's success, making sure others are aware of team accomplishments, and finding high-level sponsorship for the team. It will also strengthen your team and company as a whole. When you constantly build each member's leadership tool kit, the leadership pipeline will be full of individuals who can then move to more formal leadership roles in other virtual teams.

Best Practices for Leading Virtual Teams as a Whole

A common complaint we hear when working with members of virtual teams is that they miss out on the sense of connection that comes from working on a "real" team. As a result, you have to work even harder to ensure that these far-flung members see themselves as an actual team with common goals. Leading virtual teams as a collective entity (a team as a whole) is made especially complex by the crossing of borders and boundaries that are less prevalent in other team types. To provide some hands-on tools that you can use right away, we discuss issues related to the team as a whole using four main categories: (1) team design, team building, and team process; (2) task and company structures; (3) communication; and (4) virtuality, or the degree to which a team is really virtual.

Team Design, Team Building, and Team Process
Perhaps the most important step you can take is to focus adequate attention on *team design*. We have mentioned before that there is evidence suggesting that team design is sometimes even more critical than team coaching for maximizing team success, though both are key factors.[23] As discussed in Chapter 4, one of the most crucial ingredients for good team design is setting clear goals and expectations for a team as a whole. To help accomplish this, you should ensure that your team has a clear, engaging direction; the proper authority to manage its work; and clear performance goals for the collective team.

Although team design is difficult enough in any virtual team, it is particularly challenging in *global* virtual teams. For example, establishing a clear, engaging direction would be especially problematic when members come from different cultures and are located in various countries because there are added difficulties associated with getting all members on the same page. In addition, many global virtual teams might be focused on knowledge sharing and idea-focused tasks with longer time horizons for which a clear direction is difficult to set. For example, a virtual team tasked with coming up with a new set of best practices for customer service might have members who differ in terms of what exactly customers expect in various locations. That is, there might not be a clear-cut outcome that the team is pursuing. If the goal is discovery, as in the case of this team, rather than just completing tasks, it may be more difficult for you to motivate member engagement. We therefore encourage you to ask team members to reinforce and communicate direction, which can be facilitated in part by holding regular briefings. If a global virtual team is cross-functional, you likewise might find it more difficult to promote interdependence, particularly early in a team's life. Many members may also bring varying levels of power distance to their team, so granting the proper authority to manage work may be highly problematic because members will desire different levels of autonomy, direction, and control. Similarly, setting overall team performance goals will be important to motivate members with different cultural backgrounds to work toward common team goals.

One recommendation for motivating participation in virtual teams is to provide some level of team rewards so that there is "something in it for the team to succeed."[24] As discussed in Chapter 4, some companies offer team bonuses or other types of valued rewards to motivate beyond individual incentives. The small amount of evidence that has been accumulated on using rewards in virtual teams suggests that members will be more motivated and perform better to the extent that they receive team-based incentives[25] or a mixture of team- and individual-based rewards.[26] If monetary resources are tight, as they often are, you will likely need to get creative with regard to this form of motivation, particularly since a team dinner, celebration, or other face-to-face reward is not often feasible. Companywide recognition—including acknowledgments of the contributions of a team and its members to all company stakeholders in e-mails or web-based newsletters—may be a particularly economical way to incentivize team performance. And, of course, you also need to ensure that your teams have enough resources like information, availability of training, and basic materials to accomplish tasks.

Another key leadership action necessary for success is *team building*. For virtual teams, this represents a major challenge. Unfortunately, online tools that virtual teams can use to team-build (online video gaming anyone?) remain elusive, meaning face-to-face team building is still your best bet. Given the cost of travel and difficulty in coordinating international travel, however, this can be especially difficult for global virtual teams. We encourage you to be opportunistic about company-wide or industry conferences where it might be possible to gather as a team and, more generally, to look for creative ways (in person or otherwise) to bring your team together that help them get to know one another, build trust, and gain a shared understanding of how the team will complete its work. Be especially mindful early on to ensure everyone has a chance to learn about and discuss the style, context, goals, responsibilities, and challenges of the other members. To start this discussion, you can rely on a variety of personality and cultural value instruments to illustrate the team's diversity and prepare your team for potential trouble spots down the road. The tool we discussed in the previous chapter, GlobeSmart, is one such possibility.

Finally, you should focus on *developing and maintaining effective virtual team processes and states.* As discussed in Chapter 4, team processes include things like problem solving, decision making, conflict management, goal setting, planning, and communication. Team states include shared perceptions of team empowerment, trust, and psychological safety.

Several years ago, Yahoo's CEO made an announcement regarding the policy on working remotely and virtually stating: "To become the absolute best place to work, communication and collaboration will be important, so we need to be working side-by-side. . . . That is why it is critical that we are all present in our offices."[27] An announcement banning telecommuting and virtual work from a well-known high-tech company in Silicon Valley was startling because it went completely against the increasing trends toward virtual work over the past few decades and ignored its many presumed benefits.[28] Although various reasons for the policy have been debated, the stated rationale for invoking the change was that "people are more innovative when they're together."[29]

Despite this surprising proclamation in a high-tech world where agility and the ability to pivot are paramount, at least some evidence supports the admonition that physical separation, or geographic dispersion, can harm team innovation.[30] In light of this fact, leaders of virtual teams should try to get team members in face-to-face meetings as much as possible, particularly when engaging in idea creation or other innovative team behaviors. Again, we realize that this recommendation is often not feasible due to the high cost of travel, team member schedules, conflicting roles, or other barriers.

Fortunately, there is evidence that creating effective team states can mitigate the harmful effects of geographic dispersion on innovation and learning in virtual teams.

For example, when leaders create a climate of psychological safety in their virtual teams, the negative effects of geographic dispersion on innovation are negligible. The same positive effects of psychological safety exist for other innovation-hindering aspects of virtual teams, such as the extent to which teams use electronic communication tools (e-mail, chat), nationality diversity, and frequent membership changes.[31] In our work with global virtual communities of practice in a Fortune 100 aluminum company,[32] we also found that increasing psychological safety offset some of the process losses associated with virtual communities that are more nationally diverse.[33] The steps that we discussed in Chapter 4 that leaders can take to increase psychological safety in their teams can be used in virtual teams too.

In addition to psychological safety, in our work with the online travel reservation company, we found that highly virtual teams whose members communicated using mostly e-mail and chat were better at learning-oriented tasks when they also had high levels of team empowerment.[34] Another study also found that empowering leadership can improve team member virtual collaboration and performance, especially when members are spread out across the world.[35] In Chapter 4, we discussed the various ways in which leaders can work to increase team empowerment by using empowering leader behaviors; however, there may be important differences in increasing team empowerment for more global virtual teams compared to those that are more face-to-face.

For example, you will have to spend considerable time coaching individual team members apart from team meetings and other team interactions. In particular, geographically dispersed team members need to feel completely informed about critical company issues and events as well as be able to see how their work contributes to organizational success. Your coaching can be especially helpful in building a strong line of sight for members. Without this line of sight, all of your other efforts to encourage problem solving and set team goals will likely be wasted. As also mentioned in Chapter 4, you can try to alter social structures to help ensure better communication and coordination across teams, though in many virtual teams interactions are bound by technological means. Nevertheless, you can increase the likelihood of success by verifying that all members have adequate technology support and training on which technology is best for any particular task.[36] In sum, empowering a virtual team requires some decidedly different steps than a face-to-face team does, though the underlying goals are the same.

You should also not forget about the importance of building trust in virtual teams. Trust, as it turns out, is sometimes referred to as the "glue" of the global work space.[37] Although building trust is difficult in any team, the geographic dispersion in global virtual teams magnifies and intensifies issues of trust (and mistrust).[38] As evidence of this, recall our discussion of how trust positively increased the impact of team training on customer service in global virtual teams at a major travel reservation company.[39] In Chapter 4, we suggested that team trust can be built through either relationship-based means, such as spending time together and sharing meals, or task-based ones, such as consistently following through on requests and quickly answering e-mails. Because virtual team members will not have as many opportunities to build relationship-based trust, trust in these teams will likely take the form of task-based trust. Thus, you should reinforce timeliness and consistency of team interaction, ensure that members rapidly respond to one another when using email, chat, and other electronic communication, and encourage members to exhibit high levels of performance and share their expertise to gain legitimacy.[40] Your role in establishing and reinforcing norms regarding communication patterns is key in accomplishing these goals.

Interestingly, virtual teams may appear to have very high levels of trust early on, a phenomenon known as "swift trust," which can create a deceptively positive perception for leaders. Rest assured, however, that if it seems too good to be true, it likely is. It is thought that swift trust forms because initially there is a tendency for team members to assume they are in alignment with one another and will pursue similar goals in their company, but this type of trust is incredibly fragile.[41] One violation, even over some innocuous mistake, can destroy whatever semblance of trust the team displayed and throw you as a leader into a near impossible situation for promoting collaboration and teamwork. Because of this, we encourage you to invest in trust-building efforts early and often regardless of whether your team members appear to be enjoying high levels of swift trust on their own. In doing so, you might be able to enjoy the benefits of swift trust while simultaneously building stronger and more resilient forms of deep trust that will persist throughout your team's life cycle.

Task and Company Structures

Many virtual teams are parallel in nature—that is, they exist outside any formal structure of a single organization and are only one part of a team member's formal role responsibilities. This feature can make fully engaging members in team activities a major challenge for virtual team leaders. To encourage participation, you should look for opportunities to use task and company structures to your advantage. For example, members are often torn between responsibilities of their formal functional role and their assignment on a virtual team. And when push comes to shove, these members will typically put their formal role responsibilities ahead of those of the virtual team because, after all, they are accountable first and foremost to their formal leaders. A structural solution could be to assign each team member's formal leader as a high-level sponsor of the virtual team so that functional leaders can be more aware of what the member is doing for the virtual team.

To avoid burnout (of both the team leader and team members), predictable leadership tasks like agenda creation, meeting facilitation, knowledge management activities, overseeing electronic discussions, schedule tracking, and external presentations should be rotated among members. To create awareness of each team member's areas of expertise (again what we have been referring to as transactive memory[42]), members can pair up with one another to work on short-term projects and then rotate these pairings at different times so that each member gets to work with other members. Having a highly developed team transactive memory is important for any team, but it is critical for effective virtual team performance because members do not have the benefit of constant face-to-face reinforcement.

Communication

Virtual teams are often charged with generating novel ideas and breakthrough innovations, which makes effective communication clearly critical. Unfortunately, these teams also rely heavily on electronic communication tools, which are not always the most conducive for surfacing ideas and encouraging numerous back-and-forth iterations that cultivate creativity and innovation. You can improve the richness of these communications, however, by creating shared understandings and higher levels of trust. One specific way to accomplish these goals is to establish clear communication norms and protocols, which can aid by addressing a number of questions: How will members work together in (and outside of) meetings? Who is responsible for capturing and sharing knowledge, when will this knowledge be gathered, and by whom and how fast? How will decisions be made, and by whom? What are the behavioral norms in the team? In addition, leaders also have to negotiate roles in the team. All of this can often be decided on very early in the team's life cycle by way of a team charter, and the more that can be captured and communicated early on, the greater the chances for team success are later.[43]

We have already discussed the issue of using communication technology appropriately in virtual teams. However, there is no generally accepted set of principles for which technologies to use for which purposes, and even if there were, the rules would most likely change quite frequently.[44] One common rule of thumb that communication experts often use is that for highly controversial, emotional, or complex messages, richer communication media (e.g., face-to-face, videoconferencing) are typically better than leaner media (e.g., e-mail, chat). For routine information, the reverse is true.

Interestingly, in a study of dozens of virtual teams across many industries, researchers found that the most successful virtual teams *banned the use of e-mail* for team communication; members used it only for one-to-one member communication.[45] Other tools such as electronic discussion threads were much more efficient for communication between team members. Indeed, the French global information technology firm Atos also minimized the use of e-mail throughout its worldwide locations, relying almost completely on internal (not public, of course) social media tools for communication.[46]

In our work with the aluminum company, we found that highly nationally diverse virtual teams performed significantly better the more the team's members used richer communication media, underscoring a link between the diversity of a team and a team's need for face-to-face and videoconferencing communication.[47] We again strongly recommend that you encourage your virtual teams to meet face-to-face and use richer media, particularly when they are diverse and expected to engage in innovative processes.

When virtual teams meet using video- or audioconferencing, or some combination of these, there are several steps that leaders can take to enable effective meetings. For example, prior to an actual meeting, leaders should make sure agenda items are assigned, conflicts are identified before the meeting takes place, and time lines are known. At the beginning of each meeting, leaders should take five or ten minutes to recapture a sense of "teaminess" by discussing celebratory personal events or having members update one another on significant accomplishments. During meetings, leaders need to ensure that all members feel included, possibly by using innovative techniques such as electronic voting tools, and take steps to increase psychological safety during meetings (again, see Chapter 4). At the end of each meeting, leaders should allocate action items clearly and make sure that meeting minutes are quickly posted in knowledge repositories. Between meetings, leaders should initiate and facilitate electronic discussion threads, track progress, and follow up with one-on-one discussions with team members.

Virtuality

As we alluded to earlier and in line with Yahoo's surprising move to limit virtual work, physical proximity and face-to-face interactions can play an important role in driving innovation. In fact, a University of Michigan study found that scientists who worked in the same building were 33 percent more likely to form new collaborations than scientists who were located in different buildings. And scientists who were located on the same floor of a building were 57 percent more likely to form new collaborations than those located in different buildings.[48] These percentages may jump even higher in the newer architectural styles being used in headquarters for companies like Google, Apple, and Facebook that create environments that maximize face-to-face contact.

Obviously, virtual team members miss out on many of the benefits that are associated with working alongside other team members in more traditional offices, including serendipitous watercooler chats that can spark unanticipated idea generation and breakthrough thinking.[49] There are several things you can do to hedge against the disadvantages of very high levels of virtuality. First, as we have discussed already in this chapter, you should try to find opportunities to give your team even cursory face-to-face exposure with one another and place extra emphasis on building trust.[50]

Second, you should try to ensure your communication methods allow for as much nuance and natural interaction as possible. For example, you could use a highly rich communication tool such as Cisco System's Telepresence rooms to simulate face-to-face communication through high-definition video and realistic audio tracking. If done correctly, each room, no matter where it is in the world, will have the same tables, chairs, and paint color to simulate being in the "same room." Those encountering this tool for the first time are often surprised by how realistic these meetings can be. Although some team members will shy away from having to go to a certain room at a certain time for a virtual team meeting, there is still much to be gained from using communication tools of high fidelity and richness. We encourage you to force the issue with reluctant team members if this is a viable option for your team.

Electronic discussion threads and social media applications that hide behind company firewalls (Microsoft's Yammer is an example) or cloud computing team-based applications like Slack can also help streamline idea exchange for global virtual teams. Indeed, these have proven much more efficient for effective virtual team communication than other common tools such as e-mail.[51] Although particular tools will come and go as they always do, discussion threads and secure social media can be used to exchange valuable ideas as part of an overall global virtual team suite of tools

In short, geographically dispersed team members often miss out on the opportunistic chance meetings that their face-to-face counterparts have, but you can take certain steps to recapture some of these benefits when working virtually.

Best Practices for Leading the Subteams in a Virtual Team

Chapter 5 addressed the challenges associated with leading subteams. For a global virtual team, focusing on subteams is especially important because they can emerge, sometimes unhealthily, on faultlines relating to geographic locations and national origin.[52]

Our work with the global aluminum company demonstrated this phenomenon firsthand.[53] Of the many global virtual communities of practice we examined, some were composed of members from the same country but working in different locations in that country (the teams were still considered virtual because members rarely, if ever, met in person). For example, one of these teams was located north of Perth, Australia, with members working virtually across the different offices. Other teams were composed of two major subteams, each working in one of two different countries. Members within each country were located in the same place and worked on the same subteam, but they also had to work virtually across the subteams. For example, one of the teams had five members working in Australia in the same or a nearby office and six members working in Brazil in the same or a nearby office. Still other teams were composed of members from many different countries working in various locations. For example, one team had one member each working in Australia, Brazil, China, Jamaica, Mexico, New Zealand, Spain, Great Britain, and the United States.

If all you had to go on was country of origin and location, which of these three example teams would you guess had the lowest performance? Probably not the team of all Australians, as they have likely met face-to-face before and share a common cultural background, which thereby reduces the chances for miscommunication and misunderstanding. The third team could be a reasonable choice: it has nine team members of nine different nationalities working in nine different locations with almost no chance for any face-to-face interaction. Most communication occurs through e-mail with occasional video- and audioconferencing. Given the cultural diversity on this team and the often lean communication media used, there is obviously a lot of room for miscommunication and misunderstanding.

But, perhaps surprisingly (or maybe not given what we said about faultlines in Chapter 7), the team that might have the most difficulty performing well is the one composed of half Australians and half Brazilians. The reason is that the team will likely fracture along both nationality and location, resulting in a lot of communication *within* each subteam but very little communication *between* subteams. Members will likely express frustration about working with "those guys over there" to their same-country team members. Similarly, there will be a strong sense of loyalty and obligation within their subteams but very little across. Figure 8.1 graphically depicts the three example teams.

Our work with this company showed that same-country and highly nationally diverse teams performed at about the same level. The same-country teams enjoyed the advantage of being on the same page almost from the onset and were able to detect and react to a lot of unspoken cues like facial expressions and hand gestures. The highly diverse teams had to encounter some challenges early on, but ultimately they benefited from having more unique perspectives (an advantage, given that the key task was to come up with innovative solutions). Rather than combining the best of both worlds, however, the teams with two location-based subteams rarely performed in a healthy way. They could not (or would not) create a unified team identity needed for optimal team functioning.[54]

Other evidence reinforces our findings and supports the idea that these results were not unique to the particular company with which we worked. For example, studies have shown that the more members work across geographic boundaries, the more they experience conflict and exhibit lower levels of trust.[55] Another showed that strong subteam boundaries have a tendency

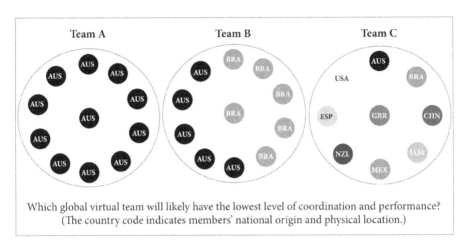

Which global virtual team will likely have the lowest level of coordination and performance?
(The country code indicates members' national origin and physical location.)

FIGURE 8.1. A Tale of Three Global Virtual Teams

Note: AUS = Australia; BRA = Brazil; CHN = China; ESP = Spain; GBR = Great Britain;
JAM = Jamaica; MEX = Mexico; NZL = New Zealand; USA = United States

to weaken overall team identification and coordination and create unhealthy
conflict.[56]

So with all of this potential for team fracturing along nationality and location faultlines, what is a virtual team leader to do? Many of the lessons from
Chapter 5 still hold, but there are a few points where necessary tweaks for this
context need to be considered. For example, we discussed in Chapter 5 how to
manage the three types of interdependencies in multisubteam systems: *within*
each subteam, *between* subteams, and *across* subteams (i.e., between the overall team and its external environment). And we also said that managing the
between-subteam interdependencies is the most challenging task for leaders.
Unfortunately, this gets even more difficult in a virtual team. The main reason
for this is that there is likely to be a natural degree of interdependence within
subteams already, particularly if they are of the same nationality and in the
same location. In contrast, due again to the high risk of virtual team fracturing along nationality or location faultlines, you will have to put much more
emphasis on leading and managing interdependence between subteams.

Previously we discussed managing the interdependence within and
between subteams as a delicate balancing act. Here, we depart from that
advice to simply say that you should always err on the side of building and
maintaining interdependence between subteams because this is most likely to
be the place where overall team functioning breaks down in virtual teams. In

terms of the behaviors needed to ensure that subteams are coordinating and integrating with one another, we again refer to the strategizing and coordinating behaviors outlined in Chapter 5.

We also previously discussed the likelihood of teams fracturing along subteam lines even if the members are not of the same nationality or located in the same place. In this discussion, we provided four steps that leaders can take to help their teams make the best use of subteams for later success. Some of these are more or less applicable in a virtual team environment. The first step—assigning subteams a specific purpose so that they work for the good of the whole team and not for their subteam's own best interests—can apply to virtual teams as well.

The second step was to rotate team members to different subteams when feasible. This might not be as easily accomplished if the team members are spread out geographically due to the costs of moving members across countries. And one of the biggest advantages of a global virtual team is to tap the expertise of people no matter where they are in the world.

The third piece of advice was to increase the number of subteams within an overall team. This is excellent advice for virtual teams. Indeed, you should do all you can to avoid the trap of having half of the team's members co-located in one country and half in another. To foster breakthrough thinking and idea generation, you should use subteams in virtual teams with members from, and located in, several different countries. The prior example with nine different members located in nine different countries suggests that unhealthy subteams are not as likely to form on the basis of nationality and/or location.

The final step—and the one we have found to be most critical for virtual team performance—is to ensure that team members, regardless of their subteam membership, have an overall sense of collective team identification. Recall the best practices for how you can create that sense of collective team identification: by creating the right mix of task and goal interdependence, showing support for and recognizing the overall team, allowing teams to develop a shared history, and increasing contact among members.[57] Thus, by tweaking these four steps outlined in Chapter 5, you will be able to more effectively manage your global virtual team's subteams. And by following the advice outlined in the entirety of this chapter, you can pump up the full 3D Team Leadership model and lead your virtual teams to success.

In summary, evidence clearly supports our contention that virtual teams really are a unique type of team. In this chapter, we have described the complexity and common leadership challenges of leading virtual teams. However, we have also demonstrated that when applying the 3D Team Leadership model to virtual teams, some of the messiness described can be made more manageable. Successfully using our approach will require patience, persistence, flexibility, and lots and lots of energy. However, the power of virtual teams is real: when led properly, they can accomplish tasks and objectives that simply cannot be done by more traditional teaming.

9 What It Takes to Be a 3D Team Leader

THROUGHOUT THIS BOOK, WE HAVE PROVIDED PRAC-
tical tips and advice aimed at helping you to focus on all three
dimensions of a team: the individuals on a team, a team as a whole, and the
subteams within an overall team. Due to the complex, dynamic, and frankly
overwhelming nature of many teams today and limitations on your resources
(e.g., time, energy, breadth of knowledge), we have also argued that you need
to shift your focus among leading and motivating these distinct dimensions at
different times. Simply put, you need to develop and demonstrate two important skills to be effective 3D team leaders: recognizing when a particular team
situation calls for which type of focus and displaying the appropriate behaviors and strategies required when leading a particular team dimension.

Perhaps unsurprisingly, our experience has shown that these two skills are
unnatural for a lot of team leaders; indeed, we have worked with many team
leaders who struggled mightily with one, and sometimes both, of these necessary attributes. In this chapter, we identify several key characteristics associated with highly successful 3D team leaders and, in doing so, convey two
critical points. First, for better or worse depending on where you fall, a small
portion of the characteristics associated with successful 3D team leaders are
rooted in relatively stable traits. So for a small number of attributes, some
leaders are just more naturally inclined to be successful 3D team leaders than
others. We view this as a head start toward being a great team leader, though,
and not an assurance.

Second, the good news and the most important takeaway, is that a majority of the attributes characterizing successful 3D team leaders reflect competencies that can be developed over time with hard work, an open mind, and clear direction. In fact, we have seen firsthand dramatic growth and change from those who have embraced and committed themselves to becoming better 3D team leaders. The latter point should not be taken lightly: if 3D Team Leadership were all about leader traits alone, we could just assess all leaders on these traits and pick the ones that scored the highest and make them 3D team leaders, leaving everyone else by the wayside. So regardless of whether you're naturally inclined toward some aspects of 3D Team Leadership or not, you can significantly improve your leadership ability and set yourself up for tremendous professional and personal success.

Before diving into the specific characteristics that enable effective 3D Team Leadership, let's first walk through two exemplar cases that demonstrate the most common mistakes that plague potential 3D team leaders.

A Tale of Two Team Leaders

We'll start with Allison. At the time of this case example, Allison worked at a large, well-known financial institution and ran a team charged with developing new products and services for commercial clients, which was primarily a business-to-business operation. Her team consisted of eight team members with similar but still distinct job responsibilities. Moreover, her team members frequently shifted between different tasks, some of which could be done relatively independently by members, whereas others required substantively more collaboration and cooperation. Up until this point, Allison had been successful in just about every job she had ever held, including those in prior organizations. As a result, management viewed her as a prototypical fast-tracker.

When we applied our 3D Team Leadership lens to Allison's approach, however, we uncovered some blemishes that could hold her back from being her best as a team leader. Our lengthy discussions with her made it clear that she never recognized when her team was shifting from (or needed to shift from) one level of interdependence to another. As a result, she maintained her focus on only one of the key dimensions of her team, the individuals, without considering whether this was the most appropriate focus.

Allison's case became more interesting as we dove deeper into her past professional experience. We uncovered that this was not her first foray as a team leader and, more importantly, that she had been successful leading several different types of teams previously. For instance, at a consumer products organization where she had worked, she and her team were recognized with several company-wide awards for their performance on a highly interdependent task. To us, this indicated that Allison possessed the skills to effectively lead a team as a whole. Right after leaving the consumer products company, and immediately on joining her current organization, Allison was put in charge of a group (notice that we use the term *group* here intentionally) of investment analysts whose job it was to scan investment markets for potential deals that the financial institution could make. Despite the fact that the financial analysts were referred to as a team, the members were working pretty much on their own, with occasional meetings designed to simply share information and update one another. Allison's boss in this assignment glowed about her performance, even noting that he fought to keep her in his part of the company when other divisions came calling. Thus, it was evident to us that Allison also had the chops for leading individuals within a group.

Returning to the current case, in Allison's role leading a team of eight people charged with developing new products and services for commercial clients, many of her skills went dormant. Based on our discussions, we believe she appropriately identified the interdependence level in the first stage of her team's life cycle, a simple information-gathering assignment, and focused her attention on leading the individuals in her team. However, she remained fixated on this dimension even as her team's demands changed. One member commented, for instance,

> Allison is a great mentor and coach, but I think she does this mainly one-on-one. In fact, I have learned a lot about this business from her. She has an incredible track record that I'd like to emulate, which is why I wanted to work for her. But if there's one thing missing, it's that I don't really feel part of a true team. We have no team goals, no team coaching, and we're all compensated pretty much individually. We seem to work as a team sometimes in spite of all of this! It's not the end of the world, but I think we could do better as a team sometimes if she focused more on teamwork.

Our conclusion is that Allison's problems had nothing to do with her ability to lead a group, a team, or something in between (i.e., subteams within an overall team). After all, her prior experiences clearly suggest otherwise. Rather, her shortfall was *not being able to recognize when her team needed what type of leadership behavior.* When our MBA students, executive education participants, and consulting clients display similar tendencies, we strive to help them develop the skills for diagnosing different team situations more effectively and accurately. Once they master this skill, their already impressive leadership repertoire becomes tremendously more versatile and valuable.

Another leader we've worked with, Jack, stands in stark contrast to Allison. When we met Jack, he was employed at a high-tech company that we've been associated with for over fifteen years and was leading a team of software engineers charged with creating unique, sophisticated software for business clients. Given the complexity of each project, Jack's team used a version of the Agile project life cycle approach. As we noted in Chapter 6, this approach required him to go through a series of iterative stages, many requiring a different level of team interdependence; sometimes the members worked very independently (like a group), other times very interdependently (like a team), and still other times with multilayered interdependence structures that required them to break apart into functionally based subteams that each carried out a specific aspect of the overall task.

Unlike Allison, Jack was quite gifted in diagnosing which stage his team was in and the level of interdependence at each stage. In fact, he even made constructive suggestions for how his team might arrange its work when members appeared confused for how to tackle a particular problem. So from an intellectual standpoint, Jack should've had a firm grasp on when each dimension deserved the most attention. However, he was clearly most comfortable in his role as a leader of teams and refused to deviate from this approach. In our interviews with Jack, he expressed confusion about why he should ever focus at all on individuals in his team or subteams. Regarding this topic, he said:

> In this company and in the software industry in general, we cannot write code and sell software without teams. The work is just too complex to be done individually. So I learned early on that if I was going to be successful in working my way up in this industry, I needed to focus on leading teams. And that's just what I do. I make sure we have team goals and that there are severe consequences for those who are not team players. I know its cliché, but I often say to my team members that "there's no 'I' in team" [*imagine our groans when we heard Jack say this*], and I really believe that. I use a version of the Agile project life cycle a lot, and I know that my team members work differently from time to time. For example, sometimes we coordinate a lot between members

when doing our work and sometimes members split off into smaller teams to get some part of the project done. I guess I could do some things differently, but at the end of the day, it's still all about the team. Leading individuals on a team just doesn't make all that much sense to me; I don't want to set a bad precedent that screws us up later. I'd rather invest in coaching, counseling, and trying to motivate my whole team to succeed. I think that works really well.

As is obvious from these statements, Jack's problem is his unwillingness to shift his leadership behavior from a focus on his overall team to a focus on his team's individuals or subteams as it goes through the Agile life cycle. To be fair to Jack, many of the leaders we work with have a natural pull toward one of the dimensions. Clearly, his particular security blanket was his team as a whole. This alone isn't an issue, but it can become a big problem when a leader refuses even to recognize that sometimes individuals and subteams are critical to team success. For instance, even in iterative approaches like Agile, a few underperforming episodes in low and multilayered interdependence phases (likely Jack's weak spots) can wreak long-term havoc on the team's eventual outputs.

Moreover, it is unreasonable to assume that all team members are rewarded and motivated in a way that team interests will usurp their own; individuals work on too many teams, have too many roles at home and at work, and are given feedback on so many criteria that 100 percent we-over-me styles simply don't work in many cases. Taken together, unnecessarily constraining your leadership focus on one dimension can severely limit your potential to be an effective team leader. When we encounter leaders who share Jack's views (and there are many of them), we first try to convince them to question their assumptions about using only one focus. Whereas Jack assumed that focusing on anything but the team would compromise his future efforts, we posited a near-opposite argument: failing to recognize the other dimensions at all severely limited his team's upward potential. Leaders like Jack stand to benefit a great deal from expanding their tool kits using the material presented in Chapters 3 to 6.

Allison's and Jack's experiences represent two of the most common and fundamental stumbling blocks to 3D Team Leadership success. Interestingly, they might have even been able to get away with these deficiencies for a long time in their careers. After all, both have great track records of success and are generally well liked in their companies. In cases like these, the costs associated with not developing as a 3D team leader can be masked by modest promotions and steady raises for several years. Missed opportunities, like being passed up for high-profile committees or senior- and executive-level positions, remain largely unknown until it becomes painfully obvious that an employee has hit a ceiling. We ended up working with both Allison and Jack in one of our executive education workshops to help them understand and apply the tenets of 3D Team Leadership. Both have reported positive results and remain on track for immense success in their careers.

We next describe a set of general competencies that can help you apply 3D Team Leadership.

What Does the Evidence Say about the Characteristics of Successful Leaders In General?

In our jobs, we constantly see lists of purportedly new leadership competencies emerge from popular list-based websites (e.g., BuzzFeed); the vast cottage industry of leadership publications, which produces literally thousands of books and e-books per year; and the organizations in which we work. From those organizations, we have found that nearly every company has its own competency model that managers use in their leadership training and development efforts. Yet although the names may change from company to company, in our experience we estimate that there is about 85 to 90 percent overlap in the actual competencies in each model.

To start the conversation, let's take a look at a classic list of evidence-based leadership competencies:[1]

- Drive—the motivation to persevere even in the face of obstacles
- Honesty and integrity—the ethical component of leadership, which includes fairness
- Leadership motivation—the desire to take on more and more leadership responsibilities
- Self-confidence—the inherent belief in one's capability to do things well
- Cognitive ability—the extent to which leaders are intelligent and have business savvy
- Knowledge of the business—the understanding of how one's industry functions and the role of the organization in it

- Creativity—the ability to generate novel and useful ideas
- Flexibility—the capability to see things from different perspectives and to change approaches and behavior to fit any situation

If you have been around leadership training programs, we have little doubt that you have seen a somewhat similar list. On the one hand, the similarity across lists is good news. Successful leadership competencies should be transferable from industry to industry and company to company. Although leaders may need to acquire some specific technical skills depending on their industry and company, they can lean on a common body of competencies when motivating and directing a team. On the other hand, the high degree of overlap can make competency models feel rather stale and staid. When we present various models in our workshops and classes, we often hear things like, "Oh, I've seen these all before" and "This is just old wine in new bottles."

Our objective throughout this book has never been to introduce a whole new set of competencies. Rather, our goal is to distill what the evidence accumulated over several decades indicates are the most relevant competencies for 3D team leaders. In other words, we want to answer the question, *What are the key essentials every 3D team leader must have to be optimally successful?*

Our research and experience point to several promising starting points. We'll begin with leader traits. Traits, in contrast to knowledge- and skill-based characteristics, are considered relatively stable. For this reason, they are often considered more useful for selection purposes than training and development. Nevertheless, even traits that have traditionally been viewed as quite stable, like personality, can change modestly over time; moreover, dedicated employees can make meaningful behavioral adjustments once they have an understanding of their tendencies (i.e., an extrovert learning to listen quietly to member feedback like Melanie in Chapter 7).[2]

The first area is personality traits; recall our discussion of the Big Five personality traits in Chapter 7.[3] Perhaps not surprisingly, extraversion—the extent to which a leader is comfortable with relationships with others and how gregarious, assertive, and sociable she or he is—explains both leader emergence (whether a person rises to leadership roles) and leader effectiveness (whether the person is successful in those roles). Similarly, conscientiousness, or the extent to which a leader is responsible, organized, dependable, and persistent and a well-known predictor of general job performance, can also explain leadership outcomes, though this relationship is more nuanced.

Namely, conscientiousness is a stronger predictor of leadership emergence compared to effectiveness, suggesting that conscientiousness may serve as a "ticket to the dance" (being conscientious is a requisite for being identified and selected as a leader), but alone may not be enough.

Furthermore, one study reported that conscientiousness was more strongly associated with leader effectiveness in nonbusiness contexts (i.e., military and student samples), which may imply it loses some of its isolated value as roles and routines become blurrier. Several scholars have also suggested highly conscientious leaders can sometimes become rigid and inflexible and have an overly perfectionist mind-set that leaves their employees feeling dissatisfied and voiceless.[4] Obviously, these are not ideal characteristics when working in today's VUCA environments. Openness to experience, again the tendency to be unconventional and imaginative and was something we indicated was critical for using the 3D Team Leadership model cross-culturally in Chapter 7, also helps determine whether leaders emerge and how effective they are. We suspect openness may be a particularly helpful trait for navigating complex teaming environments, a point to which we return later in this chapter.

As we noted previously, personality traits are hardly iron cages that enable or limit our ability to thrive in certain settings. Rather they actually just represent general motivational tendencies that tend to manifest in certain types of behaviors when unchecked;[5] you can, without question, successfully develop the behaviors and skills associated with each trait. In fact, evidence supports that individuals' personality traits change as they mature and begin to learn what behaviors increase their chances for success.[6] So, taken together, even if you do not naturally have an inclination toward extraversion, conscientiousness, and openness, you can still find success as a 3D team leader.

The second trait set that is often discussed in association with leadership effectiveness is intelligence. In short, leader intelligence matters too, but not as much as you might think. Some estimates suggest that intelligence explains only 4 to 6 percent of leadership effectiveness, depending on how you measure intelligence and leadership success.[7] Perhaps this explains why, anecdotally at least, some would describe the success of certain leaders as being in the right place at the right time or "dumb luck." Perhaps a modest level of intelligence is a prerequisite for effective leadership, but after that, other factors take over.

Finally, over a century ago, leadership researchers argued that the most successful leaders were born, not made, and that physical traits, such as being male and tall, were solid indicators of future leadership effectiveness. This theory has been used to explain in part why George Washington, quite tall for his time, was so revered.[8] Although leader gender has its own separate field of study, concluding that neither men nor women make better leaders (but at least some evidence shows that there are some systematic differences in styles),[9] one comprehensive study did show that physical height for both men and women explained about 6 percent of the variance in leadership emergence. Interestingly, height also predicted income over a person's career. For example, an individual who is 72 inches tall would earn almost $177,000 more over a thirty-year career than an individual who is 65 inches tall.[10] The study authors concluded there is actually nothing about a person's height that makes him or her a better leader, but tall people may be perceived as different by themselves and others and then ascribed certain leader success factors.

Specifically, the effect of physical attributes on leadership can be explained using several theories, including implicit leadership theory and sociobiological theory. Implicit leadership theory suggests that individuals (followers and people who select leaders, in this case) hold a vision of a prototypical leader in their minds and then respond better to actual leaders who more closely resemble this vision.[11] Interestingly, ideals of what a leader looks like can change over time, sometimes in a slow, natural progression or more suddenly because of a breakout leader that doesn't fit the mold (Margaret Thatcher, for example). Related, sociobiological views argue that traits reflecting human evolutionary advantages, such as survival, mating options, and hunting prowess, can be translated as markers of power.[12] Of course, the evidence and everyone's experience demonstrate that great leaders come in all genders, shapes, sizes, colors, and whatever other descriptive term you can think of.

Our ultimate conclusion is that although some relatively stable traits have been linked to important leadership outcomes, these relationships are not overwhelmingly large. Thus, you should be neither overjoyed nor disheartened based on your personality ratings, intelligence scores, or physical attributes. Many leadership competencies can be learned, and potentially perfected, with hard work and dedication. We turn to these next.

What Are the Specific Attributes
of Successful 3D Team Leaders?

Flexibility/Adaptability

Drawing from the list of general successful leader competencies we presented earlier in the chapter, leader flexibility/adaptability ranks near the top of our list of the most important 3D team leader competencies. Despite the widespread belief and anecdotal evidence from practitioners that flexible leaders are generally more successful in today's VUCA business environments, surprisingly little actual evidence demonstrates the important role that flexibility plays in leadership success.[13] However, given our basic premise that leaders should shift their focus among the three team dimensions depending on the level of team interdependence required at any given point in time, it makes perfect sense that flexibility should be associated with great 3D team leader success.

In the study of firefighter teams we introduced in Chapter 6, we tested this assumption. We first sought to confirm that leader flexibility was a general leader competency in the firefighter sample regardless of 3D Team Leadership principles. As expected, we found that teams that had more flexible leaders also had more effective task-related and people-related team processes, better team performance, and members who helped one another more. Next, we moved to more precise tests of the impact of leader flexibility on specific 3D Team Leadership principles. Supporting our expectations, flexible leaders were the most likely to embrace each of the three dimensions of leader focus: individuals, teams, and subteams. Moreover, the impact of flexibility on team performance was contingent on interdependence, such that more flexible leaders were even more effective in highly interdependent teams.[14]

Given its importance, we recommend that you conduct a frank assessment of your leadership flexibility. Questions to ask yourself when undergoing this assessment include: Do I explore a wide variety of approaches to my team's problems? Do I plan ahead rather than react to situations? Do I adapt well to changes in my leadership role? Do I cope with stressful events effectively? Do I maintain effective leadership in challenging circumstances?[15]

Importantly, evidence suggests that you can get the most useful information from an assessment when you compare your own self-ratings with ratings from others, such as team members, managers, and peers.[16] You might be surprised by what you find. Differences between self-and other's assessments can reveal important blind spots and help you direct your efforts toward healthier and more rapid development. In our firefighter study, for instance, many leaders viewed themselves as highly flexible, whereas their team members felt they were very inflexible. In fact, we did not find any relationship between the two viewpoints! Divergent views can emerge for many different reasons, but one recurring theme was that leaders viewed flexibility as a state of mind (meaning they rarely acted on their perceived flexibility), whereas team members cared more about observable actions. Not surprisingly, the strongest relationships between flexibility and team outcomes were based on team member ratings of flexibility.

So, is flexibility something you're born with or something you can develop over time? The answer is, as it usually is with these things, both. Yes, we do have some evidence suggesting that some leaders are born more innately flexible than others. However, evidence on the related concept of *cognitive agility*[17] suggests that flexibility-like concepts are not entirely trait based; rather, they may originally emerge from stable traits but then evolve or develop through learning and experience. In line with this premise, results from our firefighter study revealed a positive relationship between the personality trait of openness to experience and leaders' self-ratings of flexibility.

There are numerous practical guidelines for increasing your own leadership flexibility. Some of the more evidence-based approaches are (1) learning about and expanding your behavioral repertoire through multirater feedback gathering, behavioral modeling, role playing, and executive coaching; (2) developing the skills that are relevant for increased flexibility, such as emotional intelligence, situational awareness, and self-awareness; (3) enrolling in seminars and executive education courses that specifically examine leader flexibility; and (4) consistently working on balancing the behaviors that are targeted to different entities—individuals, teams, and subteams—with special attention devoted toward the actions that might be positive for one entity but have unintended negative consequences for others.[18]

In terms of other ways to develop flexibility, we have firsthand experience with a commercially available tool from ExperiencePoint, a company based in Toronto, Canada. In conjunction with the Palo Alto consulting firm IDEO, ExperiencePoint provides ExperienceInnovation, a simulation that puts teams of leaders together and has them work on skills related to design thinking. When done correctly, the simulation can increase both cognitive and behavioral flexibility. In addition, many such workshops and exercises are available to increase flexibility and adaptability (including many executive education programs). However, the effectiveness of any program depends on your willingness to embrace your newly learned skills.

A leadership attribute closely related to flexibility is self-monitoring, which refers to the extent a person monitors and regulates his or her expressive behaviors and public appearances.[19] Those who are higher in self-monitoring are very attuned to situational cues and are willing to alter their behavior to match a certain situation or role. Think of a team leader who is naturally introverted but senses in a team meeting that his or her team needs an encouraging pep talk. He or she is willing to go against his or her natural introverted tendency to deliver a rousing motivational address to the team. By contrast, those lower in self-monitoring are much less responsive to different social contexts and will stick more closely to behaviors aligned with their inner attitudes, beliefs, and traits, even if the situation clearly calls for an alternative approach.[20] In this sense, high self-monitors are chameleon-like in the way they approach different leadership situations,[21] which can be advantageous so long as they do not compromise their authenticity as leaders[22] (another important leader attribute we discuss below). Indeed, there is at least some evidence that high self-monitors are more likely to emerge as leaders than low self-monitors.[23]

Leader Switching Behavior

Another important competency that successful 3D team leaders must have is something we have coined *leader switching behavior*, which can best be described as a leader's actual behaviors that effectively signal a visible switch in his or her focus from individuals to teams to subteams (and in any order) when the situation calls for it. Note that this attribute is related to but still distinct from flexibility/adaptability. Flexibility reflects a broader concept related to a general capacity to make adjustments as needed, whereas switching behaviors reflect the extent to which this ability is put into practice for leadership. Recall that many leaders' self-assessments of their flexibility were quite different from team members' ratings, presumably because team members never saw the flexibility in action. Switching behaviors address that gap.

In our firefighter study, we confirmed that flexibility and switching behaviors were distinct but positively related concepts. Moreover, we found that when a team leader exhibited more leader switching behaviors, his or her team had more effective team processes, better team performance, and team members who helped one another more. Interestingly, we also found that leader switching behaviors explained a significant part of these outcomes *even when taking into account more established and traditional leadership concepts*, such as transformational leadership, task-focused leadership (i.e., initiating structure), and relationship-focused leadership (i.e., consideration). Thus, we are confident that the positive gains you can expect from developing strong, established leadership behaviors in a general sense can be amplified by switching the target of these behaviors across each of the dimensions described in the 3D Team Leadership model.

To conduct an honest assessment of your actual switching behaviors, ask yourself: Am I able to move effortlessly between managing individuals on my team, my team as a whole, and the subteams within my overall team across different situations? Can I effectively switch my focus among the different team dimensions? Am I effective at motivating the three entities of my team? And am I able to simultaneously balance the needs of individuals, the entire team, and the subteams? Again, we highly recommend a multirater approach to assessing leader switching behavior so you can compare your answers to those of your team members (and perhaps your boss and peers as well).

What should you do if you fall short on the leader switching dimension? Can leader switching behavior, like flexibility, be developed over time so that you become better able to make these on-the-fly adjustments in your behavior? We believe so. In fact, it might be easier to change an actual behavioral competency, like switching behavior, than a more cognitive mind-set like flexibility. Interestingly, when we first started thinking about the notion of leader switching behavior almost ten years ago, we did not see much attention toward such a leadership concept in the academic or practitioner literatures. However, brothers Chip and Dan Heath (of Stanford and Duke University, respectively) wrote an informative book, *Switch: How to Change Things When Change Is Hard*.[24] After reading their book, our reaction was, "Exactly! These principles are at the heart of leader switching behavior!"

In the book, the Heath brothers first ask you to consider whether you are a leader who wants to change your own or other people's behaviors. They then suggest that much personal change is stymied by an inherent conflict between two basic systems in our brain: the rational mind and the emotional mind. Anyone who has ever tried to get in great physical shape after a long period of not hitting the gym knows these two systems and their conflicts very well! They point out that despite the fact that the rational mind might want to change something at work (e.g., learn how to develop your ability to switch your focus between individuals, teams, or subteams), the emotional mind prefers the comfort and safety of maintaining the status quo (e.g., "I'll just keep focusing on individuals [or teams or subteams] because switching makes me uncomfortable"). Thus, the essence of their approach is to resolve this fundamental tension so that change can occur.

Their framework for how to change behavior in any situation has three steps: (1) direct the "rider" (the name the Heath brothers use for the rational side), (2) motivate the "elephant" (the name they use for the emotional side), and (3) shape the path (or make sure the situation enables change to occur). These three steps correspond to the factors that would enable a leader to improve his or her switching behavior. For example, for the rational side, you'll need to have a vision of what an effective 3D team leader looks like, which should include the ability to switch focus when the situation calls for it. Start with the end in mind, then create a list of critical moves that will help you hone your switching behavior skills. For the emotional side, it helps to have a growth mind-set ("abilities are like muscles; they can be built up with practice") rather than a fixed mind-set ("my abilities are static; I will avoid challenges so I won't fail"). This is similar to the learning versus performance orientations we discussed in Chapter 1. If you struggle here, try to make small, incremental changes rather than tackling huge ones all at once. For shaping the path, get support from those around you: your team, your boss, your peers. Let others know you're trying to develop your leadership competencies. Over time, you'll get more well-meaning feedback from those around you and the new skills will become habitual. And if other leaders in your company are also trying to improve their switching behavior, all the better. As the Heath brothers point out, the herd has a strong influence on individuals' motivation and ability to change.

Ambidextrous Leadership
The notion of ambidextrous leadership has gained traction in recent years, especially in terms of its effects on innovation.[25] Originally applied to organizations (how an entire company functions) rather than individuals, ambidexterity has also been viewed as a way to think about versatility in a leader's behavioral repertoire. The idea behind ambidextrous leadership is that no single leadership style or behavior can result in innovation in companies because innovation requires the simultaneous processes of *exploration* (i.e., experimenting, searching for alternatives, and risk taking) and

exploitation (i.e., adhering to rules, aligning processes, and avoiding risk). At certain points during the cycle of innovation, individuals and teams will be required to engage in exploration ("let's figure out a brand-new way to complete a certain process"). At other times in the innovation cycle, those same individuals and teams will be required to engage in exploitation ("let's figure out how this new process can generate maximum value in our company"). Because these two processes have inherent tensions between them, it is suggested that leaders who are ambidextrous—or those who have "the ability to foster explorative and exploitative behaviors in followers by increasing or reducing variance in their behavior and flexibly switching between those behaviors"—will be the ones most likely to lead successful innovation efforts.[26]

Similar to the notion of leaders switching between exploration and exploitation to help individuals and teams during the innovation process, our 3D Team Leadership model argues that leaders need to be open to switching their focus on different behaviors (relationship, task, and change-oriented behaviors) and each of the three dimensions in teams (these are not mutually exclusive from exploration and exploitation, mind you; they are simply another layer). We also agree with the leader ambidexterity researchers who argue that a leader's change in focus need not necessarily follow some sort of phase model or sequence. Indeed, in today's VUCA world, the requirements for leaders to change are likely to be nonlinear and complex. Thus, you need to be able to react quickly to changing circumstances and situations.

Leader ambidexterity requires a wide behavioral repertoire. In our 3D Team Leadership model, how you behave and motivate varies depending on which team dimension is the current focus. You must have the ability to think "integratively,"[27] or survive and thrive when there is tension between opposing foci (e.g., when what individuals need is different from what the teams or subteams need). This is the essence of what makes leader ambidexterity different from flexibility and leader switching behavior. Neither of the prior competencies implies anything about your ability to balance the *inherent tensions* associated with the 3D Team Leadership model.

If you are interested in rating yourself on leader ambidexterity in the context of 3D Team Leadership, you need to ask: Am I able to balance the tensions between leading the different dimensions of my team? Can I reconcile the competing goals between the three entities? Can I remain calm when faced with making tough decisions regarding the trade-offs among individuals, teams, and subteams? Do I effectively recognize the inherent tensions that exist among the dimensions?

If you determine that you fall short on leader ambidexterity, what can you do to strengthen this important leader skill? Much of the development of this attribute would be related to managing tensions and trade-offs among individuals, teams, and subteams. Those who study leader ambidexterity refer to a couple of points of leverage in honing this attribute. First, you have to develop your *behavioral complexity*, which refers to a range of behaviors that you can exhibit, along with the ability to vary the behaviors according to situational requirements (think back to self-monitoring).[28]

Second, you will also need to sharpen your *cognitive complexity*, which refers again to integrative thinking. You will need to hold the interests and needs of your individuals, teams, and subteams simultaneously in your mind and refrain from placing one above the other; instead, you need to be able to integrate the needs into an overall leadership strategy. Both of these important skills can be developed in executive training sessions specifically designed to focus on ambidexterity. Interestingly, identifying tensions between foci is often the product of interpreting subtle emotional cues from your team members. Honing the next competency we discuss, emotional intelligence, can help you get a better sense of when tensions within your team are emerging.

Emotional Intelligence

Emotional intelligence (EQ) is your ability to recognize your own and other people's emotions, discriminate among different feelings and categorize them appropriately, and use this emotional information to support your thinking and behavior. EQ is quite distinct from the other leader attributes such as flexibility, switching, and ambidexterity.[29] Rather than being related to your ability to change your focus, EQ helps you be more perceptive of team needs so that you can more precisely and effectively alter your behaviors and focus. In this sense, EQ acts as a critical diagnostic mechanism that guides how the other competencies (flexibility, switching behavior, and ambidexterity) should be applied.

Psychologist Daniel Goleman's original book on EQ proposed five distinct dimensions:[30]

- *Self-awareness*—recognizing and understanding your moods, emotions, and drives and their effects on others

- *Self-regulation*—controlling impulses and moods; thinking before acting
- *Internal motivation*—passion for working beyond money and status; pursuing goals with energy and persistence
- *Empathy*—understanding the emotional makeup of other people; treating people according to their emotional reactions
- *Social skill*—managing relationships and building networks; finding common ground and building rapport

Though EQ is incredibly popular among practitioners, scholars have vigorously debated its merits. Our intent is not to wade deeply into this debate here, yet we do note that it might not be accurate to refer to the concept of EQ as "intelligence." EQ blends elements of both traits (e.g., empathy) and abilities (e.g., social skill), some of which have little to do with actual intelligence. Others have criticized some of the EQ measures as actually capturing conformity, knowledge, or personality.

Such criticism notwithstanding, a comprehensive analysis showed that at least some measures of EQ are associated with job performance over and above other common predictors such as IQ and personality traits.[31] Other studies show that EQ can help to explain leadership effectiveness (as rated by followers),[32] as well as career success, entrepreneurial potential, health, relationship satisfaction, humor, and happiness.[33] So we have at least some evidence supporting the notion that EQ matters when it comes to work-related outcomes. Regarding 3D Team Leadership, our point here is that you have to be very much attuned to the emotions and needs of your team members, both individually and collectively. You must be able to read cues in person and at a distance as to the emotional well-being and psychological needs of your team members, particularly in complex VUCA environments. And you need to regulate your own emotions as you engage in switching your focus and balancing the inherent tensions of individuals, teams, and subteams.

You can assess your level of EQ with questions like these: Are you able to recognize and stay in touch with how you are feeling? Can you generate an emotion and then reason using that emotion? Can you understand complex emotions and how they shift from one stage to another? Can you manage your own and others' emotions? Do you have a good understanding of how others around you are feeling? Are you comfortable in a variety of social situations? Do you empathize effectively with other people? Are you motivated to work beyond money and status? Again, we encourage self-assessment and gathering others' feedback for ratings of EQ. This point is particularly important because, as in our firefighter study assessing flexibility, research has shown that the relationship between self and others' ratings of EQ is sometimes weak.[34] As a result, you will need feedback from those around you in order to accurately assess your EQ and start down the road to improvement.

Importantly, EQ appears to be relatively stable but not entirely unchangeable. Thus, even if your EQ scores seem disappointing, you can improve. Of course, your ability to improve is dependent somewhat on the dimension of EQ you're addressing. For more stable traits like empathy, it's hard to imagine going from the inability to experience the emotions of others to some sort of empathy savant, although there is at least some evidence that training can help people engage in more empathetic and altruistic behaviors. For a dimension like social skills, you can clearly get better with practice in social situations, just as you can improve your public speaking ability through training. In fact, studies have shown that social skills can improve up to 50 percent through training and development. Some research has also shown that EQ generally increases with age, one of the (few) positives that come with getting older![35]

Countless articles and websites provide steps for increasing your EQ. Our review of these materials suggests convergence around a few common practices: (1) developing a higher level of self-awareness by constantly seeking feedback and perhaps using an executive coach; (2) developing your listening skills, usually through workshops or leadership development sessions on active listening; (3) displaying more concern and interest in the people you lead, which can involve spending time with people and discussing non-work-related matters; (4) learning to better manage your and others' emotions (again a good coach would be indispensable here); and (5) making sure those around you feel heard and understood. Each of these techniques, we believe, can help you learn more about what your team is thinking and feeling, which can help you make more accurate assessments of where your focus needs to be in the 3D Team Leadership model.

Embarking on a journey to develop your 3D Team Leadership competencies will likely involve significant work and some awkward moments spent outside your natural comfort zone. As a result, you may begin to question whether you would have been better off just learning to cope with your limitations as a leader and hope for the best. *Nonsense.* In the next section, we quickly touch on one of the most important attributes you'll need to master to generate great performances and personal fulfillment: being true to yourself, or authenticity.

Authenticity

In their seminal *Harvard Business Review* article and their book, Robert Goffee and Gareth Jones posed a simple question: *"Why should anyone be led by you?"*[36] Many answers are plausible: results, strategic vision, and technical proficiencies, just to name a few. But a recurring theme stands out: Do you help people find a sense of meaning in their lives? (Recall that meaning was the most important dimension of both individual and team empowerment.) Leaders who are true to themselves, or authentic, and can help those around them feel more authentic at work are especially valuable in creating a sense of meaning. In today's VUCA environments, and especially leading the messiness inherent in teams, we believe this is especially important. You can apply 3D Team Leadership principles all you want, but if you aren't authentic, your team members will always hold something back.

Before you can learn how to develop your 3D Team Leadership skills authentically, you must first understand what *authenticity* means. Goffee and Jones described it as (1) being consistent in your words and actions (i.e., practicing what you preach), (2) adhering to a set of basic principles even as roles and situations change (i.e., the "underlying thread," which of course requires some level of balancing with our description of self-monitoring above), and (3) being comfortable with your true self.[37]

For many individuals, authenticity is an appealing and straightforward concept, but one that is remarkably hard to put into action. This is actually not all that surprising given that we are constantly being told how to behave, who our role models should be, and how we should think about problems (particularly as leaders). So after years—decades for some of us!—of not being ourselves, how do we decide what our authentic self really is? Harvard's Bill George and his colleagues have written extensively about this question. It is impossible to do this work justice in just a few paragraphs, but these are some of their fundamental steps:[38]

> *Understanding and learning from your story.* Do you have a personal narrative of your life that is consistent with but not entirely driven by objective facts and milestones? Does this narrative help you see

the source of your inspiration and values, which will then guide your leadership?

Practicing your personal values. When tested, are you able to hold firm to the value system informed from and instilled by your life story?

Keeping your intrinsic and extrinsic motivation in balance. Can you resist the temptation to measure and pursue success using outside (i.e., extrinsic) parameters (e.g., other peers, professional titles) if they do not line up with you intrinsic views of success?

Once you've got a baseline idea of what your authentic self looks like, you need to build a support network (people who know and support your authentic self), work to stay grounded (avoiding decisions that lead you away from your authentic self), and then, finally (once again!), learn to empower others.[39] The last one is highly relevant for one of our book's main premises: to handle the complex and ambiguous nature of leading teams, you have to empower others and let them carry some of the load. Ideally, you want to empower your team members in ways that allow them to pursue work as their true authentic selves.

Goffee and Jones offer several tips that leaders can use to help their members engage in their team's tasks using all of their authentic selves. These include letting members see your weaknesses, using "tough empathy" (showing passionate concern, but also giving members what they need versus what they want in terms of feedback), and revealing your differences from others in the organization, including team members.[40] These practices, when executed properly, can help members to see you as an accessible human being (not a robotic manipulator) who cares about the members on your team and the task at hand, which can engender a feeling within members that they can add significant and unique value to the team's mission.

Of course, we'd be doing you a disservice not to mention some of the tensions inherent in authenticity and authentic leadership. For one, being flexible and switching your focus might feel like a contradiction to remaining authentic. Yet authenticity is more about being consistent and principled in your values rather than specific behaviors. When viewed this way, it becomes possible for you to switch foci across the three dimensions without violating your true self. Separate from this point, it is entirely possible for an authentic leader to be a bad leader, especially if this person uses his or her authenticity as an

TABLE 9.1. The Characteristics of Successful 3D Team Leaders

Characteristics	Examples
1. Flexibility/adaptability	Leaders anticipate a team moving from a low to a high level of team interdependence and begin preparing the necessary systems and processes needed to move from a focus on individuals to a focus on a team as a whole.
2. Switching behavior	Leaders are able to move effortlessly between each of the three of dimensions of 3D Team Leadership.
3. Ambidextrous leadership	Leaders can balance the tensions between leading individuals versus their team versus their subteams. They are able to make tough decisions regarding trade-offs between the dimensions.
4. Emotional intelligence	Leaders are able to recognize and regulate their own emotions, read others' emotions, and use emotional information to support their thinking and behavior.
5. Authenticity	Leaders are (1) consistent in their words and actions (they practice what they preach), (2) adhere to a set of basic principles even as roles and situations change (i.e., the "underlying thread"), and (3) are comfortable with their true selves.

excuse for not looking for ways to get better. A leader who feels authentically disagreeable and disrespectful, for instance, runs a significant risk: members do not like jerks regardless of whether their poor behaviors are rooted in a true self!

Speaking to this issue, experts in this area acknowledge that sometimes leaders need to "manage authenticity."[41] Though the idea that authenticity needs to be managed is somewhat paradoxical, Goffee and Jones argue that leaders still have control over how much of their true selves, especially weaknesses, can be revealed at any given time. They would also suggest that in an organizational setting where buy-in is required from multiple levels (subordinates and higher-ups), it is important to demonstrate some conformity with the overarching company goals and mission (their specific advice is to "conform—but only just enough"). Finally, authenticity needs to be viewed as a dynamic concept whereby you constantly add to and reinterpret your life story. Although your core values are unlikely to change frequently, this dynamic approach to authenticity gives you the latitude to add new skills and learn new approaches that allow you to ideally present your authentic self to your followers. The point here is to *constantly strive to be a better you*. We hope this book helps you get there. We summarize these five critical success factors for 3D Team Leaders in Table 9.1.

In summary, in answer to the question, are successful 3D team leaders born or made, the answer, as it always tends to be, is yes: *they are born and made.* Based on their inherent abilities, some people naturally come around to 3D Team Leadership more quickly than others. Nevertheless, most of what makes 3D team leaders successful can be developed over time. We have discussed how the competencies of flexibility/adaptability, leader switching behavior, ambidexterity, emotional intelligence, and authenticity are the most closely tied to being an excellent 3D team leader. All five of these competencies can be improved on and strengthened with motivation, persistence, and an open mind. We strongly urge you to get multirater feedback on these five competencies and, when gaps are evident, engage in developmental experiences that strengthen your 3D Team Leadership repertoire.

1O Assessing Your 3D Team Leadership Skills

W E HOPE THAT YOU NOW HAVE A CLEAR UNDER-
standing that a team is made up of not one but three distinct
dimensions (the "I's" in a team, a team as a whole, and the subteams within
an overall team). Because of the complexity of today's teaming environment,
there is no way you can be all things to all dimensions of your teams at all
times. With your limited time and numerous responsibilities, you have to be
able to focus your team leadership behaviors where they are needed most at
any given time. The whole premise of the 3D Team Leadership approach is to
teach you how to do this effectively.

We also hope that you now realize just how widely applicable the 3D Team
Leadership approach can be. Consider for a moment the number of ways in
which you can apply the framework in your daily working life. First, if you
are leading one or more entities that have relatively stable levels of interdependence, the 3D Team Leadership approach can help you. For example, if you
are leading what is generally regarded as a group (i.e., low interdependence)
and that group does not morph into a team or a set of subteams, then the
material in Chapter 3 on leading individuals in team contexts is most applicable for you. We have included material on both intrinsic motivation (i.e.,
empowerment) and extrinsic motivation (i.e., individual reward and evaluation systems, goal setting, peer evaluations). And, don't be afraid to call your
low interdependence entity what it really is—a group. Of course, you'll have
to be brave enough to do this because the tendency today is to call everything

a team. Beyond semantics, calling a group a group will likely increase the chances that you will do the right things in your leadership and that your group's expectations will match your behavior.

If you are leading a real team and that team is not expected to change at any point into a group or a set of subteams, the material in Chapter 4 on leading teams as a whole provides you with a go-to playbook. You will find information on intrinsic motivation for teams (i.e., team empowerment) as well as the key states of trust and psychological safety that are associated with making today's complex and diverse teams successful. We also discussed the importance of designing teams to make them optimally effective. We noted the importance of transformational leadership aimed at teams as a whole to enhance team empowerment, trust, and psychological safety. We also provided practical advice on designing extrinsic motivation systems for teams, including team bonuses, special recognition, peer evaluations, and reconciling such systems with the fact that people often have multiple concurrent team memberships.

If you are leading a team composed of multiple subteams (i.e., a multi-subteam system) and your team of subteams is not expected to transition to a team as a whole or a group, then the information provided in Chapter 5 is most relevant to you. Leading a team of subteams is incredibly complex, and we highlighted the need for team leaders to be able to focus on three types of interdependence: within-subteam interdependence (between members of each subteam), between-subteam interdependence (relationships between each of the subteams themselves), and across-subteam interdependence (the relationship between an overall team of subteams and its external environment). To manage this type of multilayered interdependence, we alerted team leaders to two primary behaviors: strategizing and coordinating.

We also spoke to the importance of fostering shared mental models and managing the various goals in a multisubteam system, including both proximal and distal goals, in the form of a goal hierarchy. We warned against trying to use multiple types of financial rewards in such a complicated system, recommending the use of goals to motivate team members instead. Finally, we provided several practical tips for avoiding the harmful effects of having multiple subteams within one overall team, especially the tendency for such teams to develop faultlines that fracture the team in ways that prevent synergy.

Beyond leading stable entities that do not change over time, the second way in which our 3D Team Leadership model is applicable is if you are leading an entity that changes in levels of interdependence throughout its life cycle. In Chapter 6, we described how Tom, a senior engineering manager, was able to use the 3D Team Leadership approach when managing his global software development team that followed an Agile life cycle model. The key to understanding how to use 3D Team Leadership did not depend on the Agile model but, rather, on understanding what level of interdependence in your team is best at any point in its life cycle and then being able to change your behavior and focus to lead and motivate the correct dimension of the model.

Tom's story showed that he had all the key attributes of an effective 3D team leader described in Chapter 9: flexibility/adaptability (he was able to change his behavior to fit the situation); leader switching behavior (beyond general flexibility, Tom was able to shift his leadership focus between individuals, teams, and subteams in multiple directions); ambidexterity (he was able to balance the natural and inherent tensions that come with leading three different entities to make sure there were no competing goals between them); emotional intelligence (Tom was very good at understanding the various types of needs his team members had, and he was good at managing his own and dealing with others' emotional needs); and authenticity (although Tom was flexible, he never lost sight of who he really was as a leader, and he was able to balance flexibility with being authentic).

The third way in which the 3D Team Leadership model was applicable is that it is relevant for various types of teams. Clearly, Tom's experience in Chapter 6 demonstrated that the model lends itself readily to project teams that follow a particular life cycle. Using that life cycle, Tom was able to determine the proper focus at any given time. Tom also commented on how he adapted the model for use in project teams that did not follow a life cycle. Our research with firefighters also showed that our approach is highly applicable to action teams. Action teams tend to have bursts of very intense activity followed by periods of relative calm, in which preplanning and after-action reviews occur.

Although it was outside the specific scope of our book, the 3D Team Leadership model is also applicable to executive or top management teams, whose members sometimes work very interdependently, but likewise focus on their individual unit or division responsibilities a great deal. CEOs could use our approach to determine the right areas of focus depending on what level of interdependence is present in their teams. It could also be used with parallel teams—teams that sit outside the formal structure of a company. Our work with communities of practice and networks in various companies revealed that even though these types of entities are often group-like, there could be periods in which they operate as teams or a team of subteams. In short, our 3D Team Leadership approach is not dependent on a particular type of team; rather, what it is dependent on is a leader's ability to correctly diagnose the level of interdependence in the entities they are leading.

A fourth way in which our 3D Team Leadership model is applicable is that it does not have to be executed by a single, formal team leader. For many of today's teams, leadership responsibilities are likely to be distributed among several team members. As we discussed in Chapter 2, when we talk about a "leader's" focus, *we don't just necessarily mean one individual.* 3D Team Leadership can effectively be shared among multiple individuals in a team, and when particular individuals emerge as leaders, they can adopt the principles we have set out to help make their teams more effective.

A fifth way the 3D Team Leadership model is highly applicable is that it can be culturally flexible. As we described in Chapter 7, we have worked with teams in many countries on five continents and found that cultural differences make certain aspects of our approach more relevant than others. For example, in teams that have members with highly individualistic cultural values, including many Western countries, leaders would be wise to err on the side of focusing more on the "I"s in their teams. These team members will desire individual attention, they will want to stand out among their fellow team members, and their relationships with fellow team members will be more transactional.

On the contrary, in teams with members who have more collectivistic cultural values, leaders will want to emphasize the entire team more so than individuals. These team members will eschew individual attention, they will want to maintain and protect the harmony in their teams, and their relationships with fellow team members will be much stronger and more permanent than those from more individualistic countries. We include helpful advice that leaders can use to successfully apply the 3D Team Leadership model in any country in the world.

Finally, especially relevant for today's teams operating in VUCA environments, the 3D Team Leadership model is not bound by face-to-face team interaction. Indeed, as we described in Chapter 8, even though it gets more complex to use when your teams are global and virtual, this represents a perfect environment to use tools associated with 3D Team Leadership. Clearly, you need some finely honed diagnostic skills to keep your finger on your team's pulse. After all, you won't have the benefit of all of the nonverbal signals that are so important in minimizing miscommunication. However, as you juggle multiple responsibilities and try to motivate team members on multiple continents, the tenets of 3D Team Leadership will be vital for helping you thrive in the face of great complexity.

We hope our concluding points here are clear. Whether you are leading a stable entity or one that changes; leading a project, action, parallel, or another team type; the sole formal leader of a team or you have a team in which leadership is shared among the members; leading a team in Argentina, France, Nigeria, India, Malaysia, the United States or somewhere else; or leading a team that has members physically located in a single place or spread out all over the world, 3D Team Leadership can be tailored to maximize your team's success. We hope you will find all of the tools that you will need in our book to be the best team leader you can be, and we invite you to reach out to us to share your experiences as you use the 3D Team Leadership model to help you see teams as they really are: in 3D!

Tools to Assess Your Abilities to Be an Effective 3D Team Leader

Throughout the previous chapters discussing 3D Team Leadership, we have repeatedly encouraged you to informally assess yourself on the actions and behaviors we described that are required to be a successful 3D team leader. We also strongly urged you to be honest with yourself in terms of the types of things you do well and about the various things on which you might need more development work.

Although we strongly recommend informal reflection to all of the leaders with whom we work, we also believe in the power of more *formal assessment*, particularly that involving multirater feedback. For those of you who want to take that next important (and yes, we realize, a somewhat daunting) step of gathering information from others about your 3D Team Leadership strengths and "developmental needs" (note that we don't use the word *weaknesses*, because that implies that these cannot be improved and developed over time), this chapter is for you.

Here we present the various measures of many of the concepts related to 3D Team Leadership. Take an honest and candid look at yourself and your teams.

It is only in this way that you will be able to continue your authentic journey as a 3D team leader. We recommend that you assess all measures using a 7-point agreement-disagreement scale: 1 = Strongly Disagree; 2 = Somewhat Disagree; 3 = Slightly Disagree; 4 = Neither Agree nor Disagree; 5 = Slightly Agree; 6 = Somewhat Agree; 7 = Strongly Agree. When using these measures with a single source (e.g., yourself, your boss), you can average the scores across the various items to come up with a total score for the rater. If you are using multiple raters (e.g., team members, peers), you will need to also average the scores across these raters to calculate a total score. To interpret your results, any scores that are 3.0 or less are generally considered low, those between 3.0 and 5.0 are typically considered moderate, and those 5.0 and above are usually considered high.

One of the most important things we have asked leaders to do in this book is to figure out the level of interdependence that exists (and, more important, should exist) in the entities they lead. One key way to do this is with a task interdependence measure. Such a measure can be used for overall teams and the subteams within an overall team. Again, if interdependence is on the lower end, you probably have a group (3.0 or less on the 7-point scale), and if it is on the higher end (5.0 or more on the 7-point scale), you most likely have a team. If you fall somewhere in the middle (between 3.0 and 5.0), you can interpret this has having a hybrid entity between a group and a team.

Task Interdependence

1. To complete its tasks, the members of my team/the team I lead must constantly exchange materials, resources, and/or information.
2. To successfully accomplish work, the members of my team/the team I lead need to ensure that there is a high level of coordination between one another.
3. Without a high degree of integration of the work done by members, my team/the team I lead could not be successful.
4. Members of my team/the team I lead cannot generally work alone to complete their tasks, then put it all together relatively quickly near the end of a deadline.
5. The success of my team/the team I lead depends to a great extent on how much collaboration there is between the team members.
6. The members of my team/the team I lead constantly depend on one another to accomplish team tasks.

7. Our work features very few specialized subtasks that are best completed by individuals with specific expertise.

8. If all team members are not involved at every step of the team's task, we will likely encounter significant problems down the line.[1]

The task interdependence measure is helpful for determining whether an individual or team focus is best, but what about subteams? To date, there is no existing measure for multilayered interdependence (the optimal condition for subteam arrangements), but our measure can still be used to inform your leadership focus in these settings with one caveat: you must be sure to draw critical inferences about whether the types (and nature) of tasks your teams are working on are *best* completed by two or more collective entities within the team. Usually this means there are at least two distinct tasks (or subtasks) that need to be completed concurrently for your team to succeed. Also, remember our words of caution from earlier in the book: team members may sometimes prefer to work in subteams, especially when you have a critical mass of employees from common backgrounds, locations, or business functions, even though this is not the best arrangement for the work being done. A key leadership task is making sure work structures are determined by tasks, not other superficial factors.

Once you feel confident that your team's work is suited for subteams, you (and/or your team members) should then complete the task interdependence measure for each subteam's assignment and score each subteam separately. These scores will then give you an idea of how you should focus your efforts on each subteam. Remember that it is possible that you may need to treat one subteam as a group of individuals and another like a real team (or any other combination of the two). Also, don't forget that in these situations, at least part of your focus needs to be on coordinating the work between subteams so that your overall team ultimately produces a great final product or service.

The second measure assesses the extent to which you exhibit the behaviors associated with empowering leadership. Note that these can be individual, team, or subteam focused. You can adapt the wording to fit the target:

Empowering Leadership Behaviors

1. I give my team members/team/subteams many responsibilities.

2. I make my team members/teams/subteams responsible for what they do.

3. I ask my team members/teams/subteams for advice when making decisions.

4. I use my team members'/teams'/subteams' suggestions and ideas when making decisions.

5. I do not control my team members'/teams'/subteams' activities.

6. I encourage my team members/teams/subteams to take control of their work.

7. I allow my team members/teams/subteams to set their own goals.

8. I encourage my team members/teams/subteams to come up with their own goals.

9. I stay out of the way when my team members/teams/subteams work on performance problems.

10. I encourage my team members/teams/subteams to figure out the causes/solutions to problems.

11. I tell my team members/teams/subteams to expect a lot from themselves.

12. I encourage my team members/teams/subteams to strive for high performance.

13. I trust my team members/teams/subteams.

14. I am confident in what my team members/teams/subteams can do.[2]

In addition to empowering leadership, in Chapter 6 we also discussed the two other important leadership behaviors: those that are more task focused (i.e., initiating structure) and those that are more team member focused (i.e., consideration). The next two measures list fourteen behaviors—seven that are more task focused and seven that are more team member focused. Again, each behavior can be directed at each of the three dimensions of teams: the individuals in a team, the team as a whole, and the subteams.

Task-Focused Leader Behaviors

1. I ensure that the task performance goals for my team members/teams/subteams are clear.

2. I actively participate in how work is structured for my team members/teams/subteams.

3. I clarify task performance strategies for my team members/teams/subteams.

4. I provide task-related instructions for my team members/teams/subteams.

5. I review relevant task performance results for my team members/teams/subteams.

6. I monitor task performance for my team members/teams/subteams.

7. I will advocate for my team members/team/subteam to others inside/outside the organization to get key resources or support so we can complete our tasks.[3]

Team Member–Focused Leader Behaviors

1. I help develop solutions to relationship-related problems (i.e., personal disagreements) for my team members/teams/subteams.

2. I respond promptly to personal needs or concerns for my team members/teams/subteams.

3. I engage in actions that demonstrate respect and concern for my team members/teams/subteams.

4. Beyond my own self-interests, I strive to consider the needs and wants of my team members/teams/subteams.

5. I express trust in my team members/teams/subteams.

6. I strive to actively acknowledge the contributions of my team members/team/subteams to others who are not on the team, including upper management.

7. I actively check in and solicit feedback from my team members/teams/subteams to see how they are doing.[4]

Throughout our book, we have suggested that 3D Team Leadership is critical for increasing the level of individual, team, and subteam empowerment. The next set of items can be used for assessing empowerment levels for all three of these dimensions and can be used as an important test of how effective your leadership behaviors have been in increasing empowerment. Note that we recommend that team members themselves provide assessments of empowerment because the measure is tapping the internal beliefs and experiences of the team members. As such, they will provide the most accurate assessment. We provide three items each for the dimensions of potency, meaningfulness, autonomy, and impact.

Empowerment

1. My team members/teams/subteams feel confident (potency).
2. My team members/teams/subteams believe they can get a lot done when they work hard (potency).
3. My team members/teams/subteams believe they can be very productive when they work hard (potency).
4. My team members/teams/subteams feel that their projects are significant (meaningfulness).
5. My team members/teams/subteams believe that their tasks are worthwhile (meaningfulness).
6. My team members/teams/subteams feel that their work is meaningful (meaningfulness).
7. My team members/teams/subteams can select different ways to do their work (autonomy).
8. My team members/teams/subteams determine how things are done in their team (autonomy).
9. My team members/teams/subteams make their own choices without being told by management (autonomy).
10. My team members/teams/subteams have a positive impact on this company's customers (impact).
11. My team members/teams/subteams perform tasks that matter to this company (impact).
12. My team members/teams/subteams make a difference in this organization (impact). [5]

In Chapter 9, we discussed several key leadership characteristics that are associated with successful 3D Team Leadership, including flexibility/adaptability, switching behavior, and ambidextrous leadership. Ideally, you would have your team members, peers, and bosses rate these about you and then compare your own ratings to theirs in a multirater system.

The leader flexibility/adaptability items were originally written for general (not team) leadership and were designed to be used in a self-report fashion. We recommend that you modify them to apply more specifically to a team leadership situation and change the referents from "you" to "My/The team leader" or the person's name being rated.

Leader Flexibility/Adaptability

Over the last month, to what extent have you (use this preface for items 1–9):

1. Explored a wide variety of approaches to a problem?
2. Planned ahead rather than reacted to a situation?
3. Created multiple courses of action during planning?
4. Adapted well to changes in your work role?
5. Adjusted well to new equipment, process, or procedures in your tasks?
6. Been able to adapt your personal approach to the situation at hand?
7. Coped with stressful events effectively?
8. Maintained productivity in challenging circumstances?
9. Adapted to change with minimal stress?
10. Overall, given my work context, I would consider myself to be a flexible person. [6]

Leader Switching Behavior

1. I/my team leader am/is able to move effortlessly between managing individuals on the team, the team as a whole, and the subteams within the team across different situations.
2. I/my team leader effectively switch(es) my/his/her focus between individuals, the whole team, and subteams within the team.
3. I/my team leader am/is effective at motivating individuals, the entire team, or subteams within the team when the situation calls for it.
4. I/my team leader can seamlessly alternate my/his/her focus on individuals, the whole team, or the subteams within the team.
5. I/my team leader am/is able to simultaneously balance the needs of individuals, the entire team, and subteams within the team. [7]

Leader Ambidexterity

1. I/my team leader am/is able to a balance the tensions between leading individuals, teams, and subteams.
2. I/my team leader can reconcile the competing goals between the individuals, teams, and subteams that I/she/he lead(s).
3. I/my team leader remain(s) calm when faced with making tough decisions regarding the trade-offs between individuals, teams, and subteams.

4. I/my team leader effectively recognize(s) the inherent tensions that exist between individuals, teams, and subteams.

5. I/my team leader am/is able to make tough decisions when needed to manage the trade-offs between individuals, teams, and subteams.[8]

If you would like to assess your team's (or subteam's) performance using our generic and widely applicable measure, we invite you to use the following:

(Sub)Team Performance

1. My (sub)team/the (sub)team I lead meets or exceeds its goals.
2. My (sub)team/the (sub)team I lead completes its tasks on time.
3. My (sub)team/the (sub)team I lead makes sure that products and services meet or exceed quality standards.
4. My (sub)team/the (sub)team I lead responds quickly when problems come up.
5. My (sub)team/the (sub)team I lead is a productive team.
6. My (sub)team/the (sub)team I lead successfully solves problems that slow down work.

If you would like to assess the extent to which your team (or subteam) initiates the performance of tasks on their own without instructions from management, you can use our measure of (sub)team proactivity.[9]

(Sub)Team Proactivity

1. My (sub)team/the (sub)team I lead is excited when other teams or employees use our/its ideas.
2. My (sub)team/the (sub)team I lead believes that nothing can stop us/it from making something happen.
3. My (sub)team/the (sub)team I lead feels that it can make things happen even when the odds are against it.
4. My (sub)team/the (sub)team I lead can fix things it does not like.
5. My (sub)team/the (sub)team I lead is always looking for better ways to do something.
6. My (sub)team/the (sub)team I lead likes to overcome obstacles to our/its ideas.
7. My (sub)team/the (sub)team I lead tackles problems head-on.[10]

If you are interested in assessing the extent to which respondents feel that their (sub)team provides goods or services in a timely and quality manner to their customers, you can use our measure of (sub)team customer service:

(Sub)Team Customer Service

1. My (sub)team/the (sub)team I lead produces high-quality products/ services.
2. My (sub)team/the (sub)team I lead works out customer problems in a timely manner.
3. My (sub)team/the (sub)team I lead is very reliable when working on customer requests.
4. My (sub)team/the (sub)team I lead follows through on complaints and requests.
5. My (sub)team/the (sub)team I lead provides a satisfactory level of customer service overall.[11]

Notes

Chapter 1

1. Wageman, Ruth. "How Leaders Foster Self-Managing Team Effectiveness: Design Choices versus Hands-On Coaching." *Organization Science* 12 (2001): 559–577.

2. Conger, Jay A. "Developing Leadership Capability: What's Inside the Black Box?" *Academy of Management Executive* 18 (2004): 136–139.

3. Kozlowski, Stephen W. J., Stanton Mak, and Georgia T. Chao. "Team-Centric Leadership: An Integrative Review." *Annual Review of Organizational Psychology and Organizational Behavior* 3 (2016): 21–54.

4. Kozlowski, Stephen W. J., and Bradford S. Bell, "Work Groups and Teams in Organizations." In *Handbook of Psychology, vol. 12: Industrial and Organizational Psychology*, 2nd ed., edited by Neal Schmitt, Scott Highhouse, and Irving Weiner, 412–469. Hoboken, NJ: Wiley, 2013.

5. Mathieu, John, M. Travis Maynard, Tammy Rapp, and Lucy Gilson. "Team Effectiveness 1997–2007: A Review of Recent Advancements and a Glimpse into the Future." *Journal of Management* 34 (2008): 410–476.

6. Mathieu, John E., John R. Hollenbeck, Daan van Knippenberg, and Daniel R. Ilgen. "A Century of Work Teams in the *Journal of Applied Psychology*." *Journal of Applied Psychology* 102 (2017): 452–467.

7. Swider, Brian W., Joseph T. Liu, T. Brad Harris, and Richard G. Gardner. "Employees on the Rebound: Extending the Careers Literature to Include Boomerang Employment." *Journal of Applied Psychology* (2017): http://psycnet.apa.org/psycinfo/2017-10514-001/

8. Bennett, Nathan, and James Lemoine. "What VUCA Really Means for You." *Harvard Business Review* 92, nos. 1/2 (2014): 27.

9. Bertolli, Fabiola, Elisa Mattarelli, Matteo Vignoli, and Diego Maria Macri. "Exploring the Relationship between Multiple Team Membership and Team

Performance: The Role of Social Networks and Collaborative Technology." *Research Policy* 44 (2015): 911-924; O'Leary, Michael B., Mark Mortensen, and Anita W. Woolley. "Multiple Team Membership: A Theoretical Model of Its Effects on Productivity and Learning for Individuals and Teams." *Academy of Management Review* 36 (2011): 461–478.

10. Sargut, Gokce, and Rita G. McGrath, "Learning to Live with Complexity." *Harvard Business Review* 89, no. 9 (2011): 68–76.

11. Snowden, David J., and Mary E. Boone. "A Leader's Framework for Decision Making." *Harvard Business Review* 85, no. 11 (2007): 53–66.

12. Sargut and McGrath (2011).

13. Uhl-Bien, Mary, Bill McKelvey, and Russ Marion. "Complexity Leadership Theory: Shifting Leadership from the Industrial Age to the Knowledge Era." *Leadership Quarterly* 18 (2007): 298–318.

14. Kozlowski, Stephen W. J., Daniel J. Watola, Jaclyn M. Nowakowski, Brian H. Kim, and Isabel C. Botero. "Developing Adaptive Teams: A Theory of Dynamic Team Leadership." In *Team Effectiveness in Complex Organizations: Cross-Disciplinary Perspectives and Approaches*, edited by Eduardo Salas, Gerald F. Goodwin, and C. Shawn Burke, 113–155. New York: Routledge, 2009.

15. Kanfer, Ruth, and Phillip L. Ackerman. "Motivation and Cognitive Abilities: An Integrative/Aptitude-Treatment Interaction Approach to Skill Acquisition." *Journal of Applied Psychology* 74 (1989): 657–690.

16. Hobfoll, Stevan E. *The Ecology of Stress.* Washington, DC: Hemisphere, 1988.

17. Baumeister, Roy F., Ellen Bratslavsky, Mark Muraven, and Dianne M. Tice. "Ego Depletion: Is the Active Self a Limited Resource?" *Journal of Personality and Social Psychology* 74 (1998): 1252–1265; DeWall, C. Nathan, Roy F. Baumeister, Nicole L. Mead, and Kathleen D. Vohs. "How Leaders Self-Regulate Their Task Performance: Evidence That Power Promotes Diligence, Depletion, and Disdain." *Journal of Personality and Social Psychology* 100 (2011): 47–65.

18. Schwartz, Jeff, Udo Bohdal-Spiegelhoff, Michael Gretczko, and Nathan Sloan. *Global Human Capital Trends 2016, The New Organization: Different by Design.* Deloitte University Press.

19. Kozlowski and Bell (2013).

20. Campion, Michael A., Gina J. Medsker, and A. Catherine Higgs. "Relations between Work Group Characteristics and Effectiveness: Implications for Designing Effective Work Groups." *Personnel Psychology* 46 (2003): 823–850.

21. Kozlowski and Bell (2013).

22. Katzenbach, Jon R., and Douglas K. Smith. *The Wisdom of Teams: Creating the High-Performance Organization.* Boston: Harvard Business School Press, 1993.

23. Katzenbach and Smith (1993).

24. Tuckman, Bruce W. "Developmental Sequences in Small Groups." *Psychological Bulletin* 63 (1965): 384–389.

25. Gersick, Connie J. G. "Marking Time: Predictable Transitions in Task Groups." *Academy of Management Journal* 32 (1989): 274–309.

26. Marks, Michelle A., John E. Mathieu, and Stephen. J. Zaccaro. "A Temporally Based Framework and Taxonomy of Team Processes." *Academy of Management Review* 26 (2001): 356–376; Mathieu et al. (2017).

27. Hackman, Richard J. *Leading Teams: Setting the Stage for Great Performances.* Boston: Harvard Business School Press, 2002.

28. Hackman (2002, 42).

29. Hackman (2002, 50).

30. Wageman, Ruth, Heidi Gardner, and Mark Mortensen. "The Changing Ecology of Teams: New Directions for Teams Research." *Journal of Organizational Behavior* 33 (2012): 305.

31. Wageman et al. (2012, 306).

32. Wageman et al. (2012, 312).

33. Hackman, Richard J. "From Causes to Conditions in Group Research." *Journal of Organizational Behavior* 33 (2012): 428.

34. Hackman (2012, 439).

35. Hill, Linda. *Managing Your Team.* Boston: Harvard Business School Publishing, 1995.

36. Hill, Linda A., and Kent Linebeck. *Being the Boss: The 3 Imperatives for Becoming a Great Leader.* Boston: Harvard Business Review Press, 2011.

37. Hill (1995, 10).

38. Tajfel, Henri. "Social Psychology of Intergroup Relations." *Annual Review of Psychology* 33 (1982): 1–39.

39. Turner, John C., Michael A. Hogg, Penelope J. Oakes, Stephen D. Reicher, and Margaret S. Wetherell. *Rediscovering the Social Group: A Self-Categorization Theory.* Cambridge, MA: Basil Blackwell, 1987.

40. Brewer, Marilyn B. "The Social Self: On Being the Same and Different at the Same Time." *Personality and Social Psychology Bulletin* 17 (1991): 475–482.

41. Hirschhorn, Larry. *Managing in the New Team Environment: Skills, Tools, and Methods* Lincoln, NE: Authors Choice Press, 2002.

42. Hill (1995, 10).

43. Janis, Irving L. *Groupthink: Psychological Studies of Policy Decisions and Fiascoes.* Boston: Wadsworth, 1982.

44. Tjosvold, Deon, and Haifa F. Sun. "Understanding Conflict Avoidance: Relationship, Motivations, Actions, and Consequences." *International Journal of Conflict Management* 13 (2002): 142–164.

45. Gigone, Daniel, and Reid Hastie. "The Common Knowledge Effect: Information Sharing and Group Judgment." *Journal of Personality and Social Psychology* 65 (1993): 959–974.

46. De Dreu, Carsten K. W., and Laurie R. Weingart. "Task versus Relationship Conflict, Team Performance, and Team Member Satisfaction: A Meta-Analysis." *Journal of Applied Psychology* 88 (2003): 741–749.

47. Hill (1995, 11).

48. Sitkin, Sim B. "Learning through Failure: The Strategy of Small Losses." In *Research in Organizational Behavior,* Vol. 14, edited by Larry L. Cummings and Barry M. Staw, 231–266. Greenwich, CT: JAI Press, 1992.

49. Babineaux, Ryan, and John Krumboltz. *Fail Fast, Fail Often: How Losing Can Help You Win*. New York: Penguin, 2013.

50. VandeWalle, Don, and Larry L. Cummings. "A Test of the Influence of Goal Orientation on the Feedback-Seeking Process." *Journal of Applied Psychology* 82 (1997): 390–400.

51. VandeWalle, Don, Steven P. Brown, William L. Cron, and John W. Slocum Jr. "The Influence of Goal Orientation and Self-Regulation Tactics on Sales Performance: A Longitudinal Field Test." *Journal of Applied Psychology* 84 (1999): 249–259.

52. Hill (1995, 11).

53. LeRoy, Sophie. "Why Is It So Hard to Do My Work? The Challenge of Attention Residue When Switching between Work Tasks." *Organizational Behavior and Human Decision Processes* 109 (2009): 168–181.

54. Carson, Jay B., Paul E. Tesluk, and Jennifer A. Marrone. "Shared Leadership in Teams: An Investigation of Antecedent Conditions and Performance." *Academy of Management Journal* 50 (2007): 1217–1234; Pearce, Craig, and Jay A. Conger. *Shared Leadership: Reframing the Hows and Whys of Leadership*. Thousand Oaks, CA: Sage, 2003.

55. Harris, T. Brad, Ning Li, Wendy R. Boswell, Xin-an Zhang, and Zhitao Xie. "Getting What's New from Newcomers: Empowering Leadership, Creativity, and Adjustment in the Socialization Context." *Personnel Psychology* 67 (2014): 567–604.

Chapter 2

1. McArgle, Megan. "How 'Groupidity' Blew Up the Space Shuttle." *Bloomberg View*, April 3, 2014. https://www.bloomberg.com/view/articles/2014-04-03/how-groupidity-blew-up-the-space-shuttle.

2. Tuckman, Bruce W. "Developmental Sequence in Small Groups." *Psychological Bulletin* 63 (1965): 384–399.

3. De Dreu, Carsten K. "When Too Little or Too Much Hurts: Evidence for a Curvilinear Relationship between Task Conflict and Innovation in Teams." *Journal of Management* 32 (2006): 83–107; Farh, Jing-Li L., Cynthia Lee, and Crystal I. Farh. "Task Conflict and Team Creativity: A Question of How Much and When." *Journal of Applied Psychology* 95 (2010): 1173–1180.

4. Lau, Dora C., and J. Keith Murnighan. "Demographic Diversity and Faultlines: The Compositional Dynamics of Organizational Groups." *Academy of Management Review* 23 (1998): 325–340.

5. Mathieu, John E., John R. Hollenbeck, Daan van Knippenberg, and Daniel R. Ilgen. "A Century of Work Teams in the *Journal of Applied Psychology*." *Journal of Applied Psychology* 102 (2017): 452–467.

6. O'Neill, Elizabeth. "The Leo Burnett Company, Ltd.: Virtual Team Management" (Case 9B03M052). London, Ontario: Ivey Business School Publishing, 2003.

7. Mathieu, John E., Travis M. Maynard, Thomas Rapp, and Lucy Gilson. "Team Effectiveness 1997–2007: A Review of Recent Advancements and a Glimpse into the Future." *Journal of Management* 34 (2008): 410–476; Mathieu et al. (2017).

8. Burke, C. Shawn, Kevin C. Stagl, Cameron Klein, Gerald F. Goodwin, Eduardo Salas, and Stanley M. Halpin. "What Types of Leadership Behaviors Are Functional in Teams? A Meta-Analysis." *Leadership Quarterly* 17 (2006): 288–307.

9. McGrath, Joseph. E. *Leadership Behavior: Some Requirements for Leadership Training.* Washington, DC: U.S. Civil Service Commission, Office of Career Development, 1962, 5.

10. Morgeson, Frederick P., D. Scott DeRue, and Elizabeth P. Karam. "Leadership in Teams: A Functional Approach to Understanding Leadership Structures and Processes." *Journal of Management* 36 (2010): 5–39.

11. Schutz, William, C. "The Ego, FIRO Theory and the Leader as Completer." In *Leadership and Interpersonal Behavior,* edited by Luigi Petrullo and Bernard M. Bass, 61. New York: Holt, Rinehart & Winston, 1961.

12. Zaccaro, Stephen J., Andrea L. Rittman, and Michelle A. Marks. "Team Leadership." *Leadership Quarterly* 12 (2001): 451–483.

13. Santos, Joaquim P., Antonio Caetano, and Susana M. Tavares. "Is Training Leaders in Functional Leadership a Useful Tool for Improving the Performance of Leadership Functions and Team Effectiveness?" *Leadership Quarterly* 26 (2015): 470–484.

14. Hirschhorn, Larry. *Managing in the New Team Environment: Skills, Tools, and Methods.* Reading, MA: Addison-Wesley, 1991.

15. Hirschhorn, Larry. *Managing in the New Team Environment: Skills, Tools, and Methods.* Lincoln, NE: Authors Choice Press, 2002.

16. Manz, Charles C., David E. Keating, and Anne Donnellon. "Preparing for an Organization Change to Employee Self-Management: The Managerial Transition." *Organizational Dynamics* 19 (1990): 15–26.

17. Hirschhorn (1991, 16).

18. Mathieu, John E., Michelle A. Marks, and Stephen J. Zaccaro. "Multi-Team Systems." In *International Handbook of Work and Organizational Psychology,* edited by Neal Anderson, Deniz Ones, Handan K. Sinangil, and Chockalingam Viswesvaran, 289–313. London: Sage, 2001.

19. Harris, T. Brad, and Bradley L. Kirkman. "Teams and Proactivity." In *Proactivity at Work: Making Things Happen in Organizations,* edited by Uta Bindl and Sharon Parker, 530–558. New York: Routledge, 2017.

20. Hackman, J. Richard. "The Design of Work Teams." In *Handbook of Organizational Behavior,* edited by Jay W. Lorsch, 315–342. Englewood Cliffs, NJ: Prentice Hall, 1987.

21. Barker, James R. "Tightening the Iron Cage: Concertive Control in Self-Managing Teams." *Administrative Science Quarterly* 38 (1993): 408–437.

22. Barker (1993, 408).

23. Barker (1993, 408).

24. Van Knippenberg, Daan, Carsten K. De Dreu, and Astrid C. Homan. "Work Group Diversity and Group Performance: An Integrative Model and Research Agenda." *Journal of Applied Psychology* 89 (2004): 1008–1022.

25. Van Knippenberg et al. (2004).

26. Javidan, Mansour, Peter W. Dorfman, Mary Sully de Luque, and Robert J. House. "In the Eye of the Beholder: Cross Cultural Lessons in Leadership from Project GLOBE." *Academy of Management Perspectives* 20 (2006): 67–90.

27. Cappelli, Peter. "Why We Love to Hate HR . . . and What HR Can Do about It." *Harvard Business Review* 93, nos. 7–8 (2015): 54–61.

28. Macky, Keith, Dianne Gardner, and Stewart Forsyth. "Generational Differences at Work: Introduction and Overview." *Journal of Managerial Psychology* 23 (2008): 857–861.

29. Twenge, Jeanne M. "A Review of the Empirical Evidence on Generational Differences in Work Attitudes." *Journal of Business and Psychology* 25 (2010): 201–210.

30. Roberts, Brent W., Grant Edmonds, and Emily Grijalva. "It Is Developmental Me, Not Generation Me: Developmental Changes Are More Important Than Generational Changes in Narcissism—Commentary on Trzesniewski and Donnellan." *Perspectives on Psychological Science* 5 (2010): 97–102.

31. Tajfel, Henri. "Social Psychology of Intergroup Relations." *Annual Review of Psychology* 33 (1982): 1–39.

32. Gibson, Cristina B., and Freek Vermeulen. "A Healthy Divide: Subgroups as a Stimulus for Team Learning Behavior." *Administrative Science Quarterly* 48 (2003): 202–239.

33. Bezrukova, Katerina, Chester S. Spell, David Caldwell, and Jerry M. Burger. "A Multilevel Perspective on Faultlines: Differentiating the Effects of Between Group- and Organizational-Level Faultlines." *Journal of Applied Psychology* 101 (2016): 86–107.

34. O'Leary, Michael B., and Mark Mortensen. "Go (Con)figure: Subgroups, Imbalance, and Isolates in Geographically Dispersed Teams." *Organization Science* 21 (2010): 115–131.

35. Chiu, Chia-Yen, Bradley P. Owens, and Paul E. Tesluk. "Initiating and Utilizing Shared Leadership in Teams: The Role of Leader Humility, Team Proactive Personality, and Team Performance Capability." *Journal of Applied Psychology* 101 (2016): 1705–1720; D'Innocenzo, Lauren, John E. Mathieu, and Michael R. Kukenberger. "A Meta-Analysis of Different Forms of Shared Leadership-Team Performance Relations." *Journal of Management* 42 (2016): 1964–1991.

36. Carson, Jay B., Paul E. Tesluk, and Jennifer A. Marrone. "Shared Leadership in Teams: An Investigation of Antecedent Conditions and Performance." *Academy of Management Journal* 50 (2007): 1217–1234.

37. Bell, Bradford S., and Stephen W. J. Kozlowski. "A Typology of Virtual Teams: Implications for Effective Leadership." *Group and Organization Management* 27 (2002): 14–49; Kozlowski, Stephen W. J., Stanley M. Gully, Earl R. Nason, and Eleanor M. Smith. "Developing Adaptive Teams: A Theory of Compilation and Performance across Levels and Time." In *The Changing Nature of Work and Performance: Implications for Staffing Personnel Actions and Development,* edited by Daniel R. Ilgen and Elaine D. Pulakos, 240–292. San Francisco: Jossey-Bass, 1999.

38. Kirkman, Bradley L., and John E. Mathieu. "The Dimensions and Antecedents of Team Virtuality." *Journal of Management* 31 (2005): 700–718.

39. Hackman (2002).

40. Edmondson, Amy C., Richard M. Bohmer, and Gary P. Pisano. "Speeding Up Team Learning," *Harvard Business Review* 79, no. 9 (2001): 125–134; Edmondson, Amy C., Richard M. Bohmer, and Gary P. Pisano. "Disrupted Routines: Team Learning and New Technology Implementation in Hospitals." *Administrative Science Quarterly* 46 (2001): 685–716.

Chapter 3

1. Hackman, Richard J. *Leading Teams: Setting the Stage for Great Performances.* Boston: Harvard Business School Press, 2002, 43.

2. Nembhard, Ingrid M., and Amy C. Edmondson. "Making It Safe: The Effects of Leader Inclusiveness and Professional Status on Psychological Safety and Improvement Efforts in Health Care Teams." *Journal of Organizational Behavior* 27 (2006): 941–966.

3. Fugate, Mel, Gregory E. Prussia, and Angelo J. Kinicki. "Managing Employee Withdrawal during Organizational Change: The Role of Threat Appraisal." *Journal of Management* 38 (2012): 890–914.

4. Burris, Ethan R., James R. Detert, and Dan S. Chiaburu. "Quitting before Leaving: The Mediating Effects of Psychological Attachment and Detachment on Voice." *Journal of Applied Psychology* 93 (2008): 912–922; Klotz, Anthony C., and Ryan D. Zimmerman. "On the Turning Away: An Exploration of the Employee Resignation Process." In *Research in Personnel and Human Resources Management,* edited by M. Ronald Buckley, Anthony R. Wheeler, and Jonathan R. B. Halbesleben, 51–119. Bingley, UK: Emerald, 2015.

5. Menon, Tanya, and Leigh Thompson. *Stop Spending, Start Managing: Strategies to Transform Wasteful Habits.* Boston: Harvard Business Review Press, 2016.

6. Anand, Smriti, Jia Hu, Robert C. Liden, and Prajya R. Vidyarthi. "Leader-Member Exchange: Recent Research Findings and Prospects for the Future." In *The Sage Handbook of Leadership*, edited by Alan Bryman, David Collison, Keith Grint, Mary Uhl-Bien, and Brad Jackson, 311–325. Thousand Oaks, CA: Sage, 2011; Greenberg, Jerald, and Jason A. Colquitt, *Handbook of Organizational Justice.* Mahwah, NJ: Erlbaum, 2005.

7. Heath, Chip, and Dan Heath. *Switch: How to Change Things When Change Is Hard.* New York: Broadway, 2010.

8. Pfeffer, Jeffrey. *SAS Institute (A): A Different Approach to Incentives and People Management Practices in the Software Industry.* Palo Alto, CA: Stanford University, 1998.

9. Society for Human Resource Management. "Employee Job Satisfaction and Engagement: The Road to Economic Recovery—2014." Alexandria, VA: Society for Human Resource Management, 2014.

10. Deci, Edward L., and Richard M. Ryan. "Cognitive Evaluation Theory: Perceived Causality and Perceived Competence." In *Intrinsic Motivation and Self-Determination in Human Behavior*, edited by Edward L. Deci and Richard M. Ryan, 43–85. New York: Springer Science + Business Media, 1985; Deci, Edward L., Richard Koestner, and Richard M. Ryan. "A Meta-Analytic Review of Experiments Examining the Effects of Extrinsic Rewards on Intrinsic Motivation." *Psychological Bulletin* 125 (1999): 627–668.

11. Menon and Thompson (2016).

12. Wong, Sut I., and Steffen R. Giessner. "The Thin Line between Empowering and Laissez-Faire Leadership: An Expectancy-Match Perspective." *Journal of Management* (in press); Lewin, Kurt, Ronald Lippit, and Ralph K. White. "Patterns of Aggressive Behavior in Experimentally Created Social Climates." *Journal of Social Psychology* 10 (1939): 271–301.

13. Hackman (2002).

14. Blanchard, Kenneth, John P. Carlos, and Alan Randolph. *Empowerment Takes More Than a Minute.* San Francisco: Berrett-Koehler, 1996.

15. Blanchard, Kenneth, and Spencer Johnson. *The One Minute Manager.* New York: Morrow, 1982.

16. Thomas, Kenneth W., and Betty A. Velthouse. "Cognitive Elements of Empowerment: An 'Interpretive' Model of Intrinsic Task Motivation." *Academy of Management Review* 15 (1990): 666–681.

17. Thomas and Velthouse (1990).

18. Thomas and Velthouse (1990).

19. Thomas and Velthouse (1990).

20. Thomas and Velthouse (1990).

21. Humphrey, Stephen E., Jennifer D. Nahrgang, and Frederick P. Morgeson. "Integrating Motivational, Social, and Contextual Work Design Features: A Meta-Analytic Summary and Theoretical Extension of the Work Design Literature." *Journal of Applied Psychology* 92 (2007): 1332–1356.

22. Seibert, Scott E., Gang Wang, and Stephen H. Courtright. "Antecedents and Consequences of Psychological and Team Empowerment in Organizations: A Meta-Analytic Review." *Journal of Applied Psychology* 96 (2011): 981–1003.

23. Argyris, Chris. "Empowerment: The Emperor's New Clothes." *Harvard Business Review* 76, no. 3 (1998): 98–105.

24. Kirkman, Bradley L., and Benson Rosen. "Beyond Self-Management: Antecedents and Consequences of Team Empowerment." *Academy of Management Journal* 42 (1999): 58–74.

25. Arnold, Josh A., Sharon Arad, Jonathan A. Rhoades, and Fritz Drasgow. "The Empowering Leadership Questionnaire: The Construction and Validation of a New Scale for Measuring Leader Behaviors." *Journal of Organizational Behavior* 21 (2000): 249–269.

26. Sharma, Payal, and Bradley L. Kirkman. "Leveraging Leaders: A Literature Review and Future Lines of Inquiry for Empowering Leadership Research." *Group and Organization Management* 40 (2015): 193–237.

27. Zhang, Xiaomeng, and Kathryn M. Bartol. "Linking Empowering Leadership and Employee Creativity: The Influence of Psychological Empowerment, Intrinsic Motivation, and Creative Process Engagement." *Academy of Management Journal* 53 (2010): 107–128.

28. Pacheco, G., and Don Webber. "Job Satisfaction: How Crucial Is Participative Decision Making?" *Personnel Review* 45 (2016): 183–200.

29. Edwards, Joseph, Michael Snowden, and Jamie Halsall. "Coaching Works! A Qualitative Study Exploring the Effects of Coaching in a Public Sector Organization." *Journal of Social Sciences Research* 2 (2016): 88–92.

30. Heslin, Peter, Don Vanderwalle, and Gary Latham. "Engagement in Employee Coaching: The Role of Managers' Implicit Person Theory." *Personnel Psychology* 59 (2006): 871–902.

31. Latham, Gary P. "Theory and Research on Coaching Practices." *Australian Psychologist* 42 (2007): 268–270.

32. Goleman, Daniel. *Emotional Intelligence: Why It Can Matter More Than IQ.* New York: Bantam, 2006; Goleman, Daniel, Richard Boyatzis, and Annie McKee. *Primal Leadership: Unleashing the Power of Emotional Intelligence.* Boston: Harvard Business Press, 2013.

33. Seibert et al. (2011).

34. Edmondson, Amy. "Psychological Safety and Learning Behavior in Work Teams." *Administrative Science Quarterly* 44 (1999): 350–383.

35. Hackman, J. Richard, and Greg R. Oldham. *Work Redesign.* Reading, MA: Addison-Wesley, 1980.

36. Weber, Lauren, and Rachel Feintzeig "Companies Say No to Having an HR Department." *Wall Street Journal* April 9, 2014; Cappelli, Peter. "Why We Love to Hate HR . . . and What HR Can Do about It," *Harvard Business Review* 93, nos. 7/8 (2015): 54–61.

37. Parker, Sharon K., Frederick P. Morgeson, and Gary Johns. "One Hundred Years of Work Design Research: Looking Back and Looking Forward." *Journal of Applied Psychology* 102 (2017): 403–420.

38. Butler, Timothy, and James Waldroop. "Job Sculpting: The Art of Retaining Your Best People." *Harvard Business Review* 77, no. 5 (1999): 144–152.

39. Butler and Waldroop (1999).

40. Tims, Maria, and Arnold B. Bakker. "Job Crafting: A New Model of Individual Job Redesign." *South African Journal of Industrial Psychology* 36 (2010): 1–9; Tims, Maria, Arnold B. Bakker, and Daantje Derks. "Development and Validation of the Job Crafting Scale." *Journal of Vocational Behavior* 80 (2012): 173–186; Tims, Maria, Derks, Daantjie, and Arnold B. Bakker. "Job Crafting and Its Relationship with Person-Job Fit and Meaningfulness: A Three-Wave Study." *Journal of Vocational Behavior* 92 (2016): 44–53.

41. Weick, Karl E. *Sensemaking in Organizations,* vol. 3. Thousand Oaks, CA: Sage, 1995.

42. Dulebohn, James H., William H. Bommer, Robert C. Liden, Robyn L. Brouer, and Gerald R. Ferris. "A Meta-Analysis of Antecedents and Consequences of

Leader-Member Exchange: Integrating the Past with an Eye toward the Future." *Journal of Management* 38 (2012): 1715–1759.

43. Dulebohn et al. (2012).

44. Graen, George B., and Mary Uhl-Bien. "Relationship-Based Approach to Leadership: Development of Leader-Member Exchange (LMX) Theory of Leadership over 25 Years: Applying a Multi-Level Multi-Domain Perspective." *Leadership Quarterly* 6 (1995): 219–247.

45. Liden, Robert C., Berrin Erdogan, Sandy J. Wayne, and Raymond T. Sparrowe. "Leader-Member Exchange, Differentiation, and Task Interdependence: Implications for Individual and Group Performance." *Journal of Organizational Behavior* 27 (2006): 723–746.

46. Harris, T. Brad, Ning Li, and Bradley L. Kirkman. "Leader–Member Exchange (LMX) in Context: How LMX Differentiation and LMX Relational Separation Attenuate LMX's Influence on OCB and Turnover Intention." *Leadership Quarterly* 25 (2014): 314–328.

47. Hooper, Danica T., and Robin Martin. "Beyond Personal Leader–Member Exchange (LMX) Quality: The Effects of Perceived LMX Variability on Employee Reactions." *Leadership Quarterly* 19 (2008): 20–30.

48. Huang, Xu, Robert P. Wright, Warren C. K. Chiu, and Chao Wang. "Relational Schemas as Sources of Evaluation and Misevaluation of Leader–Member Exchanges: Some Initial Evidence." *Leadership Quarterly* 19 (2008): 266–282.

49. Mortensen, Mark, Anita Williams Woolley, and Michael O'Leary. "Conditions Enabling Effective Multiple Team Membership," In *Virtuality and Virtualization*, edited by Kevin Crowston, Sandra Sieber, and Eleanor Wynn, 215–228. Boston: Springer, 2007.

50. Erdogan, Berrin, and Talya N. Bauer. "Differentiated Leader-Member Exchanges: The Buffering Role of Justice Climate." *Journal of Applied Psychology* 95 (2010): 1104–1120.

51. Rogers, Robert. W. *Realizing the Promise of Performance Management.* Pittsburgh, PA: Development Dimensions International, 2004.

52. Olson, Elizabeth G. "Microsoft, GE, and the Futility of Ranking Employees." *Fortune*, November 18, 2013. http://fortune.com/2013/11/18/microsoft-ge-and-the-futility-of-ranking-employees/.

53. Aguinis, Herman. "The Best and the Rest: Revisiting the Norm of Normality of Individual Performance." *Personnel Psychology* 65 (2012): 79–119.

54. Olson (2013).

55. Kerr, Steven. "On the Folly of Rewarding A, While Hoping for B." *Academy of Management Journal* 18 (1975): 769–783.

56. Nisen, Max. "How Millennials Forced GE to Scrap Performance Reviews." *Atlantic*, August 18, 2015. http://www.theatlantic.com/politics/archive/2015/08/how-millennials-forced-ge-to-scrap-performance-reviews/432585/.

57. Welbourne, Teresa M., Diane E. Johnson, and Amir Erez. "The Role-Based Performance Scale: Validity and Analysis of a Theory-Based Measure." *Academy of Management Journal* 41 (1998): 540–555.

58. King, Jr., Ralph T. "Jeans Therapy: Levi's Factory Workers Are Assigned to Teams and Morale Takes a Hit—Infighting Rises, Productivity Falls as Employees Miss the Piecework System—It's Not the Same Company." *Wall Street Journal*, May 20, 1998, A1.

59. Li, Ning, Xiaoming Zheng, T. Brad Harris, Xin Liu, and Bradley L. Kirkman. "Recognizing 'Me' Benefits 'We': Investigating the Positive Spillover Effects of Formal Individual Recognition in Teams." *Journal of Applied Psychology* 101 (2016): 925–939; Kirkman, Bradley L., Ning Li, Xiaoming Zheng, Brad Harris, and Xin Liu. "Teamwork Works Best When Top Performers Are Rewarded," *Harvard Business Review*, May 18, 2016, https://hbr.org/2016/03/teamwork-works-best-when-top-performers-are-rewarded.

60. Kanfer, Ruth, and Gilad Chen. "Motivation in Organizational Behavior: History, Advances, and Prospects." *Organizational Behavior and Human Decision Processes* 136 (2016): 6–19.

61. Moran, Gwen. "The Pros and Cons of Peer Review," *Entrepreneur*, January 16, 2013. https://www.entrepreneur.com/article/225518; Saavedra, Richard, and Seog K. Kwun. "Peer Evaluation in Self-Managing Teams." *Journal of Applied Psychology* 78 (1993): 450–462.

62. Banks, George C., John H. Batchelor, Anson Seers, Ernest H. O'Boyle Jr., Jeffrey M. Pollack, and Kim Gower. "What Does Team-Member Exchange Bring to the Party? A Meta-Analytic Review of Team and Leader Social Exchange." *Journal of Organizational Behavior* 35 (2014): 273–295.

63. Weick (1995).

64. Ancona, Deborah G. "Outward Bound: Strategies for Team Survival in an Organization." *Academy of Management Journal* 33 (1990): 334–365; Ancona, Deborah G., and David F. Caldwell. "Bridging the Boundary: External Activity and Performance in Organizational Teams." *Administrative Science Quarterly* 37 (1992): 634–665; Marrone, Jennifer A. "Team Boundary Spanning: A Multilevel Review of Past Research and Proposals for the Future." *Journal of Management* 36 (2010): 911–940.

65. Hambrick, Donald C. "Environmental Scanning and Organizational Strategy." *Strategic Management Journal* 3 (1982): 159–174.

66. Walker, Alan G., and James W. Smither. "A Five-Year Study of Upward Feedback: What Managers Do with Their Results Matters." *Personnel Psychology* 52 (1999): 393–423.

Chapter 4

1. Michaelsen, Larry K., Warren E. Watson, and Robert H. Black. "A Realistic Test of Individual versus Group Consensus Decision Making." *Journal of Applied Psychology* 74 (1989): 834–839.

2. Hackman, J. R. "The Design of Work Teams." In *Handbook of Organizational Behavior*, edited by Jay W. Lorsch, 315–342. Englewood Cliffs, NJ: Prentice-Hall, 1987; Michaelsen et al. (1989).

3. Coutu, Diane, "Why Teams Don't Work" (an Interview with Richard Hackman)." *Harvard Business Review* 87, no. 5 (2009): 98–105.

4. Marks, Michelle A., John E. Mathieu, and Stephen J. Zaccaro. "A Temporally-Based Framework and Taxonomy of Team Processes." *Academy of Management Review* 26 (2001): 356–376.

5. Marks et al. (2001).

6. Marks et al. (2001).

7. Morgeson, Frederick P., D. Scott DeRue, and Elizabeth P. Karam. "Leadership in Teams: A Functional Approach to Understanding Leadership Structures and Processes." *Journal of Management* 36 (2010): 5–39.

8. Mathieu, John E., John R. Hollenbeck, Daan van Knippenberg, and Daniel R. Ilgen. "A Century of Work Teams in the *Journal of Applied Psychology*." *Journal of Applied Psychology* 102 (2017): 452–467..

9. Gersick, Connie J. G., and J. Richard Hackman. "Habitual Routines in Task-Performing Groups." *Organizational Behavior and Human Decision Processes* 47 (1990): 65–97; Zijlstra, Fred R. H., Mary J. Waller, and Sybil I. Phillips. "Setting the Tone: Early Interaction Patterns in Swift-Starting Teams as a Predictor of Effectiveness." *European Journal of Work and Organizational Psychology* 21 (2012): 749–777.

10. Feldman, Daniel C. "The Development and Enforcement of Group Norms." *Academy of Management Review* 9 (1984): 47–53.

11. Smith-Jentsch, Kimberly A., Gwendolyn E. Campbell, Dana M. Milanovich, and Angelique M. Reynolds. "Measuring Teamwork Mental Models to Support Training Needs Assessment, Development, and Evaluation: Two Empirical Studies." *Journal of Organizational Behavior* 22 (2001): 179–194; Mathieu, John E., Tonia S. Heffner, Gerald F. Goodwin, Eduardo Salas, and Janis A. Cannon-Bowers. "The Influence of Shared Mental Models on Team Process and Performance." *Journal of Applied Psychology* 85 (2000): 273–283; Mohammed, Susan, Lori Ferzandi, and Katherine Hamilton. "Metaphor No More: A 15-Year Review of the Team Mental Model Construct." *Journal of Management* 36 (2010): 876–910.

12. Marks, Michelle A., Stephen J. Zaccaro, and John E. Mathieu. "Performance Implications of Leader Briefings and Team-Interaction Training for Team Adaptation to Novel Environments." *Journal of Applied Psychology* 85 (2000): 971–986; Smith-Jentsch, Kimberly A., Janis A. Cannon-Bowers, Scott I. Tannenbaum, and Eduardo Salas. "Guided Team Self-Correction Impacts on Team Mental Models, Processes, and Effectiveness." *Small Group Research* 39 (2008): 303–327.

13. Gurtner, Andrea, Franziska Tschan, Norbert K. Semmer, and Christof Nägele. "Getting Groups to Develop Good Strategies: Effects of Reflexivity Interventions on Team Process, Team Performance, and Shared Mental Models." *Organizational Behavior and Human Decision Processes* 102 (2007): 127–142.

14. Kirkman, Bradley L., and Benson Rosen. "Beyond Self-Management: The Antecedents and Consequences of Team Empowerment." *Academy of Management Journal* 42 (1999): 58–74.

15. Kirkman and Rosen (1999).

16. Kirkman and Rosen (1999).

17. Kirkman and Rosen (1999).

18. Kirkman, Bradley L., and Benson Rosen. "Powering Up Teams." *Organizational Dynamics* 28 (2000): 48–66.

19. Kirkman and Rosen (1999).

20. Maynard, M. Travis, John E. Mathieu, Lucy L. Gilson, Ernest H. O'Boyle, and Konstantin P. Cigularov. "Drivers and Outcomes of Team Psychological Empowerment: A Meta-Analytic Review and Model Test." *Organizational Psychology Review* 3 (2013): 101–137; Seibert, Scott E., Gang Wang, and Stephen H. Courtright. "Antecedents and Consequences of Psychological and Team Empowerment in Organizations: A Meta-Analytic Review." *Journal of Applied Psychology* 96 (2011): 981–1003.

21. Maynard et al. (2013).

22. Stewart, Gregory L. "A Meta-Analytic Review of Relationships between Team Design Features and Team Performance." *Journal of Management* 32 (2006): 29–54.

23. Chen, Gilad, Bradley L. Kirkman, Ruth Kanfer, Donald Allen, and Benson Rosen. "A Multilevel Study of Leadership, Empowerment, and Performance in Teams." *Journal of Applied Psychology* 92 (2007): 331–346.

24. D'Innocenzo, Lauren, Margaret M. Luciano, John E. Mathieu, M. Travis Maynard, and Gilad Chen. "Empowered to Perform: A Multilevel Investigation of the Influence of Empowerment on Performance in Hospital Units." *Academy of Management Journal* 59 (2016): 1290–1307.

25. Cummings, Larry L., and Philip Bromiley. "The Organizational Trust Inventory (OTI): Development and Validation." In *Trust in Organizations: Frontiers of Theory and Research*, edited by Roderick M. Kramer and Thomas R. Tyler, 302–330. Thousand Oaks, CA: Sage, 1996.

26. Edmondson, Amy C. "Psychological Safety and Learning Behavior in Work Teams." *Administrative Science Quarterly* 44 (1999): 350–383.

27. Pelled, L. H., Kathleen M. Eisenhardt, and Katherine R. Xin. "Exploring the Black Box: An Analysis of Work Group Diversity, Conflict, and Performance." *Administrative Science Quarterly* 44 (1999): 1–28.

28. De Dreu, Carsten K. W., and Laurie R. Weingart. "Task versus Relationship Conflict, Team Performance, and Team Member Satisfaction: A Meta-Analysis." *Journal of Applied Psychology* 88 (2003): 741–749.

29. Homan, Astrid C., John R. Hollenbeck, Stephen E. Humphrey, Daan van Knippenberg, Daniel R. Ilgen, and Gerben A. Van Kleef. "Facing Differences with an Open Mind: Openness to Experience, Salience of Intragroup Differences, and Performance of Diverse Work Groups." *Academy of Management Journal* 51 (2008): 1204–1222; van Knippenberg, Daan, Carsten K. W. De Dreu, and Astrid C. Homan. "Group Diversity and Group Performance: An Integrative Model and Research Agenda." *Journal of Applied Psychology* 89 (2004): 1008–1022; van Knippenberg, Daan, and Julija Mell. "Past, Present, and Potential Future of Team Diversity Research: From Compositional Diversity to Emergent Diversity." *Organizational Behavior and Human Decision Processes* 136 (2016): 135–145.

30. De Jong, Bart A., Kurt T. Dirks, and Nicole Gillespie. "Trust and Team Performance: A Meta-Analysis of Main Effects, Moderators, and Covariates." *Journal of Applied Psychology* 101 (2016): 1134–1150.

31. Edmondson, Amy C. *Teaming: How Organizations Learn, Innovate, and Compete in the Knowledge Economy.* San Francisco: Jossey-Bass, 2012; Frazier, M. Lance, Stav Fainschmidt, Ryan L. Klinger, Amir Pezeshkan, and Veselina Vracheva. "Psychological Safety: A Meta-Analytic Review and Extension." *Personnel Psychology* 70 (2017): 113–165; Sanner, Bret and J. Stuart Bunderson. "When Feeling Safe Isn't Enough: Contextualizing Models of Safety and Learning in Teams." *Organizational Psychology Review* 5 (2015): 224–243.

32. Mortensen, Mark, Anita Williams Woolley, and Michael O'Leary. "Conditions Enabling Effective Multiple Team Membership." In *Virtuality and Virtualization*, edited by Kevin Crowston, Sandra Sieber, and Eleanor Wynn, 215–228. Boston: Springer, 2007.

33. Gigone, Daniel, and Reid Hastie. "The Common Knowledge Effect: Information Sharing and Group Judgment." *Journal of Personality and Social Psychology* 65 (1993): 959–974.

34. Stasser, Garold, and Dennis Stewart. "Discovery of Hidden Profiles by Decision-Making Groups: Solving a Problem versus Making a Judgment." *Journal of Personality and Social Psychology* 63 (1992): 426–434.

35. McAllister, Daniel J. "Affect- and Cognition-Based Trust as Foundations for Interpersonal Cooperation in Organizations." *Academy of Management Journal* 38 (1995): 24–59.

36. Kirkman, Bradley L., Benson Rosen, Cristina B. Gibson, Paul E. Tesluk, and Simon O. McPherson. "Five Challenges to Virtual Team Success: Lessons from Sabre, Inc." *Academy of Management Executive* 16 (2002): 67–79.

37. Kirkman et al. (2002).

38. Rachel Mendelowitz. "For Leaders, Soft Is the New Strong (McChrystal Group Report)." *Medium*, April 25, 2016. https://medium.com@mccrystalgroup/for-leaders-soft-is-the-new-strong-2a38910eac97#.8jz0y36se

39. Edmondson (2012); Edmondson, Amy C., Richard M. Bohmer, and Gary Pisano. "Disrupted Routines: Team Learning and New Technology Adaptation." *Administrative Science Quarterly* 46 (2001): 685–716.

40. Mathieu, John E., and Tammy L. Rapp. "Laying the Foundation for Successful Team Performance Trajectories: The Roles of Team Charters and Performance Strategies." *Journal of Applied Psychology* 94 (2009): 90–103.

41. Edmondson (2012).

42. Sharma, Payal, and Bradley L. Kirkman. "Leveraging Leaders: A Literature Review and Future Lines of Inquiry for Empowering Leadership Research." *Group and Organization Management* 40 (2015): 193–237.

43. Rapp, Tammy L., Lucy L. Gilson, John E. Mathieu, and Thomas Ruddy. "Leading Empowered Teams: An Examination of the Role of External Team Leaders and Team Coaches." *Leadership Quarterly* 27 (2016): 109–123.

44. Maynard et al. (2013); Seibert et al. (2011)

45. Hackman, Richard J. *Leading Teams: Setting the Stage for Great Performances.* Boston: Harvard Business School Press, 2002; Wageman, Ruth. "How Leaders Foster Self-Managing Team Effectiveness: Design Choices versus Hands-On Coaching." *Organization Science* 12 (2001): 559–577.

46. Campbell, David. *If You Don't Know Where You're Going, You'll Probably End Up Somewhere Else.* Allen, TX: Thomas More, 1974.

47. Brandon, David P., and Andrea B. Hollingshead. "Transactive Memory Systems in Organizations: Matching Tasks, Expertise, and People." *Organization Science* 15 (2004): 633–644; Wegner, Daniel M. "Transactive Memory: A Contemporary Analysis of the Group Mind," In *Theories of Group Behavior,* edited by Brian Mullen and George R. Goethals, 185–208. New York: Springer-Verlag, 1987.

48. Austin, John R. "Transactive Memory in Organizational Groups: The Effects of Content, Consensus, Specialization, and Accuracy on Group Performance." *Journal of Applied Psychology* 88 (2003): 866–878.

49. Brandon and Hollingshead (2004); Majchrzak, Ann, Sirkka L. Jarvenpaa, and Andrea B. Hollingshead. "Coordinating Expertise among Emergent Groups Responding to Disasters." *Organization Science* 18 (2007): 147–161; Woolley, Anita Williams, Margaret E. Gerbasi, Christopher F. Chabris, Stephen M. Kosslyn, and J. Richard Hackman. "Bringing In the Experts: How Team Composition and Collaborative Planning Jointly Shape Analytic Effectiveness." *Small Group Research* 39 (2008): 352–371.

50. Mortensen et al. (2007).

51. Wood, Robert E., Anthony J. Mento, and Edwin A. Locke. "Task Complexity as a Moderator of Goal Effects: A Meta-Analysis." *Journal of Applied Psychology* 72 (1987): 416–425.

52. Heckhausen, Heinz. *Motivation in Action.* Berlin: Springer-Verlag, 1991; Kanfer, Ruth, Michael Frese, and Russell E. Johnson. "Motivation Related to Work: A Century of Progress." *Journal of Applied Psychology* 102 (2017): 338–355.

53. Michaelsen, Larry K., Warren E. Watson, and Robert H. Black. "A Realistic Test of Individual versus Group Consensus Decision Making." *Journal of Applied Psychology* 74 (1989): 834–839.

54. McChrystal, Stanley. *Team of Teams: New Rules of Engagement for a Complex World.* New York: Penguin, 2015.

55. Seibert et al. (2011).

56. Maynard et al. (2013).

57. Bass, Bernard M., David A. Waldman, Bruce J. Avolio, and Michael Bebb. "Transformational Leadership and the Falling Dominoes Effect." *Group and Organization Management,* 12 (1987): 73–87.

58. van Knippenberg, Daan, and Sim B. Sitkin. "A Critical Assessment of Charismatic-Transformational Leadership Research: Back to the Drawing Board?" *Academy of Management Annals* 7 (2013): 1–60.

59. Bass, Bernard M. *Leadership and Performance beyond Expectations.* New York: Free Press, 1985.

60. Judge, Timothy A., and Ronald F. Piccolo. "Transformational and Transactional Leadership: A Meta-Analytic Test of Their Relative Validity." *Journal of Applied Psychology* 89 (2004): 755–768; Lowe, Kevin B., K. Galen Kroeck, and Nagaraj Sivasubramaniam. "Effectiveness Correlates of Transformational and Transactional Leadership: A Meta-Analytic Review of the MLQ Literature." *Leadership Quarterly* 7 (1996): 385–415.

61. Wu, Joshua B., Anne S. Tsui, and Angelo J. Kinicki. "Consequences of Differentiated Leadership in Groups." *Academy of Management Journal* 53 (2010): 90–106.

62. Conroy, Samantha A., and Nina Gupta. "Team Pay-For-Performance: The Devil is in the Details." *Group and Organization Management* 41 (2016): 32–65.

63. Garbers, Yvonne, and Udo Konradt. "The Effect of Financial Incentives on Performance: A Quantitative Review of Individual and Team-Based Financial Incentives." *Journal of Occupational and Organizational Psychology* 87 (2014): 102–137.

64. Conroy and Gupta (2016)

65. Pearsall, Matthew J., Michael S. Christian, and Aleksander P. J. Ellis. "Motivating Interdependent Teams: Individual Rewards, Shared Rewards, or Something in Between?" *Journal of Applied Psychology* 95 (2010): 183–191.

66. Wageman, Ruth. "Interdependence and Group Effectiveness." *Administrative Science Quarterly* 40 (1995): 145–180.

67. Wageman (1995, 175).

68. Kirkman, Bradley L., and Debra L. Shapiro. "Understanding Why Team Members Won't Share: An Examination of Factors Affecting Employee Receptivity to Team-Based Rewards." *Small Group Research* 31 (2000): 175–209.

69. Kirkman and Rosen (1999).

70. Erez, Amir, Jeffrey A. LePine, and Heather Elms. "Effects of Rotated Leadership and Peer Evaluations on the Functioning and Effectiveness of Self-Managed Teams: A Quasi-Experiment." *Personnel Psychology* 55 (2002): 929–948.

Chapter 5

1. Lau, Dora C., and J. Keith Murnighan. "Demographic Diversity and Faultlines: The Compositional Dynamics of Organizational Groups." *Academy of Management Review* 23 (1998): 325–340.

2 Mathieu, John E., John R. Hollenbeck, Daan van Knippenberg, and Daniel R. Ilgen. "A Century of Work Teams in the *Journal of Applied Psychology.*" *Journal of Applied Psychology* 102 (2017): 452–467.

3. Gibson, Cristina B., and Jennifer L. Gibbs. "Unpacking the Concept of Virtuality: The Effects of Geographic Dispersion, Electronic Dependence, Dynamic Structure, and National Diversity on Team Innovation." *Administrative Science Quarterly* 51 (2006): 451–495.

4. Katzenbach, Jon R., and Douglas K. Smith. *The Wisdom of Teams: Creating the High-Performance Organization.* Boston: Harvard Business School Press, 1993.

5. Gibson, Cristina B., and Freek Vermeulen. "A Healthy Divide: Subgroups as a Stimulus for Team Learning Behavior." *Administrative Science Quarterly* 48 (2003): 202–239.

6. Mathieu, John E., Michelle A. Marks, and Stephen J. Zaccaro. "Multi-Team Systems." In *International Handbook of Work and Organizational Psychology*, vol. 1, *Personnel Psychology*, edited by Neal Anderson, Deniz Ones, Handan K. Sinangil, and Chockalingam Viswesvaran, 290. London: Sage, 2001.

7. Mathieu et al. (2017)

8. Zaccaro, Stephen J., Michelle A. Marks, and Leslie A. DeChurch (eds.). *Multiteam Systems: An Organization Form for Dynamic and Complex Environments*. New York: Routledge, 2012.

9. Luciano, Margaret M., Leslie A. DeChurch, and John E. Mathieu. "Multiteam Systems: A Structural Framework and Meso-Theory of System Functioning," *Journal of Management* (2015): http://journals.sagepub.com/doi/abs/10.1177/0149206315601184.

10. Marks, Michelle A., Leslie A. DeChurch, John E. Mathieu, Frederick J. Panzer, and Alexander Alonso. "Teamwork in Multiteam Systems." *Journal of Applied Psychology* 90 (2005): 964–971.

11. Boswell, Wendy R., John B. Bingham, and Alexander J. S. Colvin. "Aligning Employees through 'Line of Sight.'" *Business Horizons* 49 (2006): 499–509.

12. De Vries, Thomas A., John R. Hollenbeck, Robert B. Davison, Frank Walter, and Gerben S. Van Der Vegt. "Managing Coordination in Multiteam Systems: Integrating Micro and Macro Perspectives." *Academy of Management Journal* 59 (2016): 1823–1844.

13. DeChurch, Leslie A., and Michelle A. Marks. "Leadership in Multiteam Systems." *Journal of Applied Psychology* 91 (2005): 311–329.

14. Marks, Michelle A., John E. Mathieu, and Stephen J. Zaccaro. "A Temporally Based Framework and Taxonomy of Team Processes." *Academy of Management Review* 26 (2001): 356–376.

15. Marks et al. (2001).

16. Ancona, Deborah. *X-Teams: How to Build Teams That Lead, Innovate, and Succeed*. Boston, MA: Harvard Business School Publishing, 2007; DeChurch, Leslie A., C. Shawn Burke, Marissa L. Shuffler, Rebecca Lyons, Daniel Doty, and Eduardo Salas. "A Historiometric Analysis of Leadership in Mission Critical Multiteam Environments." *Leadership Quarterly* 22 (2011): 152–169.

17. DeChurch et al. 2011).

18. DeChurch et al. (2011, 160).

19. DeChurch et al. (2011, 160).

20. DeChurch et al. (2011, 160).

21. DeChurch et al. (2011, 160).

22. DeChurch et al. (2011, 160).

23. De Vries et al. (2016).

24. Luciano et al. (in press).

25. Marrone, Jennifer. A., Paul E. Tesluk, and Jay B. Carson. "A Multilevel Investigation of Antecedents and Consequences of Team Member Boundary-Spanning Behavior." *Academy of Management Journal* 50 (2007): 1423–1440.

26. Ancona, Deborah G., and David F. Caldwell. "Bridging the Boundary: External Activity and Performance in Organizational Teams." *Administrative Science Quarterly* 37 (1992): 634–665.

27. Marks et al. (2005).

28. DeChurch et al. (2011, 160).

29. Mathieu et al. (2001, 300).

30. Luciano et al. (in press).

31. Mathieu et al. (2001, 302).

32. Mathieu, John E., Tonia S. Heffner, Gerald F. Goodwin, Eduardo Salas, and Janis A. Cannon-Bowers. "The Influence of Shared Mental Models on Team Process and Performance." *Journal of Applied Psychology* 85 (2000): 273–283.

33. Luciano et al. (in press).

34. Marks, Michelle A., Stephen J. Zaccaro, and John E. Mathieu. "Performance Implications of Leader Briefings and Team-Interaction Training for Team Adaptation to Novel Environments." *Journal of Applied Psychology* 85 (2000): 971–986.

35. Cannon-Bowers, Janis A., Eduardo Salas, and Sharolyn Converse. "Shared Mental Models in Expert Team Decision Making." In *Individual and Group Decision Making: Current Issues*, edited by N. John Castellan Jr., 221–246. Hillsdale, NJ: Erlbaum, 1993.

36. Cannon-Bowers et al. (1993).

37. Cannon-Bowers et al. (1993).

38. Marks et al. (2000).

39. Mathieu et al. (2001, 309).

40. Kanfer, Ruth, Michael Frese, and Russell E. Johnson. "Motivation Related to Work: A Century of Progress." *Journal of Applied Psychology* 102 (2017): 338–355; Wood, Robert E., Anthony J. Mento, and Edwin A. Locke. "Task Complexity as a Moderator of Goal Effects: A Meta-Analysis." *Journal of Applied Psychology* 72 (1987): 416–425.

41. Tajfel, Henri. "Social Psychology of Intergroup Relations." *Annual Review of Psychology* 33 (1982): 1–39; Tajfel, Henri, and John C. Turner. "The Social Identity of Intergroup Behavior." In *Psychology and Intergroup Relations*, edited by Stephen Worchel and William Austin, 7–24. Chicago: Nelson-Hall 1986.

42. Luciano et al. (in press).

43. Carton, Andrew M., and Jonathan N. Cummings. "A Theory of Subgroups in Work Teams." *Academy of Management Review* 37 (2012): 441–470; Carton, Andrew M., and Jonathan N. Cummings. "The Impact of Subgroup Type and Subgroup Configurational Properties on Work Team Performance." *Journal of Applied Psychology* 98 (2013): 732–758; Gibson and Vermeulen (2003).

44. Austin, John R. "Transactive Memory in Organizational Groups: The Effects of Content, Consensus, Specialization, and Accuracy on Group Performance." *Journal*

of Applied Psychology 88 (2003): 866–878; Brandon, David P., and Andrea B. Hollingshead. "Transactive Memory Systems in Organizations: Matching Tasks, Expertise, and People." *Organization Science* 15 (2004): 633–644.

45. Marks, Michelle. A., Mark J. Sabella, C. Shawn Burke, and Stephen J. Zaccaro. "The Impact of Cross-Training on Team Effectiveness." *Journal of Applied Psychology* 87 (2002): 3–13.

46. Marks et al. (2000).

47. Luciano et al. (in press).

48. Carton and Cummings (2012).

49. Sui, Yang, Hui Wang, Bradley L. Kirkman, and Ning Li. "Understanding the Curvilinear Relationships between LMX Differentiation and Team Coordination and Performance." *Personnel Psychology* 69 (2016): 559–597.

50. Van der Vegt, Gerben S., and J. Stuart Bunderson. "Learning and Performance in Multidisciplinary Teams: The Importance of Collective Team Identification." *Academy of Management Journal* 48 (2005): 532–547.

51. Van der Vegt and Bunderson (2005, 545).

Chapter 6

1. Mathieu, John E., John R. Hollenbeck, Daan van Knippenberg, and Daniel R. Ilgen. "A Century of Work Teams in the *Journal of Applied Psychology*." *Journal of Applied Psychology* 102 (2017): 452–467; Mathieu, John, M. Travis Maynard, Tammy Rapp, and Lucy Gilson. "Team Effectiveness 1997–2007: A Review of Recent Advancements and a Glimpse into the Future." *Journal of Management* 34 (2008): 410–476.

2. Lindsley, Dana H., Daniel J. Brass, and James B. Thomas. "Efficacy-Performance Spirals: A Multilevel Perspective." *Academy of Management Review* 3 (1995): 645–678.

3. Saavedra, Richard, P. Christopher Earley, and Linn Van Dyne. "Complex Interdependence in Task-Performing Groups." *Journal of Applied Psychology* 78 (1993): 61–72; Thompson, James D. *Organizations in Action: Social Science Bases of Administrative Theory*. New Brunswick, NJ: Transaction, 1967.

4. Gully, Stanley M., Dennis J. Devine, and David J. Whitney. "A Meta-Analysis of Cohesion and Performance Effects of Level of Analysis and Task Interdependence." *Small Group Research* 26 (1995): 497–520; Liden, Robert C., Sandy J. Wayne, and Lisa K. Bradway. "Task Interdependence as a Moderator of the Relation between Group Control and Performance." *Human Relations* 50 (1997): 169–181.

5. Parker, Sharon K., Frederick P. Morgeson, and Gary Johns. "One Hundred Years of Work Design Research: Looking Back and Looking Forward." *Journal of Applied Psychology* 102 (2017): 403–420.

6. Huntford, Roland. *The Last Place on Earth*. New York: Modern Library, 1999.

7. Collins, Jim, and Morten T. Hansen. *Great by Choice*. New York: HarperCollins, 2011.

8. Huntford (1999): 150–151.

9. Bass, Bernard M. *The Bass Handbook of Leadership: Theory, Research, and Managerial Implications*, 4th ed. New York: Free Press, 2008.

10. Yukl, Gary, Angela Gordon, and Tom Taber. "A Hierarchical Taxonomy of Leadership Behavior: Integrating a Half Century of Behavior Research." *Journal of Leadership & Organizational Studies* 9 (2002): 15-32.

11. Judge, Timothy A., Ronald A. Piccolo, and Remus Ilies. "The Forgotten Ones? The Validity of Consideration and Initiating Structure in Leadership Research." *Journal of Applied Psychology* 89 (2004): 36-51.

12. Kim, Gene, Kevin Behr, and George Spafford. *The Phoenix Project: A Novel about IT, DevOps, and Helping Your Business Win*. Portland, OR: IT Revolution Press, 2013.

13. Cooper, Robert G. "Agile-Stage-Gate Hybrids: The Next Stage for Product Development." *Research-Technology Management* 59 (2016): 21-29.

14. Erdogan, Berrin, and Talya N. Bauer. "Differentiated Leader-Member Exchanges: The Buffering Role of Justice Climate." *Journal of Applied Psychology* 95 (2010): 1104–1120.

15. Seibert, Scott E., Gang Wang, and Stephen H. Courtright. "Antecedents and Consequences of Psychological and Team Empowerment in Organizations: A Meta-Analytic Review." *Journal of Applied Psychology* 96 (2011): 981–1003.

16. Banks, George, Krista N. Engerman, Courtney E. Williams, and Melissa R. Medaugh. "A Meta-Analytic Review and Future Research Agenda of Charismatic Leadership." *Leadership Quarterly* (in press).

Chapter 7

1. Javidan, Mansour, Peter W. Dorfman, Mary Sully de Luque, and Robert J. House. "In the Eye of the Beholder: Cross Cultural Lessons in Leadership from Project GLOBE." *Academy of Management Perspectives* 20 (2006): 67–90.

2. Kirkman, Bradley L., Cristina B. Gibson, and Debra L. Shapiro. "'Exporting' Teams: Enhancing the Implementation and Effectiveness of Work Teams in Global Affiliates." *Organizational Dynamics* 30 (2001): 12–29.

3. Gibson, Cristina B., and Mary Zellmer-Bruhn. "Metaphor and Meaning: An Intercultural Analysis of the Concept of Teamwork." *Administrative Science Quarterly* 46 (2001): 274–303.

4. Gibson and Zellmer-Bruhn (2001).

5. Nardon, Luciara, and Richard M. Steers. "The Culture Theory Jungle: Divergence and Convergence in Models of National Culture." In *Cambridge Handbook of Culture, Organizations, and Work*, edited by Rabi S. Bhagat and Richard M. Steers, 3–22. Cambridge: Cambridge University Press, 2009.

6. Hofstede, Geert. *Culture's Consequences: Comparing Values, Behaviors, Institutions, and Organizations across Nations*. Thousand Oaks, CA: Sage, 2001.

7. Javidan et al. (2006).

8. Kirkman, Bradley L., Kevin B. Lowe, and Cristina B. Gibson. "A Quarter Century of *Culture's Consequences*: A Review of Empirical Research Incorporating Hofstede's Cultural Values Framework." *Journal of International Business Studies* 37 (2006):

285–320; Kirkman, Bradley L., Kevin B. Lowe, and Cristina B. Gibson. "A Retrospective on *Culture's Consequences*: The 35-Year Journey." *Journal of International Business Studies* 48 (2017): 12–29.

9. Oyserman, Daphna, Heather M. Coon, and Markus Kemmelmeier. "Rethinking Individualism and Collectivism: Evaluation of Theoretical Assumptions and Meta-Analyses." *Psychological Bulletin* 128 (2002): 3–72.

10. Weinberg, Corey. "Why American B-School Students Can't Stand Teamwork." *Bloomberg BusinessWeek,* June 16, 2014. http://www.bloomberg.com/news/articles/2014–06–06/why-american-business-students-dislike-working-in-teams.

11. Earley, P. Christopher. "Social Loafing and Collectivism: A Comparison of the United States and the People's Republic of China." *Administrative Science Quarterly* 34 (1989): 565–581.

12. Kirkman, Bradley L., and Debra L. Shapiro. "Understanding Why Team Members Won't Share: An Examination of Factors Affecting Employee Receptivity to Team-Based Rewards." *Small Group Research* 31 (2000): 175–209.

13. Kirkman, Bradley L., and Debra L. Shapiro. "The Impact of Employee Cultural Values on Productivity, Cooperation, and Empowerment in Self-Managing Work Teams." *Journal of Cross-Cultural Psychology* 32 (2001a): 597–617.

14. Kirkman, Bradley L., and Debra L. Shapiro. "The Impact of Cultural Values on Job Satisfaction and Organizational Commitment in Self-Managing Work Teams: The Mediating Role of Employee Resistance." *Academy of Management Journal* 44 (2001b): 557–569.

15. Kirkman and Shapiro (2001b).

16. Kirkman et al. (2001).

17. http://www.aperianglobal.com/learning-solutions/online-learning-tools/globesmart/.

18. Hofstede (2001).

19. Taras, Vas, Piers Steel, and Bradley L. Kirkman. "Improving National Cultural Indices Using a Longitudinal Meta-Analysis of Hofstede's Dimensions." *Journal of World Business* 47 (2012): 329–341.

20. Taras, Vas, Bradley L. Kirkman, and Piers Steel. "Examining the Impact of *Culture's Consequences*: A Three-Decade, Multi-Level, Meta-Analytic Review of Hofstede's Cultural Value Dimension." *Journal of Applied Psychology* 95 (2010): 405–439.

21. Gelfand, Michele J., Lisa H. Nishii, and Jana L. Raver. "On the Nature and Importance of Cultural Tightness-Looseness." *Journal of Applied Psychology* 91 (2006): 1226.

22. Gelfand, Michele J., et al. "Differences between Tight and Loose Cultures: A 33-Nation Study." *Science* 332 (2011): 1100.

23. Szkudlarek, Betina, Jeanne McNett, Laurence Romani, and Henry Lane. "The Past, Present, and Future of Cross-Cultural Management Education: The Educators' Perspective." *Academy of Management Learning and Education* 12 (2013): 477–493.

24. Hofstede (2001).

25. Friedman, Thomas L. *The World Is Flat: A Brief History of the Twenty-First Century*. New York: Farrar, Straus, and Giroux, 2005.

26. Taras, Vas, Piers Steel, and Bradley L. Kirkman. "Is the World Really Flat (or Flattening)? A Meta-Analytic Test of National Cultural Convergence and Modernization Theories." Paper presented at the annual Academy of International Business Southeast USA conference, Miami, FL, October 23–25, 2014.

27. Inglehart, Ronald, and Christian Welzel. "Changing Mass Priorities: The Link between Modernization and Democracy." *Perspectives on Politics* 8 (2010): 551–567.

28 Crair, Ben. "Maniac Killers of the Bangalore IT Department: Why Is India Obsessed with Crimes Committed by Software Engineers?" *BloombergBusinessweek*, February 15, 2017. https://www.bloomberg.com/news/features/2017-02-15/maniac-killers-of-the-bangalore-it-department.

29. Rein, Shaun. *The End of Copycat China: The Rise of Creativity, Innovation, and Individualism in Asia* (Hoboken, NJ: Wiley, 2014).

30. Ralston, David A., Carolyn P. Egri, Sally Stewart, Robert H. Terpstra, and Yu Kaicheng. "Doing Business in the 21st Century with the New Generation of Chinese Managers: A Study of Generational Shifts in Work Values in China." *Journal of International Business Studies* 30 (1999): 415–428.

31. Sima, Yangzi, and Peter C. Pugsley. "The Rise of a 'Me Culture' in Postsocialist China: Youth, Individualism and Identity Creation in the Blogosphere." *International Communication Gazette* 72 (2010): 287–306.

32. Li, Ning, Xiaoming Zheng, T. Brad Harris, Xin Liu, and Bradley L. Kirkman. "Recognizing 'Me' Benefits 'We': Investigating the Positive Spillover Effects of Formal Individual Recognition in Teams." *Journal of Applied Psychology* 101 (2016): 925–939.

33. Ralston et al. (1999).

34. Grant, Adam. "Goodbye to the MBTI, the Fad That Won't Die." *Psychology Today*, September 18, 2013.

35. Kirkman and Shapiro (2001).

36. Hofstede (2001).

37. Taras, Vas, Piers Steel, and Bradley L. Kirkman. "Does Country Equal Culture? Beyond Geography in the Search for Cultural Entities." *Management International Review* 56 (2016): 455–487.

38. Osland, Joyce S., and Allan Bird. "Beyond Sophisticated Stereotyping: Cultural Sensemaking in Context." *Academy of Management Executive* 14 (2000): 65–77.

39. Osland and Bird (2000, 65).

40. Zhang, Xin-an, Ning Li, and T. Brad Harris. "Putting Non-Work Ties to Work: The Case of Guanxi in Supervisor–Subordinate Relationships." *Leadership Quarterly* 26 (2015): 37–54.

41. Kirkman, Bradley L., Gilad Chen, Jing-Li Farh, Zhen Xiong Chen, and Kevin B. Lowe. "Individual Power Distance Orientation and Follower Reactions to Transformational Leaders: A Cross-Level, Cross-Cultural Examination." *Academy of Management Journal* 52 (2009): 744–764. Kirkman, Bradley L., Debra L. Shapiro, Shuye

Lu, and Daniel P. McGurrin. "Culture and Teams." *Current Opinion in Psychology* 8 (2016): 137–142.

42. Neeley, Tsedal, and Thomas J. Delong. "Managing a Global Team: Greg James at Sun Microsystems, Inc. (A)." Case #9-409-003. Boston: Harvard Business School Publishing, 2009.

43. Stahl, Gunter K., Martha L. Maznevski, Andreas Voigt, and Karsten Jonsen. "Unraveling the Effects of Cultural Diversity in Teams: A Meta-Analysis of Research on Multicultural Work Groups." *Journal of International Business Studies* 41 (2010): 690–709.

44. Earley, P. Christopher, and Elaine Mosakowski "Creating Hybrid Team Cultures: An Empirical Test of Transnational Team Functioning." *Academy of Management Journal* 43 (2000): 26–49.

45. Kirkman, Bradley L., John L. Cordery, John E. Mathieu, Benson Rosen, and Michael Kukenberger. "Global Organizational Communities of Practice: The Effects of Nationality Diversity, Psychological Safety and Media Richness on Community Performance." *Human Relations* 66 (2013): 333–362.

46. Koch, Pamela Tremain, Bradley Koch, Tanya Menon, and Oded Shenkar. "Cultural Friction in Leadership Beliefs and Foreign-Invested Enterprise Survival." *Journal of International Business Studies* 47 (2016): 453–470.

47. Godart, Frederic C., William W. Maddux, Andrew V. Shipilov, and Adam D. Galinsky. "Fashion with a Foreign Flair: Professional Experiences Abroad Facilitate the Creative Innovations of Organizations." *Academy of Management Journal* 58 (2015): 195–220.

48. Earley, P. Christopher, and Elaine Mosakowski. "Cultural Intelligence." *Harvard Business Review* 82, no. 10 (2004): 140.

49. Chao, Melody M., Riki Takeuchi, and Jing-Lih Farh. "Enhancing Cultural Intelligence: The Roles of Implicit Culture Beliefs and Assumptions." *Personnel Psychology* 70 (2017): 257–292.

50. Earley and Mosakowski (2004).

51. McCall, Morgan M., and George P. Hollenbeck. *Developing Global Executives: The Lessons of International Experience.* Boston, MA: Harvard Business School Publishing, 2002.

52. Roberts, Brent W., Jing Luo, Daniel A. Briley, Philip I. Chow, Rong Su, and Patrick L. Hill. "A Systematic Review of Personality Trait Change Through Intervention." *Psychological Bulletin* 143 (2017): 117–141.

53. Kirkman et al. (2016).

Chapter 8

1. Dulebohn, James H., and Julia E. Hoch. "Virtual Teams in Organizations." *Human Resource Management Review* (2017): http://www.sciencedirect.com/science/article/pii/S1053482216300961; Gibson, Cristina B., Laura Huang, Bradley L. Kirkman, and Debra L. Shapiro. "Where Global and Virtual Meet: The Value of Examining

the Intersection of These Elements in Twenty-First Century Teams." *Annual Review of Organizational Psychology and Organizational Behavior* 1 (2014): 217–244.

2. Ivanaj, Sylvester, and Claire Bozon. *Managing Virtual Teams*. Cheltenham, UK: Elgar, 2016.

3. Neeley, Tsedal, and Thomas J. Delong. "Managing a Global Team: Greg James at Sun Microsystems, Inc. (A)," Case #9-409-003. Boston: Harvard Business School Publishing, 2009.

4. Haas, Martine, and Mark Mortensen. "The Secrets of Great Teamwork." *Harvard Business Review* 94, no. 6 (2016): 70-76.

5. Kirkman, Bradley L., Cristina B. Gibson, and Kwanghyun Kim. "Across Borders and Technologies: Advancements in Virtual Teams Research." In *Oxford Handbook of Industrial and Organizational Psychology*, vol. 1, edited by Stephen W. J. Kozlowski, 789–858. New York: Oxford University Press, 2012.

6. Blackburn, Richard S., Stacie A. Furst, and Benson Rosen. "Building a Winning Virtual Team." In *Virtual Teams That Work: Creating the Conditions for Virtual Team Effectiveness*, edited by Cristina B. Gibson and Susan G. Cohen, 95–120. San Francisco: Jossey-Bass, 2003.

7. Hardin, Andrew M., Mark A. Fuller, and Robert M. Davison. "I Know I Can, But Can We? Culture and Efficacy Beliefs in Global Virtual Teams." *Small Group Research* 38 (2007): 130–155.

8. Krumm, Stefan, Jens Kanthak, Kai Hartmann, and Guido Hertel. "What Does It Take to Be a Virtual Team Player? The Knowledge, Skills, Abilities, and Other Characteristics Required in Virtual Teams." *Human Performance* 29 (2016): 123–142.

9. Bell, Suzanne T., Anton J. Villado, Marc A. Lukasik, Larisa Belau, and Andrea L. Briggs. "Getting Specific about Demographic Diversity Variable and Team Performance Relationships: A Meta-Analysis." *Journal of Management* 37 (2011): 709–743; Horwitz, Sujin K., and Irwin B. Horwitz. "The Effects of Team Diversity on Team Outcomes: A Meta-Analytic Review of Team Demography." *Journal of Management* 33 (2007): 987–1015.

10. Cummings, Jonathon N., Sara Kiesler, Reza Bosagh Zadeh, and Aruna D. Balakrishnan. "Group Heterogeneity Increases the Risks of Large Group Size: A Longitudinal Study of Productivity in Research Groups." *Psychological Science* 24 (2013): 880–890.

11. Gilson, Lucy L., M. Travis Maynard, Nicole C. Jones Young, Matti Vartiainen, and Marko Hakonen. "Virtual Teams Research: 10 Years, 10 Themes, and 10 Opportunities." *Journal of Management* 41 (2015): 1313–1337; Ruggieri, Stefano. "Leadership in Virtual Teams: A Comparison of Transformational and Transactional Leaders." *Social Behavior and Personality* 37 (2009): 1017–1021.

12. Kirkman, Bradley L., Benson Rosen, B., Cristina B. Gibson, Paul E. Tesluk, and Simon O. McPherson. "Five Challenges to Virtual Team Success: Lessons from Sabre, Inc." *Academy of Management Executive* 16 (2002): 67–79.

13. Gajendran, Ravi S., and Aparna Joshi. "Innovation in Globally Distributed Teams: The Role of LMX, Communication Frequency, and Member Influence on Team Decisions." *Journal of Applied Psychology* 97 (2012): 1252–1261.

14. Bosch-Sijtsema, Petra. "The Impact of Individual Expectations and Expectation Conflict on Virtual Teams." *Group and Organization Management* 32 (2007): 358–388.

15. Walther, Joseph B., and Ulla Bunz. "The Rules of Virtual Groups: Trust, Liking, and Performance in Computer-Mediated Communication." *Journal of Communication* 55 (2005): 828–846.

16. Dineen, Brian R. "TeamXchange: A Team Project Experience Involving Virtual Teams and Fluid Team Membership." *Journal of Management Education* 29 (2005): 593–616.

17. Holtbrügge, Dirk, Katrin Schillo, Helen Rogers, and Carina Friedmann. "Managing and Training for Virtual Teams in India." *Team Performance Management* 17 (2011): 206–223.

18. Rosen, Benson, Stacie A. Furst, and Richard Blackburn. "Training for Virtual Teams: An Investigation of Current Practices and Future Needs." *Human Resource Management* 45 (2007): 229–247.

19. Kanawattanachai, Prasert, and Youngjin Yoo. "The Impact of Knowledge Coordination on Virtual Team Performance over Time." *MIS Quarterly* 31 (2007): 783–808.

20. Charlier, Steven D., Greg L. Stewart, Lindsey M. Greco, and Cody J. Reeves. "Emergent Leadership in Virtual Teams: A Multilevel Investigation of Individual Communication and Team Dispersion Antecedents." *Leadership Quarterly* 27 (2016): 745–764.

21. Gibson, Cristina B., Jennifer L. Gibbs, Taryn Stanko, Paul E. Tesluk, and Susan G. Cohen. "Including the 'I' in Virtuality and Modern Job Design: Extending the Job Characteristics Model to Include the Moderating Effect of Individual Experiences of Electronic Dependence and Co-Presence." *Organization Science* 22 (2011): 1481–1499.

22. Hoegl, Martin, and Miriam Muethel. "Enabling Shared Leadership in Virtual Project Teams: A Practitioner's Guide." *Project Management Journal* 47 (2016): 7–12.

23. Wageman, Ruth. "How Leaders Foster Self-Managing Team Effectiveness: Design Choices versus Hands-On Coaching." *Organization Science* 12 (2001): 559–577.

24. Martins, Luis L., Lucy L. Gilson, and M. Travis Maynard. "Virtual Teams: What Do We Know and Where Do We Go from Here?" *Journal of Management* 30 (2004): 805–835.

25. Quigley, Narda R., Paul E. Tesluk, Edwin A. Locke, and Kathryn M. Bartol. "A Multilevel Investigation of the Motivational Mechanisms Underlying Knowledge Sharing and Performance." *Organization Science* 18 (2007): 71–88.

26. Bryant, Stephanie M., Susan M. Albring, and Uday Murthy. "The Effects of Reward Structure, Media Richness and Gender on Virtual Teams." *International Journal of Accounting Information Systems* 10 (2009): 190–213.

27. Pepitone, Julianne. "Marissa Mayer: Yahoos Can No Longer Work From Home. *CNNMoney.com*, February 25, 2013. (http://money.cnn.com/2013/02/25/technology/yahoo-work-from-home/index.html)

28. Gajendran, Ravi S., and David A. Harrison. "The Good, the Bad, and the Unknown about Telecommuting: Meta-Analysis of Psychological Mediators and Individual Consequences." *Journal of Applied Psychology* 92 (2007): 1524–1541.

29. Whitelocks, Sadie. "'People are More Innovative When They're Together': Mayer Finally Addresses Unpopular Work-from-Home Ban." *DailyMail.com*, April 19, 2013. (http://www.dailymail.co.uk/femail/article-2311875/People-innovative-theyre-Yahoo-CEO-Marissa-Mayer-finally-addresses-unpopular-work-home-ban.html)

30. Gibson, Cristina B., and Jennifer L. Gibbs. "Unpacking the Concept of Virtuality: The Effects of Geographic Dispersion, Electronic Dependence, Dynamic Structure, and National Diversity on Team Innovation." *Administrative Science Quarterly* 51 (2006): 451–495.

31. Gibson and Gibbs (2006).

32. Cordery, John L., Christine Soo, Bradley L. Kirkman, Benson Rosen, and John E. Mathieu. "Leading Parallel Global Virtual Teams: Lessons from Alcoa." *Organizational Dynamics* 38 (2009): 204–216.

33. Kirkman, Bradley L., John L. Cordery, John E. Mathieu, Benson Rosen, and Michael Kukenberger. "Global Organizational Communities of Practice: The Effects of Nationality Diversity, Psychological Safety and Media Richness on Community Performance." *Human Relations* 66 (2013): 333–362.

34. Kirkman, Bradley L., Benson Rosen, Paul E. Tesluk, and Cristina B. Gibson. "The Impact of Team Empowerment on Virtual Team Performance: The Moderating Role of Face-to-Face Interaction." *Academy of Management Journal* 47 (2004): 175–192.

35. Hill, N. Sharon, and Kathryn M. Bartol. "Empowering Leadership and Effective Collaboration in Geographically Dispersed Teams." *Personnel Psychology* 69 (2016): 159–198.

36. Kirkman et al. (2006).

37. O'Hara-Devereaux, Mary, and Robert Johansen. *Global Work: Bridging Distance, Culture, and Time*. San Francisco: Jossey-Bass, 1994.

38. Kirkman et al. (2002).

39. Kirkman et al. (2006).

40. Kirkman et al. (2002).

41. Crisp, C. Brad, and Sirkka L. Jarvenpaa. "Swift Trust in Global Virtual Teams: Trusting Beliefs and Normative Actions." *Journal of Personnel Psychology* 12 (2013): 45–56.

42. Austin, John R. "Transactive Memory in Organizational Groups: The Effects of Content, Consensus, Specialization, and Accuracy on Group Performance." *Journal of Applied Psychology* 88 (2003): 866–878.

43. Mathieu, John E., and Tammy L. Rapp. "Laying the Foundation for Successful Team Performance Trajectories: The Roles of Team Charters and Performance Strategies." *Journal of Applied Psychology* 94 (2009): 90–103.

44. Marlow, Shannon L., Christina N. Lacerenza, and Eduardo Salas. "Communication in Virtual Teams: A Conceptual Framework and Research Agenda." *Human Resource Management Review* (2017): http://www.sciencedirect.com/science/article/pii/S1053482216300973.

45. Majchrzak, Ann, Arvind Malhotra, Jeffrey Stamps, and Jessica Lipnack. "Can Absence Make a Team Grow Stronger?" *Harvard Business Review* 82, no. 5 (2004): 131–137.

46. Matlack, Carol. "One Company Tries Life without (Much) E-Mail." *Bloomberg BusinessWeek*, October 8, 2015.

47. Kirkman et al. (2013).

48. Owen-Smith, Jason, Felichism Kabo, Margaret Levenstein, Richard Price, and Gerald Davis. "A Tale of Two Buildings: Socio-Spatial Significance of Innovation" (Technical Report). Ann Arbor: University of Michigan, 2012.

49. Harris, Michael S., and Karri Holley. "Constructing the Interdisciplinary Ivory Tower: The Planning of Interdisciplinary Spaces on University Campuses." *Planning for Higher Education* 36 (2008): 34–43.

50. Kirkman et al. (2002).

51. Majchrzak et al. (2004).

52. Neeley and Delong (2009).

53. Kirkman et al. (2013).

54. Earley, P. Christopher, and Elaine Mosakowski. "Creating Hybrid Team Cultures: An Empirical Test of Transnational Team Functioning." *Academy of Management Journal* 43 (2000): 26–49.

55. Newell, Sue, Donald Chand, and Gary David. "An Analysis of Trust among Globally Distributed Work Teams in an Organizational Setting." *Knowledge and Process Management* 14 (2007): 158–168; Polzer, Jeffrey T., C. Brad Crisp, Sirkka L. Jarvenpaa, and Jerry W. Kim. "Extending the Faultline Model to Geographically Dispersed Teams: How Colocated Subgroups Can Impair Group Functioning." *Academy of Management Journal* 49 (2006): 679–692.

56. O'Leary, Michael B., and Mark Mortensen. "Go (Con)figure: Subgroups, Imbalance, and Isolates in Geographically Dispersed Teams." *Organization Science* 21 (2010): 115–131.

57. Van der Vegt, Gerben S., and J. Stuart Bunderson. "Learning and Performance in Multidisciplinary Teams: The Importance of Collective Team Identification." *Academy of Management Journal* 48 (2005): 532–547.

Chapter 9

1. Kirkpatrick, Shelly A., and Edwin A. Locke. "Leadership: Do Traits Matter?" *Academy of Management Executive* 5 (1991): 48–60.

2. Roberts, Brent W., and Wendy F. DelVecchio. "The Rank-Order Consistency of Personality Traits from Childhood to Old Age: A Quantitative Review of Longitudinal Studies." *Psychological Bulletin* 126 (2000): 3–25; Roberts, Brent W., Kate E. Walton, and Wolfgang Viechtbauer. "Patterns of Mean-Level Change in Personality Traits across the Life Course: A Meta-Analysis of Longitudinal Studies." *Psychological Bulletin* 132 (2006): 1–25; Roberts, Brent W., Jing Luo, Daniel A. Briley, Philip I. Chow, Rong Su, and Patrick L. Hill. "A Systematic Review of Personality Trait Change through Intervention." *Psychological Bulletin* 143 (2017): 117–141.

3. Judge, Timothy A., Joyce E. Bono, Remus Ilies, and Megan W. Gerhardt. "Personality and Leadership: A Qualitative and Quantitative Review." *Journal of Applied Psychology* 87 (2002): 765–780.

4. Hogan, Robert, and Joyce Hogan. "Assessing Leadership: A View from the Dark Side." *International Journal of Selection and Assessment* 9 (2001): 40–51; Judge, Timothy A., Ronald F. Piccolo, and Tomek Kosalka. "The Bright and Dark Sides of Leader Traits: A Review and Theoretical Extension of the Leader Trait Paradigm." *Leadership Quarterly* 20 (2009): 855–875.

5. Hogan, Joyce, and Brent Holland. "Using Theory to Evaluate Personality and Job-Performance Relations: A Socioanalytic Perspective." *Journal of Applied Psychology* 88 (2003): 100–112.

6. Hogan, Robert, and Brent W. Roberts. "A Socioanalytic Model of Maturity." *Journal of Career Assessment* 12 (2004): 207–217; Roberts et al. (2006).

7. Judge, Timothy A., Amy E. Colbert, and Remus Ilies. "Intelligence and Leadership: A Quantitative Review and Test of Theoretical Propositions." *Journal of Applied Psychology* 89 (2004): 542–552.

8. Rubenzer, Steven J., and Thomas R. Faschingbauer. *Personality, Character, and Leadership in the White House: Psychologists Assess the Presidents.* Lincoln, NE: Potomac Books, 2004.

9. Eagly, Alice H., and Blair T. Johnson. "Gender and Leadership Styles: A Meta-Analysis." *Psychological Bulletin* 108 (1990): 233–256.

10. Judge, Timothy A., and Daniel M. Cable. "The Effect of Physical Height on Workplace Success and Income: Preliminary Test of a Theoretical Model." *Journal of Applied Psychology* 89 (2004): 428–441.

11. Epitropaki, Olga, and Robin Martin. "Implicit Leadership Theories in Applied Settings: Factor Structure, Generalizability, and Stability over Time." *Journal of Applied Psychology* 89 (2004): 293–310; Kenney, Robert A., Beth M. Schwartz-Kenney, and Jim Blascovich. "Implicit Leadership Theories: Defining Leaders Described as Worthy of Influence." *Personality and Social Psychology Bulletin* 22 (1996): 1128–1143.

12. Van Vugt, Mark. "Evolutionary Origins of Leadership and Followership." *Personality and Social Psychology Review* 10 (2006): 354–371.

13. Kaiser, Robert B., and Darren V. Overfield. "Assessing Flexible Leadership as a Mastery of Opposites." *Consulting Psychology Journal: Practice and Research* 62 (2010): 105–118; Yukl, Gary, and Rubina Mahsud. "Why Flexible and Adaptive Leadership Is Essential." *Consulting Psychology Journal: Practice and Research* 62 (2010): 81–93; Zaccaro, Stephen J., Roseanne J. Foti, and David A. Kenny. "Self-Monitoring and Trait-Based Variance in Leadership: An Investigation of Leader Flexibility across Multiple Group Situations." *Journal of Applied Psychology* 76 (1991): 308–315.

14. Harris, T. Brad. "The Functionality of Focus: An Investigation into the Interactive Effects of Leader Focus and Task Interdependence." PhD diss., Texas A&M University, 2012.

15. Jones, Renae A., Alannah E. Rafferty, and Mark A. Griffin. "The Executive Coaching Trend: Towards More Flexible Executives." *Leadership and Organization Development Journal* 27 (2006): 584–596.

16. London, Manuel, and James W. Smither. "Can Multi-Source Feedback Change Perceptions of Goal Accomplishment, Self-Evaluations, and Performance-Related Outcomes? Theory-Based Applications and Directions for Research." *Personnel Psychology* 48 (1995): 803–839.

17. Good, Darren J. "Explorations of Cognitive Agility: A Real Time Adaptive Capacity." PhD diss., Case Western Reserve University, 2009.

18. Yukl and Mahsud (2010).

19. Snyder, Mark. "Self-Monitoring of Expressive Behavior." *Journal of Personality and Social Psychology* 30 (1974): 526–537.

20. Fuglestad, Paul T., and Mark Snyder. "Status and the Motivational Foundations of Self-Monitoring." *Social and Personality Psychology Compass* 4 (2010): 1031–1041.

21. Bedeian, Arthur G., and David V. Day. "Can Chameleons Lead?" *Leadership Quarterly* 15 (2004): 687–718.

22. Goffee, Rob, and Gareth Jones. "Managing Authenticity: The Paradox of Great Leadership." *Harvard Business Review* 83, no.12 (2005): 85–94.

23. Eby, Lillian. T., Jailza Cader, and Carrie L. Noble "Why Do High Self-Monitors Emerge as Leaders in Small Groups? A Comparative Analysis of the Behaviors of High versus Low Self-Monitors." *Journal of Applied Social Psychology* 33 (2003): 1457–1479.

24. Heath, Chip, and Dan Heath. *Switch: How to Change Things When Change Is Hard.* New York: Broadway Books, 2010.

25. Rosing, Kathrin, Michael Frese, and Andreas Bausch. "Explaining the Heterogeneity of the Leadership-Innovation Relationship: Ambidextrous Leadership." *Leadership Quarterly* 22 (2011): 956–974.

26. Rosing et al. (2011, 957).

27. Rosing et al. (2011, 969).

28. Hooijberg, Robert. "A Multidirectional Approach toward Leadership: An Extension of the Concept of Behavioral Complexity." *Human Relations* 49 (1996): 917–946.

29. Zaccaro, Stephen J., Janelle A. Gilbert, J., Kirk K. Thor, and Michael D. Mumford. "Leadership and Social Intelligence: Linking Social Perceptiveness and Behavioral Flexibility to Leader Effectiveness." *Leadership Quarterly* 2 (1991): 317–331.

30. Goleman, Daniel. *Emotional Intelligence: Why It Can Matter More Than IQ.* New York: Bantam Books, 2006.

31. Joseph, Dana L., and Daniel A. Newman. "Emotional Intelligence: An Integrative Meta-Analysis and Cascading Model." *Journal of Applied Psychology* 95 (2010): 54–78.

32. Law, Kenneth S., Chi-Sum Wong, and Lynda J. Song. "The Construct and Criterion Validity of Emotional Intelligence and Its Potential Utility for Management Studies." *Journal of Applied Psychology* 89 (2004): 483–496.

33. Chamorro-Premuzic, Tomas. "Can You Really Improve Your Emotional Intelligence?" *Harvard Business Review*, May 29, 2013. https://hbr.org/2013/05/can-you-really-improve-your-em

34. Chamorro-Premuzic (2013).

35. Chamorro-Premuzic (2013).

36. Goffee, Robert, and Gareth Jones. "Why Should Anyone Be Led by You?" *Harvard Business Review* 78, no. 5 (2000): 62–70; Goffee, Robert, and Gareth Jones. *Why Should Anyone Be Led by You?* Boston: Harvard Business School Publishing, 2006.

37. Goffee and Jones (2006).

38. George, Bill. *Authentic Leadership: Rediscovering the Secrets to Creating Lasting Value.* San Francisco: Jossey-Bass, 2003; George, Bill, Peter Sims, Andrew N. McLean, and Diana Mayer. "Discovering Your Authentic Leadership." *Harvard Business Review* 85, no. 2 (2007): 129–138.

39. George et al. (2007).

40. Goffee and Jones (2000).

41. Goffee and Jones (2006).

Chapter 10

1. Original items created by the authors of this book.

2. Kirkman, Bradley L., and Benson Rosen. "Beyond Self-Management: The Antecedents and Consequences of Team Empowerment." *Academy of Management Journal* 42 (1999): 58–74.

3. Harris, T. Brad. "The Functionality of Focus: An Investigation into the Interactive Effects of Leader Focus and Task Interdependence." PhD diss., Texas A&M University, 2012.

4. Harris (2012).

5. Kirkman, Bradley L., Benson Rosen, Paul E. Tesluk, and Cristina B. Gibson. "The Impact of Team Empowerment on Virtual Team Performance: The Moderating Role of Face-to-Face Interaction." *Academy of Management Journal* 47 (2004): 175–192.

6. Reprinted with permission from *Emerald Group Publishing Limited*, from Jones, Renae A., Alannah E. Rafferty, and Mark A. Griffin. "The Executive Coaching Trend: Towards More Flexible Executives." *Leadership & Organization Development Journal* 27 (2006): 584–596. Copyright © 2006 by Emerald Group Publishing Limited all rights reserved.

7. Harris (2012).

8. Original items created by the authors of this book.

9. Kirkman and Rosen (1999).

10. Kirkman and Rosen (1999).

11. Kirkman and Rosen (1999).

Index

Page numbers in *italics* indicate a table or chart. Book titles will be found under the author's name.

action processes, 85
action teams, 151–53
after-action reviews or project reviews (team retrospectives), 133–34
Agile model: competencies of 3D team leaders, case study in, 225–26; concept of, 43; project teams case study, 154–55, 157–62, 164–67, 246; "scrum of scrums," 128
Allstate, 6
ambidextrous leadership, 235–37, *242*, 246, 253, 254–55
ambiguity, tolerance of (uncertainty avoidance), 172, 181–82, *185*
Amundsen, Roald, 149–51, 156, 168
Anthony, Carmelo, 91
Apollo 13 (film), 25, 134
Apple, 110, 216
Argentina, power distance in, 179, 180
assessment: formal assessment, 248; self-assessment tools, 248–56
authenticity, as 3D team leader competency, 240–42, *242*, 246
authority: of team as a whole, 106, 163; of team leader versus team member discretion and authority, 20–21

autonomy: for individuals in teams, 68, 73; self-assessment tools, 252–53; for team as a whole, 88–89, *89*

Babineaux, Ryan, 19
behavioral complexity, 237
behavioral interdependence, 16
behavioral theories about teams and team leadership, 8
Belgium, power distance in, 179
Bird, Allan, 190
Blanchard, Ken: *Empowerment Takes More Than a Minute*, 56; *The One Minute Manager* (with Spencer Johnson), 56
bonuses and pay. *See* extrinsic motivation
boundary spanning, 81
Braveheart (film), 25

Campbell, David, *If You Don't Know Where You're Going, You'll Probably End Up Somewhere Else*, 104
Capelli, Peter, 40
caring leaders. *See* concern and caring, leaders displaying

case studies: of competencies of 3D
      team leaders, 223–27; fire and rescue
      (action) teams, 151–53, 231, 232, 233;
      South Pole race (1911-1912), 149–51,
      168. *See also* project team case study
change-oriented leadership. *See*
      transformational leadership
characteristics of successful leaders. *See*
      competencies of 3D team leaders
China, cultural factors in, 187–88, 190–
      92
choice, as dimension of empowerment,
      57–58, *58*
"clear boundaries," Hackman on, 14
coaching: concept of, 4; for individuals
      on teams, 62–63, *65*; in project team
      case study, 156–57; for team as a
      whole, 99, *101*; for virtual teams,
      212–13. *See also* training
cognitive agility, 232
cognitive complexity, 237
collective team identification for
      subteams, 140–42, 220
collectivism versus individualism, as
      cultural issue, 39–40, 172–73, 174–
      78, *185*, 204, 247
communication issues for virtual teams,
      214–17
communities of practice, 2
company structures and systems. *See*
      corporate structures and systems
compensation. *See* extrinsic motivation
competence/potency: for individuals
      in teams, *58*, 58–59; self-assessment
      tools, 252–53; for team as a whole,
      88, *89*, 90–91
competencies of 3D team leaders, 222–
      43; ambidextrous leadership, 235–37,
      242, 246, 253, 254–55; authenticity,
      240–42, *242, 246*; case studies, 223–
      27; of culturally diverse teams, 195–
      99; EQ (emotional intelligence), 237–
      40, *242, 246*; flexibility/adaptability,

198–99, 231–33, *242*, 246, 253–54;
      intelligence and, 229; personality
      traits and, 198, 228–29, 232, 238;
      physical attributes and gender,
      229–30; self-assessment, 248–56;
      self-monitoring, 233; successful
      leadership generally, 227–30;
      switching behavior, 233–35, *242*, 246,
      253, 254; of virtual teams, 202–3
competition and conflict, healthy, versus
      support, *17*, 18–19
complexity theory, 8
composition of team, 107–8, *109*
concern and caring, leaders displaying:
      for individuals on teams, 63–64, *65*;
      in project team case study, 157; for
      team as a whole, 100–101, *101*
conflict and competition, healthy, versus
      support, *17*, 18–19
Confucian dynamism (long-term versus
      short-term orientation), 172
conscientiousness, 228–29
conservation of resources theory, 8
consideration (relationship-based or
      person-based leadership; team
      member-focused leader behaviors),
      30, 152–53, *153*, 252
Cook, Frederick, 149
coordinating efforts for subteams, 123–
      24, 127–29, *130*, 160–61
corporate structures and systems:
      empowerment of individuals in
      teams and, 64–72, *73*; empowerment
      of team as a whole and, 101–8, *109*;
      in project team case study, 157–58;
      virtual teams and, 214. *See also*
      perceived organizational support;
      supportive organizational climate;
      trust, organizational
CQ (cultural intelligence), 195–98, 200
cross-cultural teams. *See* cultural issues
cross-training and rotating subteam
      members, 139–40, 220

cultural issues, 169–200; applicability of 3D team leadership concept to, 247; best practices for leading culturally diverse teams, 192–99; changes in, 186–88; Confucian dynamism (long-term versus short-term orientation), 172; CQ (cultural intelligence), 195–98, 200; future orientation, 173; generational differences and team leadership, 40–41; GlobeSmart tool, 180, 194, 211; individualism versus collectivism, 39–40, 172–73, 174–78, *185*, 204, 247; indulgence versus restraint, 172; information on specific country-by-country values, 184; non-geographic factors, 189–90; paradoxes of, 190–91; power distance (importance of status and hierarchy), 172, 178–81, *185*; quantity/quality of life (masculine/feminine) differences, 172, 173, 183, *185*; significance of, 184–86; stereotyping, 188–92; team as a whole, ability to focus on, 39–40; team concept, differences in, 170–71; tightness-looseness, cultural, 185–86; training in, 196–97; transformational leadership and, 191–92; uncertainty avoidance (tolerance of ambiguity), 172, 181–82, *185*; value frameworks for understanding, 171–73; for virtual teams, 204, 217–19, *219*

DeChurch, Leslie, 120
decision-making, encouraging participation in: for individuals on teams, 61–62, 65; in project team case study, 156; for team as a whole, 98–99, *101*
"delimited authority," Hackman on, 14–15
design, work/team: concept of, 4; for individuals on teams, 67–72, *73*; in project team case study, 163–64; for team as a whole, 104–8, *109*; virtual teams, 209–10
direction for team, clarity of, 104–5, *109*, 163
diversity, 107–8, 192–99
Duncan, Tim, 91
dynamic settings, optimizing team performance in, 148

Edmondson, Amy, *Teaming: How Organizations Learn, Innovate, and Compete in the Knowledge Economy*, 97
ego depletion theory, 8
emotional intelligence (EQ), 237–40, *242*, 246
empowerment: power distance, cultural differences in, 179–81; self-assessment in, 250–51, 252–53; of subteams, 43–44; uncertainty avoidance, cultural differences in, 182; of virtual teams, 208, 212–13
empowerment of individuals in teams, 55–75; benefits of, 59–60; building high-quality relationships, 72–75, 158; confusion, cynicism, and suspicion about, 55–57; corporate structures and systems, leveraging, 64–72, *73*; defined and described, 57–59, *58*; as gold standard for intrinsic motivation, 55–56; leader behavior and, 60–64, *65*; in project team case study, 156–58; relationship to whole team empowerment, 93; reward, recognition, and performance review programs, 76–82
empowerment of team as a whole: corporate structures and systems, leveraging, 101–8, *109*; defined and described, 87–92, *89*; evidence

for effectiveness of, 92–93; leader behavior increasing, 97–101, *101*; in project team case study, 162–63; transformational leadership and, 110–11

environmental scanning, 81

EQ (emotional intelligence), 237–40, *242, 246*

Evans, Teddy, 150

executives. *See* senior management

ExperienceInnovation, 232

ExperiencePoint, 232

external boundary spanning, 81

extraversion, 228

extrinsic motivation: for individuals on teams, 54–55, 76–82; in project team case study, 158–59, 161; for subteams, 134–37; for team as a whole, 111–17

Facebook, 154

face-to-face interaction versus virtual teams, 22–23, 201–2, 216–17

family-based team concept in Philippines, 170–71

faultlines between subteams, 28–29, 119, 137–42, 220

feedback systems, 68–69, *73*

feminine/masculine (quality/quantity of life) cultural differences, 172, 173, 183, *185*

Finland, power distance in, 178–79, 181

fire and rescue teams, 151–53, 231, 232, 233

flexibility/adaptability, 198–99, 231–33, *242, 246,* 253–54

focus issues, 143–68; appropriate interdependence level, determining, 144–48; at center of 3D team leadership concept, 3–4, 8, 29–30, 34; dynamic settings, optimizing team performance in, 148; fire and rescue (action) teams case study,

151–53; individuals in teams, when to focus on, 53; interdependence as key to, 143–44; in project teams, 154–68 (*See also* project team case study); shifting focus, 166–68; South Pole race (1911-1912) case study, 149–51, 168; subteams, when to focus on, 119–20; task-focused and person-focused behavior, 30, 152–53, *153,* 251–52; team as a whole, when to focus on, 83–84

forced ranking system ("rank-and-yank"), 76–77

Friedman, Tom, 186

functional team leadership (leader as completer approach), 30–31

future orientation, as cultural issue, 173

GE, 76, 110

Gelfand, Michele, 185

gender of leaders, 230

generational differences and team leadership, 40–41

George, Bill, 240

Gersick, Connie, 12

Gerstner, Lou, 110

Gibson, Cristina, 170, 171, 180

global cultures. *See* cultural issues

Global Leadership and Organizational Behavior Effectiveness program (GLOBE), 172–73, 184

global virtual teams. *See* virtual teams

GlobeSmart tool, 180, 194, 211

goal alignment: of individual and team goals, 106–7; for subteams, 122

goal hierarchy for subteams, 129–31, 136, 245

goal interdependence, 10

goal setting: for individuals on teams, 79–80; SMART goals, 79, 82, 106, 135; for subteams, 135–36, 138, 220; for team as a whole, 106–7, *109,* 163

Goffee, Robert, 240, 241, 242

Goleman, Daniel, 237–38
Google, 154, 216
groupidity, 26, 119
groups versus teams, 9–13, 38, 224,
    244–45
guanxi, 191

Hackman, Richard: on individuals in
    teams, 51, 56; *Leading Teams: Setting
    the Stage for Great Performances,* 13–
    16; on team as a whole, 104, 106, 107
Heath, Chip and Dan, *Switch: How to
    Change Things When Change Is
    Hard,* 234–35
hierarchy and status (power distance),
    172, 178–81, *185*
Hill, Linda, *Being the Boss: The 3
    Imperatives for Becoming a Great
    Leader,* 17
Hirschhorn, Larry, *Managing in the New
    Team Environment: Skills, Tools, and
    Methods,* 31–33, 37
Hofstede, Geert, 172–73, 181, 184, 186–
    87, 189
Hoosiers (film), 25
House, Bob, 172
human resources (HR): cultural
    value assessment by, 180; goal-
    setting programs, 80; work design,
    leveraging, 69
Huntford, Roland, 150

IBM, 6, 110
idealized influence, 110–11, 164–65
identity, individual versus team, *17,*
    17–18
IDEO, 232
impact of work: for individuals in teams,
    58; self-assessment tools, 252–53; for
    team as a whole, 88, *89,* 89–90
India, information technology workers
    and cultural change in, 186
individualism versus collectivism, as

cultural issue, 39–40, 172–73, 174–
    78, *185,* 204, 247
individualized consideration, 110
individuals in teams, 51–82; best
    practices for leading and motivating,
    53–55; culturally diverse teams,
    leading, 193; Hirschhorn and
    3D model compared, *32,* 32–35;
    identity, individual versus team,
    as classic team tension, *17,* 17–18;
    individualism versus collectivism,
    as cultural issue, 176–77; life cycles
    of teams and, 53; with low levels of
    interdependence, 53; project teams
    case study, 155–59; virtual teams,
    205–9; "we over me" mindset, as
    pitfall, 25–26, 35–38, 51–52; when to
    focus on, 53. *See also* empowerment
    of individuals in teams
indulgence versus restraint, as cultural
    issue, 172
information-sharing: for individuals on
    teams, 63, *65;* in project team case
    study, 157; for team as a whole, 99–
    100, *101*
in-group collectivism, 173
initiating structure (task-based
    leadership/task-focused leader
    behaviors), 30, 152–53, *153,* 251–52
inspirational motivation, 110, 111, 164–
    65
institutional collectivism, 173
integrity, 199
intellectual stimulation, 110
intelligence: CQ (cultural intelligence),
    195–98, 200; EQ (emotional
    intelligence), 237–40, *242,* 246; as
    successful leader characteristic, 229
interdependence: across-subteam
    interdependence, *125,* 126, 127;
    appropriate interdependence level,
    determining, 144–48; between-
    subteam interdependence, *125,*

127; changing face of teams and, 16, 245–56; focus issues, as key to, 143–44; of groups versus teams, 10–11; identifying optimal type of, 49; individuals in teams with low levels of, 53; multilayered interdependence between and across subteams, 41–42, 118, 123–24, *125*, 219; self-assessment in, 249–50; team as a whole, when to focus on, 83–84; types of, 11, 16; virtual teams and, 202; within-subteam interdependence, *125*, 127
interpersonal processes, 85
intrinsic motivation, 54–55. *See also specific entries at* empowerment
Iverson, Allen, 91

James, LeBron, 91
Japan, cultural factors in, 174, 188, 190
Jobs, Steve, 110
Johansen, Hjalmar, 150
Johnson, Spencer, and Ken Blanchard, *The One Minute Manager,* 56
Jones, Gareth, 240, 241, 242
journal briefings, 133

Katzenbach, Jon, and Douglas Smith, *The Wisdom of Teams,* 11, 119
Kerr, Steve, 77
Krumboltz, John, 19

leader as completer approach (functional team leadership), 30–31
leader switching behavior, 233–35, *242*, 246, 253, 254
leader-member exchange (LMX), 72–74, 80, 81, 140
leaders. *See* 3D team leadership; competencies of 3D team leaders; teams and team leadership
learning from mistakes versus successful performance, *17*, 19–20

Leo Burnett Company, 28–29
Levi Strauss, 77–78, 112
life cycles of teams: concept of, 12–13; individuals in teams, when to focus on, 53; project team case study, 155, 159, 162, 165, 166–67; subteams, when to focus on, 120; team as a whole, when to focus on, 83–84, 85–86
LMX (leader-member exchange), 72–74, 80, 81, 140
long-term versus short-term orientation (Confucian dynamism), 172

macromanagement, 56
Malaysia, power distance in, 180
Marks, Michelle, 85, 120
masculine/feminine (quantity/quality of life) cultural differences, 172, 173, 183, *185*
Mathieu, John, 85, 120
meaningfulness: for individuals on teams, *58, 59*; self-assessment tools, 252–53; for team as a whole, 88, *89*, 91–92
Mendelowitz, Rachel, 96
Menon, Tanya, 56
mental models. *See* shared mental models
micromanagement, 56
Microsoft, 76
mistakes, learning from, versus successful performance, *17*, 19–20
monetary rewards. *See* extrinsic motivation
multilayered interdependence between and across subteams, 41–42, 118, 123–24, *125*, 219
multiple team leadership and membership, coping with, 1–3, 21–22
multisubteam systems. *See* subteams
multiteam systems, 120–21. *See also* subteams

mutual accountability, 10
Myers-Briggs personality test, 189

Ohio State University leadership
    research, 152
openness to experience, 198, 199, 229,
    232
organizational structures and systems.
    See corporate structures and systems
Osland, Joyce, 190
outcome interdependence, 10

paradoxes, cultural, 190–91
pay and bonuses. *See* extrinsic
    motivation
peer evaluations, 80
perceived organizational support: for
    individuals in teams, 65–66, *73*; in
    project team case study, 157–58; for
    team as a whole, 102–3, *109*
performance goals. *See specific entries*
    at goal
performance reviews: for individuals
    in teams, 76–82; peer evaluations,
    80; self-assessment tools, 248–
    56; for subteams, 133–34; team
    retrospectives (after-action reviews
    or project reviews), 133–34
personality testing, 184–85, 189
personality traits of leaders, 198, 228–
    29, 232, 238
person-based or relationship-based
    leadership (consideration; team
    member-focused leader behaviors),
    30, 152–53, *153*, 252
Philippines: family-based team concept in,
    170–71; power distance in, 179, 180
physical attributes of leaders, 229–30
potency. *See* competence/potency
power distance (importance of status
    and hierarchy), 172, 178–81, *185*
project reviews or after-action reviews
    (team retrospectives), 133–34

project team case study, 154–68; Agile
    model, 154–55, 157–62, 164–67, 246;
    competencies of 3D team leader in,
    246; empowerment practices, 156–
    58, 162–63; extrinsic motivation,
    158–59, 161; individuals in teams,
    155–59; life cycles of, 155, 159, 162,
    165, 166–67; shared mental models,
    161; shifting focus in, 166–68;
    subteams, 159–61; team as a whole,
    162–65; transformational leadership
    in, 164–65; waterfall-type models,
    154, 160
Prudential Insurance, 6
psychological safety of team as a whole:
    concept of, 95, 96–97; cultural
    diversity of team and, 194–95;
    defined, 94; importance of, 81, 94;
    leadership behaviors providing, 97–
    101; leveraging corporate structures
    and systems to increase, 101–8, *109*;
    in project team case study, 162–63;
    transformational leadership and,
    110–11; for virtual teams, 212
punctuated equilibrium, 12

quantity/quality of life (masculine/
    feminine) cultural differences, 172,
    173, 183, *185*

"rank-and-yank" (forced ranking
    system), 76–77
recognition programs. *See* reward and
    recognition programs
relationship-based leadership
    (consideration; team member
    focused leader behaviors; person-
    based leadership), 30, 152–53, *153*,
    252
relationship-based trust, 95
Remember the Titans (film), 25
resilience, 199
resource allocation theory, 8

resources for teams, 105–6, *109*, 163
restraint versus indulgence, as cultural
    issue, 172
reward and recognition programs: for
    individuals on teams, 76–82; for
    subteams, 134–37; for teams as a
    whole, 105, 111–17, 163; for virtual
    teams, 210
role-modeling, as leader behavior: for
    individuals on teams, 61, 65; for
    team as a whole, 98, *101*
rotating and cross-training subteam
    members, 139–40, 220
Russo, David, 54

Sara Lee, 6
SAS Institute, 54
Scott, Robert Falcon, 149–51, 168
"scrum of scrums," 128, 162
self-assessment tools, 248–56
self-monitoring, 233
senior management: failure to embrace
    team concept, 26–28; teams for, 2,
    246–47
sensemaking, 70–71, 81, 117, 191
Shapiro, Debra, 180
shared leadership environment, 3D
    team leadership in, 45–47
shared mental models: in project team
    case study, 161; for subteams, 131–34,
    139, 161, 245; for team as a whole, 86
short-term versus long-term orientation
    (Confucian dynamism), 172
SHRM (Society of Human Resource
    Management), 54
size of team, 108, *109*, 164, 205
skill variety, 67, *73*
SMART goals, 79, 82, 106, 135
Smith, Douglas, and Jon Katzenbach,
    The Wisdom of Teams, 11, 119
social identity theory, 17
Society of Human Resource
    Management (SHRM), 54

sociopolitical support: for individuals
    in teams, 64–66, *73*; in project team
    case study, 157–58; for team as a
    whole, 102–3, *109*
South Korea, cultural change in, 187
South Pole race (1911–1912), 149–51, 168
sports-oriented team metaphors, 170–71
sprint teams, 43, 107, 133, 154, 162, 166
stability of teams, 15, 108, *109*
status and hierarchy (power distance),
    172, 178–81, *185*
Steel, Piers, 184
stereotyping, cultural, importance of
    avoiding, 188–92
strategizing efforts for subteams, 123–
    27, *130*, 160–61
structural interdependence, 16
subteams, 118–42; across-subteam
    interdependence, *125*, 126, 127; best
    practices for leading and motivating,
    42, 44–45, 121; between-subteam
    interdependence, *125*, 127; collective
    team identification and, 140–42,
    220; coordinating efforts, 123–24,
    127–29, *130*, 160–61; cross-training
    and rotating members, 139–40, 220;
    customer service assessment, 256;
    defined, 118, 120–21; empowerment
    of, 43–44; extrinsic motivation for,
    134–37; faultlines and faultline
    avoidance, 28–29, 119, 137–42, 220;
    goal alignment, 122; goal hierarchy,
    129–31, 136, 245; goal setting,
    135–36, 138, 220; Hirschhorn and
    3D model compared, *32*, 32–35;
    individual leadership of each
    subteam, 122–23; individualism
    versus collectivism, as cultural issue,
    177–78; life cycles of teams and,
    120; multilayered interdependence
    between and across, 41–42, 118,
    123–24, *125*, 219; number within
    overall team, increasing, 140, 220;

performance assessment, 255; proactive establishment of, 42–43, 119; proactivity assessment, 255; project teams case study, 159–61; self-assessment tools, 255–56; shared mental models for, 131–34, 139, 161, 245; South Pole race (1911-1912) as example of, 150, 151; strategizing efforts, 123–27, 130, 160–61; of virtual teams, 217–20, 219; when to focus on, 119–20; within-subteam interdependence, 125, 127

successful performance versus learning from mistakes, 17, 19–20

support versus healthy conflict and competition, 17, 18–19

supportive organizational climate: for individuals in teams, 64–65, 73; in project team case study, 157–58; for team as a whole, 102, 109

swift trust, 213

switching behavior, 233–35, 242, 246, 253, 254

Taras, Vas, 184

task identity, 67, 73

task interdependence, 10, 105, 109, 163, 249–50

task mental model, 131–32

task significance, 67–68, 73

task-based leadership (task-focused leader behaviors; initiating structure), 30, 152–53, 153, 251–52

task-based trust, 95–96

team as a whole, 83–117; best practices for leading and motivating, 84–86; corporate structures and systems leveraged for good of, 101–8, 109; culturally diverse teams, leading, 193–94; extrinsic motivation for, 105, 111–17; Hirschhorn and 3D model compared, 32, 32–35; individualism versus collectivism,

as cultural issue, 176–77; interdependence levels and, 83–84; leader behavior and, 97–111; life cycles of teams and, 83–84, 85–86; over- or under-emphasizing, as pitfall, 26–28, 38–41; project team case study, 162–65; virtual teams, 209–17; when to focus on, 83–84; work processes of, 85–86, 211–14. See also empowerment of team as a whole; psychological safety of team as a whole; trust of team as a whole

team building, 210–11

team design. See design, work/team

team interaction model, 132–33

team interaction training, 133

team member exchange (TMX), 80

team member-focused leader behaviors (person-based or relationship-based leadership; consideration), 30, 152–53, 153, 252

team mental model, 132

team of teams. See subteams

team retrospectives (after-action reviews or project reviews), 133–34

"team task," Hackman on, 14

teams and team leadership: advantages and purpose of 3D model, 3–5; behavioral theories about, 8; changing face of, 6–7, 7, 13–16; in complex environments, 7–9; definition of leadership, 5–6; definition of team, 10; groups versus teams, 9–13, 38, 224, 244–45; life cycles of, 12–13 (See also life cycles of teams); multiple team leadership and membership, coping with, 1–3, 21–22; tensions of, 16–23, 17, 236. See also 3D team leadership

"there is no I in team" mindset, 25–26, 35–38, 51–52

Thompson, Leigh, 56

3D team leadership, 25–50; across

cultures, 169–200 (*See also* cultural issues); applicable situations, 244–48; coaching teams, 4; competencies of, 222–43 (*See also* competencies of 3D team leaders); defined, 3–5; focus at center of, 3–4, 8, 29–30, 34 (*See also* focus issues); Hirschhorn's model compared, 31–33; multiple team leadership and membership, coping with, 1–3; other leadership concepts compared, 30–31; pitfalls as impetus for developing, 25–29; in shared leadership environment, 45–47; South Pole race (1911-1912) as example of, 149–51, 168; three aspects of, 31–35, *32*, 47–50 (*See also* individuals in teams; subteams; team as a whole); for virtual teams, 201–21 (*See also* virtual teams)

TMX (team member exchange), 80

"token teaming," 27

top management. *See* senior management

training: cross-training and rotating subteam members, 139–40, 220; in cultural issues, 196–97; team interaction training, 133; for virtual teams, 207–8, 212–13. *See also* coaching

transactive memory system, 106

transformational leadership: cultural issues and, 191–92; defined and described, 30, 110; in project team case study, 164–65; team as a whole and, 110–11

transition processes, 85

trust, organizational: for individuals on teams, 66, *73*, 81; in project team case study, 157–58; for team as a whole, 103–4, *109*

trust of team as a whole: concept of, 94–96; defined, 94; importance of, 81, 94; leadership behaviors providing, 97–101; leveraging corporate structures and systems to increase, 101–8, *109*; in project team case study, 162–63; relationship-based trust, 95; swift trust, 213; task-based trust, 95–96; transformational leadership and, 110–11; for virtual teams, 213

trust within team and training effectiveness, 208

Tuckman, Bruce, 12

turnover of team members, 23

uncertainty avoidance (tolerance of ambiguity), 172, 181–82, *185*

United States, cultural factors in, 187, 190–92

University of Michigan collaboration research, 216

U.S. Olympic men's basketball team (2004), 90–91

virtual teams, 201–21; applicability of 3D team leadership concept to, 247–48; characteristics of successful team leaders of, 202–3; communication issues for, 214–17; creation and establishment of, 203–5; cultural issues and, 204, 217–19, *219*; empowerment of, 208, 212–13; face-to-face interaction versus, 22–23, 201–2, 216–17; individuals in, 205–9; interdependence issues, 202; relationship issues in, 201–2; reward and recognition programs for, 210; size of, 205; subteams, 217–20, *219*; team as a whole, leading, 209–17; time zone differences, 48, 156, 202

VUCA (volatile, uncertain, complex, and ambiguous) conditions: competencies of 3D team leadership and, 229, 231, 236, 240, 247; cultural issues and, 169; defined,

CPSIA information can be obtained
at www.ICGtesting.com
Printed in the USA
BVHW031106111219
566311BV00004B/30/P

6; dynamic settings, optimizing team performance in, 148; fire and rescue teams working in, 151; goal-setting in, 107; Hackman's essential features of teams and, 14, 15; in project team case study, 165; shared leadership in, 47; South Pole race (1911-1912) as example of, 149; subteams in, 119, 138, 142; successful performance versus learning from mistakes in, 19; team as a whole in, 86, 94, 96, 107; virtual teams in, 205

Wade, Dwayne, 91
Wageman, Ruth, 104, 106, 107, 113

Washington, George, 230
waterfall-type models, 154, 160
"we over me" mindset, 25–26, 35–38, 51–52
Welch, Jack, 110
whole team. *See* team as a whole
work design. *See* design, work/team
work processes of team as a whole, 85–86, 211–14

Xerox, 113

Yahoo, 76, 211, 216

Zaccaro, Stephen, 85, 120
Zellmer-Bruhn, Mary, 170, 171